Andy Gröning

The Sukhoi Su-27
Russia's Air Superiority, and Multi-role Fighter

1977 TO THE PRESENT

Schiffer Publishing Ltd

4880 Lower Valley Road • Atglen, PA 19310

Copyright © 2018 by Schiffer Publishing Ltd.

Originally published as *Su-27* by Motorbuch Verlag, Stuttgart, Germany © 2017 Motorbuch Verlag

Translated from the German by David Johnston

Library of Congress Control Number: 2018937194

Designed by Matthew Goodman
Type set in Aurora & Helvetica Neue

ISBN: 978-0-7643-5637-7

Printed in China

Published by Schiffer Publishing, Ltd.
4880 Lower Valley Road
Atglen, PA 19310
Phone: (610) 593-1777; Fax: (610) 593-2002
E-mail: Info@schifferbooks.com
Web: www.schifferbooks.com

For our complete selection of fine books on this and related subjects, please visit our website at www.schifferbooks.com. You may also write for a free catalog.

Schiffer Publishing's titles are available at special discounts for bulk purchases for sales promotions or premiums. Special editions, including personalized covers, corporate imprints, and excerpts, can be created in large quantities for special needs. For more information, contact the publisher.

We are always looking for people to write books on new and related subjects. If you have an idea for a book, please contact us at proposals@schifferbooks.com.

Contents

CHAPTER 7:
Weapons   164

Color Profiles   186

Appendices   218

Dimitri Yuriev

Foreword

The first prototype of the Sukhoi Su-27 family took to the skies for the first time in 1977, and when its true performance was eventually determined, there was disappointment. At that time, therefore, few suspected that the redesigned T-10S would someday become an opponent feared by its adversaries in every air force. Less well-known than its smaller sister the MiG-29, the Su-27 and its derivatives would demonstrate their performance capabilities at airshows in various parts of the world. It would perform maneuvers previously thought to be impossible (the exception was the MiG-29, which was capable of the same maneuvers), and in the case of the Su-27 this was even more impressive because it was about thirty to fifty percent larger than other fighters (with the exception of the F-14 Tomcat and F-15 Eagle). Even today, thirty-five years after the maiden flight by the redesigned T-10S, the basic design of the Su-27 still makes it a rival that opponents must take seriously, a position it will be able to maintain in the present and future thanks to the use of modern technology.

The Su-27 played a vital role in the air defense units of the Soviet Union. It and its little sister the MiG-29 combined unsurpassed maneuverability with a powerful radar and weaponry. It also possessed an enormous range, greater than that of any previous fighter aircraft of the USSR. This made the Su-27 and its developments among the most capable combat aircraft in the world. Western air forces, in particular, would learn this for themselves during various exercises. While Western pilots knew about the huge Su-27's outstanding maneuverability, pilots who engaged it were frequently impressed and surprised to discover just how lethal this huge fighter was, even in close-in maneuvering combat.

I would like to express my sincere thanks to all those who helped me complete this book. Pride of place, of course, goes to my wife and my son. My wife showed great understanding for my time-consuming work on the book and the time it took away from my family. My son took great care to correct spelling errors, his efforts resulting in the text being "pre-edited." My heartfelt thanks to them both.

The search for photos made up a substantial part of my work. In this I received help from various Russian, White Russian, and Ukrainian armaments manufacturers. These were JSC Sukhoi and its KnAAZ manufacturing plant, UAC (United Aircraft Corporation), the Irkut Corporation, UEC (United Engine Corporation), the JSC 558 Aircraft Repair Plant, the Arsenal SDP State Enterprise, NPP Zvezda, and the Russian Defense Ministry. Alexey Mayer helped me a great deal in overcoming the language difficulties associated with contacting Russian companies, *spasiba*.

The majority of the photographs came from private individuals. They were: Alexey Micheyev, Charles Agnew, Hugh Dodsun, Oleg Revin, Peng Chen, Rob Schleiffert, Sergey Chaikovsky, Chris Lofting, Svido Stanislav, Dimitri Yuriyev, Andrey Zinchuk, Gilles Dennis, Olav C. the With, Resa Wahyu Giang, Jose Ramirez, Nguyen Phuong, Wojciech Kowalski, Malcom Nason, Sergey Burdin, Vitaly Kuzmin, and Vladislav Perminov. Manfred Meyer contributed his outstanding color drawing of the aircraft carrier *Tbilisi*, demonstrating great trust in sending it to me, many thanks. Frank Krüger, I thank you for your artwork. The last, even though the amount of work he put into the book is second only to my own, is Talgat Ashimov. Completely uncomplicated and very accommodating, he created the outstanding color profiles at the end of the book.

Andy Gröning,
Potsdam, Germany, 2017

CHAPTER 1
Takeoff to the Fourth Generation

The T-10 Project

The United States launched its Fighter Experimental (FX) Program, which was to create a next-generation fighter aircraft, in 1966. Since the end of the Second World War, aircraft had been designed to fly faster, higher, and further. The new type was therefore to be a heavy type with Mach 3 capability. The Americans realized, however, particularly during the Vietnam War, that they needed a type that had a capable radar and guided weapons, but which also possessed a high degree of maneuverability for aerial combat. For a while the F-4 Phantom had better weapons and electronics than the MiG-21, it was inferior to the Soviet fighter in close-in maneuvering combat. The new aircraft was to combine the positive characteristics of both types. A specification was issued to American aircraft manufacturers, and the F-15 emerged as victor.

At the same time a requirement was issued for a lighter type, which resulted in the F-16 and F-18. Those on the other side of the Iron Curtain were of course aware of this situation, and information received about the FX program, in part from the Western press but also through secret activities, soon allowed them to form a rough picture of the future F-15. In addition to the technology, the Americans also changed their offensive doctrine. The Vietnam War also showed that operations at medium and high altitudes increased the risk of being shot down by surface-to-air missiles. This was only possible, however, if a ground radar could detect the aircraft in the air. They would therefore have to fly under the radar to avoid detection or remain undetected for as long as possible.

In the early 1970s, radar coverage over the European part of the USSR was quite good, which could not be said of northern Russia or Siberia and the Far East. While the Soviets stepped up the building of radar and control installations,

First integral designs in the early 1970s. *JSC Sukhoi*

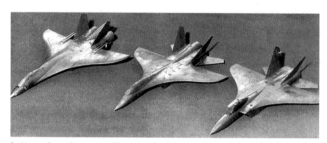
Integral and conventional wind tunnel models. *JSC Sukhoi*

they also needed an aircraft that could locate and engage low-flying aircraft. The Su-15 was modernized and the MiG-25 was developed into the MiG-31. In terms of radar and weaponry, the MiG-31 was definitely capable of engaging all modern Western combat aircraft; but the aircraft had been designed as a long-range interceptor, not a dogfighter. The new fighter was to combine both heavy armament and a highly-developed target acquisition system paired with long range and outstanding close combat capabilities.

The Soviets created their own program in 1969, and all three Soviet design bureaus for fighter aircraft (Mikoyan, Sukhoi, and Yakovlev) began working on the new design. Sukhoi actually had its hands full in 1969—the first flight of the Su-24 was imminent, and the *Opytnoye Konstruktorskoye Buro* (Experimental Design Bureau, or OKB) was heavily involved in work on the T-4 (an aircraft similar to the Tu-144 which was to carry missiles and function as a high-speed reconnaissance aircraft), the T-4MS, Su-25, and the modernization of the Su-15 and Su-17.

In the Sukhoi OKB, in 1969, Vladimir Antonov (not to be confused with the designer of transport aircraft with the same name) began the first studies into a new fighter concept. Based on this, V. Antonov, Oleg Samoylovich, and Valery Nikolayenko created the origins of the "integral layout," in which the wings and fuselage blended into a single lifting body. This layout had already been used theoretically in development of the T-4MS, successor to the T-4. The lift-drag ratio was considerably improved and the space available for equipment, systems, and fuel was also significantly increased. Furthermore, the wing roots were extended to the forward fuselage (LERX – Leading Edge Root Extensions). These created better flow characteristics over the wing surface at high angles of attack. Twin vertical tails were adopted. The engines were housed separately in nacelles beneath the aft fuselage. The wingtips were made oval in shape, as it was assumed that this would be necessary to achieve the desired agility. The wing had an ogival leading edge.

One particular feature was the unstable layout of the T-10 project. The designers believed that if the aircraft's center of gravity was not in the same place as the center of lift, it would improve agility. This was displaced along the Su-27's longitudinal axis, and without computer support it would have created such a strong and sudden pitching moment that the pilot would not have been able to control the aircraft. The pilot would have to possess extraordinary skill to fly an unstable aircraft with a conventional control system. At the time, it was said that it was equivalent to trying to ride a bicycle while sitting backwards on the bike on the hood of a moving automobile. The only solution was a computer-assisted fly-by-wire control system. Such a system was designed and flight tested in the Sukhoi T-4.

Although encouraging results had been achieved with one of the first designs in wind tunnel tests at the TsAGI (Central Aerohydrodynamic Institute), there were leading people at the institute who were very skeptical about the new integral concept and therefore rejected it. The reason may have been information obtained about the F-15 to the effect that it had a less integral layout. Sukhoi therefore formed a second team to design a more conventional aerodynamic configuration, which was completed in 1971. The wings and fuselage were not as strongly melded, the engines were located close together in the tail, and rectangular air intakes were positioned on the sides of the fuselage. When a conventional model was tested at the TsAGI, no advantages were found compared to the integral design. Gradually the heads of the institute recognized the potential of the unstable layout and called for its adoption.

In 1971, the Defense Ministry issued a first general catalogue of requirements for a future fighter aircraft. The OKBs had begun their work in advance of officialdom. Both the integral and conventional concepts had an estimated weight of about 39,700 pounds. To achieve a thrust-to-weight ratio greater than one, engines were required that would be capable of producing more than 22,500 pounds of thrust. No operational engines in that class existed at that time, but they were under development. Subsequent information was therefore based on calculations and faith that the performance figures promised by the engine manufacturers would prove correct. Finally the TsIAM (Central Research Institute for Aviation Engine Development) evaluated the documents submitted by the engine developers and recommended the AL-31F for the T-10.

In 1972, the defense ministry and the air force command were jointly working on the future doctrine for their combat aircraft. They came to realize that they needed several different types for different roles if they were to be able to meet the growing requirements on a future battlefield. This was certainly influenced in part by the fact that the USA had decided on two fighter types, a light and a heavy one. Mikoyan, Sukhoi, and Yakovlev submitted their studies for assessment. Mikoyan first submitted only its conventional design, while Sukhoi submitted both of its variants.

Soon afterward Mikoyan also submitted its integral design. Yakovlev failed in the second phase of the competition and withdrew. In the beginning, there was actually just one specification for one combat aircraft type, but as it was realized that two different designs were better, Mikoyan made a proposal that they should develop both a light and a heavy type. In 1972, Mikoyan was officially given the task of developing the MiG-29 and Sukhoi the Su-27. Total weight became a sticking point for Sukhoi. Information was received from aircraft equipment subcontractors that the weight of the avionics was greater than what had been projected and it was realized that gross weight was now higher than originally calculated.

First prototype T-10 in 1977. *JSC Sukhoi*

As well, plans called for the aircraft to possess a ten percent superiority in performance over the F-15. In particular, it was to be capable of significantly higher g loads than any previous fighter. To achieve the desired range (also greater than the F-15), an equivalent amount of extra fuel would have to be carried. Ultimately the increased weight would either exceed the airframe's structural strength, or they would have to consider a reduction in the aircraft's agility. Both were unacceptable and the designers considered the use of carbon fiber materials. These had a superior strength-to-weight ratio than the aluminum alloys used in aircraft construction. However, problems were encountered in the manufacture of carbon fiber parts and this method was not used on the T-10. Another way had to be found to make the airframe structure strong enough to meet all requirements. Sukhoi turned to the use of titanium. Titanium is also much lighter than steel but is several times stronger. Here, too, however, problems were encountered. Titanium tends to hydrogen embrittlement, for example if it is exposed to hydrogen during manufacture (welding). Hydrogen atoms are diffused into the metal lattice of the titanium and reduce its strength, comparable to normal corrosion. The Soviet metal industry developed special procedures to prevent this embrittlement. A large proportion of titanium was used in the T-10 in structurally important areas.

From 1970 until 1975, the Sukhoi collective investigated several different undercarriage and air intake designs. For example there was a box-shaped intake under the fuselage, similar to that of the present-day Eurofighter. This type of intake was also found on the Mikoyan E-8 prototypes built in 1962. Also considered were separate cylindrical air intakes with cone-shaped openings. In 1975, the design work on the T-10 was largely finalized and construction of the first prototypes began. The integral layout had finally been adopted

for the T-10: the wing and central fuselage formed a single combined lifting body, the engines were housed in individual rectangular gondolas and extended from the central fuselage to the end of the tail. There was sufficient space between the engines for additional weapons to be mounted there one behind the other. The intake entrances had variable ramps to control the flow of air in keeping with airspeed.

The vertical tail consisted of two fins, which were mounted absolutely vertically and attached centrally above the two engine compartments. The horizontal tail consisted of all-moving slab tailplanes (tailerons). Prominent leading edge root extensions, ogival in shape, formed the junction between the fuselage and wings. The wingtips were also curved. As the fuselage and wings formed a very large common surface, there was a boundary layer fence atop each wing. These were to prevent the air flowing around the wing from moving outward. The radar was located in the nose cone, the canopy bulged from the fuselage, providing an excellent all-round view but slightly increased drag. The nosewheel undercarriage was situated beneath the cockpit and retracted rearward. The main undercarriage was mounted at the junction of outer engine air intakes to the wing and retracted forward.

One of the first prototypes was ready at the beginning of 1977, but without the new AL-31F power plants, which were not yet ready for service (see engine chapter). Fitted in their place were two AL-21F-3 engines, which produced less thrust but were even heavier. After taxi trials were completed, the LII (the Gromov Flight Research Institute in Zhukovski) authorized the first flight. This was made by the T-10-1 on May 20, 1977. The aircraft was flown by Sukhoi's chief test pilot, Vladimir Ilyushin (son of the aircraft designer of the same name). Flight characteristics and controllability were tested and no weapons system was installed.

The second prototype, the T-10-2, followed in 1978. It crashed the same year, killing pilot Evgeni Soloviev. The crash occurred during a low-altitude test flight near the speed of sound. The aircraft reacted differently than Soloviev expected to a control input and the aircraft reached such high negative g values that it ultimately broke up in the air. It was found that the fly-by-wire system was responsible and it was redesigned.

In 1979, the T-10-3 and T-10-4 prototypes became available and they were designed for the AL-31F, which by then was available. The first flights were delayed because the LII did not consider the AL-31F sufficiently developed to fly. The T-10-3 and T-10-4 finally made their first flights in 1979.

T-10-1 with the distinctive undercarriage arrangement and thickened undersides of the engine air intakes. *JSC Sukhoi*

Beginning with the T-10-3, the vertical tails were splayed outward. Later the T-10-3 was further modified for possible aircraft carrier use and was transferred to the NITKA field (ground installation with deck landing system) in the Crimea. In addition to flight testing of the AL-31F, the T-10-4 was used for radar trials.

A total of eleven prototypes of the T-10 series were built by 1982: T-10-1 to T-10-6, and T-10-9 to T-10-11, two airframes being used for static testing, and of the nine flying aircraft only two flew with the AL-31F. The tailerons, vertical tails, and the wings all had anti-flutter weights.

T-10S

In 1979, it seemed certain that the later Su-27 would enter quantity production and go into service with air defense units. Mikhail Simonov, head of the T-10 program opposed this energetically. Various conditions that had made themselves apparent during development and design prior to the T-10's maiden flight were the reason why. For one, the engine materials problem with the associated loss of thrust and simultaneous increase in fuel consumption was obvious. The increased weight of the avionics produced a shift in the T-10's center of gravity, which caused the aircraft to become statically stable. The instability was required, however, to ensure significantly greater agility in air combat. The new air-to-air missiles were also going to be heavier than originally planned. Calculations revealed that with these factors they were going to be about ten to twenty percent below the requirements that had been set for the new generation of fighters.

As well, simulations showed that in its present condition the Su-27 would not be the equal of the F-15. Therefore, the T-10 could not be continued in its current configuration and had to be redesigned. This was mainly true of the aerodynamic layout. Basic performance figures such as maximum range and speed could be achieved by increasing internal fuel capacity and reducing drag. The latter would be accomplished if the aircraft accessory gearboxes installed on the AL-31Fs were moved to the top of the engines, reducing the diameter of the engine nacelles.

Improvement in aerodynamics at high angles of attack was achieved by installing Krueger flaps on the wings and a modified arrangement of the vertical tails. Mainly, however, a redesign of the wing-fuselage area, the engine nacelles, and the complete tail section was viewed as vital if the design was to survive. As Simonov rejected production of the T-10 concept even though the state had already authorized it, he not surprisingly became the focus of considerable anger. However, he believed that Sukhoi had been given the contract to develop a fighter aircraft that could defeat all conceivable enemy aircraft.

Then Minister of the Aviation Industry, Vassily Kazakov, had a different view. It was his opinion that they should begin production and use the experience gained in operating the aircraft to allow improvements to flow continuously as production went on. Enormous sums had been spent preparing for series production, and stopping it all to begin many things over from the beginning was unthinkable to the minister. More than a few officials supported his views. Simonov replied to Ivan Silayev, the Deputy Minister of the Aviation Industry, that they could produce an average fighter aircraft, like the T-10 was at that moment, in quantity and deliver it to the air force. And it there were to be no hostilities, then no consequences would follow with respect to the defense of the country. But if a war should develop between the blocks, the T-10 concept would not be capable of making an important contribution in defending the Soviet Union against an air attack, according to Simonov. He received the necessary support from Ivan Silayev to radically redesign the T-10 so that the air defense would receive a more capable fighter.

Initial planning began in 1975–76, and by 1979, the process was well under way. The project, now dubbed the T-10S, exhibited the following changes: the leading edge of the wing no longer had a double curve, in other words the transition from the LERX to the leading edge of the wing was straight, as was the wing leading edge itself. The rounded wingtips also disappeared and the wings were capped vertically. The anti-flutter weight was replaced by a launch rail on the wingtip, increasing the number of missile launch rails from the original eight to ten. Whereas the original T-10 had separate ailerons and flaps, on the T-10S these were combined into a single component, so-called flaperons (flaps/ailerons). The leading edge of the wing was also changed and Krueger flaps were introduced. This improved lift at high angles of attack, as well as during takeoff and landing. Wing area was increased. To further reduce drag, the canopy profile was changed, and the transfer of the aircraft accessory gearboxes to the tops of the engines eliminated the bulges under the engine fairings, which also reduced drag. Some weight was also saved. The configuration of the engine air intakes remained largely unchanged, but a movable inner grille was installed. It covered the air intake during takeoff and landing and prevented foreign objects from entering. The undersides of the air intakes received variable doors. The internal tanks were changed and the tail "stinger" was enlarged to hold additional fuel, resulting in an internal fuel capacity of 20,723 pounds. The tail surfaces were also changed. The vertical tails were now installed on the outsides of the engine compartments, which resulted in improved technical access to the engines and the accessory gearboxes atop the power plants. The optimal position for the horizontal tail surfaces, however, was determined by the air flow produced by the leading edge root extensions at increasing angles of attack. This improved longitudinal stability and controllability at high angles of attack and in

sideslips. To combat possible wing stall, the horizontal tail surfaces were installed under the vertical tails (though not until during the course of testing). The horizontal tail roots now housed the hydraulic drives for the tailerons, which produced less drag than before. The undercarriage also underwent changes. The forward-opening undercarriage doors served as speed brakes on the T-10S, but this interfered with the airflow to the tailerons and caused shaking. This was addressed by making the undercarriage doors open parallel to the longitudinal axis. The main undercarriage legs now locked down at the lower edges of the air intakes. This allowed a simplified structure and reduced the space required when retracted, which again resulted in reduced drag. To avoid the danger of foreign objects thrown up by the nosewheel while taxiing being sucked into the air intakes, it was decided to move the nosewheel leg aft by several feet. This also resulted in improved maneuverability while taxiing. In addition, the nosewheel now retracted forward. The undercarriage was beefed up to accept the increased weight of the T-10S.

The Sukhoi OKB worked closely with the SibNIA, the Siberian Aviation Research Institute, which played a similar role to the TsAGI. Numerous investigations of the T-10S were carried out there. Flight trials would be required to determine if all of the design changes that had been made were the correct ones. The first prototype of the T-10S was completed in 1981, and on April 20, 1981, Vladimir Ilyushin took the aircraft up on its first test flight.

Despite this, prototypes of the original T-10 were built until 1982. When the decision was made not to pursue the T-10 concept and instead pursue the T-10S project, it was also clear that much time would have to pass before they could conduct thorough testing of the T-10S with all its elements, including weapons and avionics. Until then they used the prototypes of the T-10 series to test the aircraft systems. Difficulties were also encountered during testing of the T-10S. When the T-10-7 (first T-10S prototype) undertook a long-range flight in 1981, to determine its maximum range on internal fuel, it ran out of fuel and crashed! Vladimir Ilyushin was able to escape by ejecting, but he never flew again as a test pilot.

The T-10-12, the second prototype of the T-10S, also had a short life, crashing in 1981. Pilot Alexander Komarov (not to be confused with the cosmonaut Vladimir Komarov, who was killed in 1967, during testing of the first Soyuz capsule) was

Prototype T-10-17 with full missile armament. Apart from the horizontal tips of the vertical tails, the prototype is equivalent to the present-day Su-27. *JSC Sukhoi*

killed in the crash. Although no official cause was given, it was suspected that the flight data recorder, which was installed in the avionics bay in the LERX, separated during a test flight at maximum speed. It seems to have damaged important structural components, breaking up in midair.

There was another crash in 1983. Nikolai Sadovnikov was flying the T-10-17 at maximum speed, this time at low level. Parts of the wing broke away, damaging the vertical tail surfaces. Sadovnikov landed the aircraft safely, enabling the cause to be revealed. At about the same time, the same thing happened to the T-10-21, but it was lost. A calculation error was discovered and the area of the Krueger flaps was reduced. These components were probably exposed to excessive loads if extended during certain maneuvers.

During further testing, certain areas of the airframe and wing, as well as the vertical tails, were reinforced. The latter were changed in shape and size. The tail "stinger" was lengthened and increased in diameter, making room for additional fuel. Scale models were used to investigate behavior at high angles of attack and stall characteristics. Some of these were launched from the ground by rockets, while others were dropped from a Tu-16LL (former medium-range bomber, which was used as an engine testbed by the NII) from high altitude.

Development and testing of the weapons and avionics systems are described separately. Testing was officially concluded in 1985, and the overall results of the trials confirmed Simonov's decision not to produce the T-10 and instead take a chance on the radical conversion into the T-10S.

CHAPTER 2
Overview of Prototypes

T-10-1: First prototype, used to check flight characteristics, controllability, and the control system.

T-10-2: Crashed after a few flights due to an error in the fly-by-wire system (overloading the airframe, which subsequently broke up).

T-10-3: First prototype with AL-31F engines, used for engine trials, later tests at the NITKA complex for a carrier variant.

T-10-4: Second prototype with AL-31F power plants (the T-10-3 and T-10-4 were the only T-10 prototypes with AL-31F engines), radar testing.

T-10-5 to T-10-11 (excluding the -7 and -8): testing of internal systems for the future T-10S.

T-10-7: First prototype of the T-10S, ran out of fuel and crashed during a long-range test flight.

T-10-8: Used for static testing of the T-10S.

T-10-12: Second prototype of the T-10S, crashed because of airframe damage during high-speed flight.

T-10-14 to T-10-27: Numerous tests of the overall design and systems.

T-10-15: Converted for record-setting flights and renamed P-42.

T-10-20: Tests to determine maximum range, for which all unnecessary avionics and weapons systems were removed, resulting in an increased fuel load of 28,440 pounds.

T-10-24: First tests with canards.

T-10-25: Testing of a carrier variant, tests at the NIKTA complex.

In 1979, the west obtained its first images of the new aircraft from an American reconnaissance satellite. Initially designated RAM-K, the aircraft was photographed at the testing facility at Zhukovsky. The USA still thought that this was the town of Ramenskoye, which was close to Zhukovsky, resulting in the designation RAM- being assigned to other aircraft photographed there, as no other designation was known for the prototypes. The Su-27 was later given the NATO reporting name "Flanker."

P-42 record-setting aircraft. *JSC Sukhoi*

"P-42" Record-Setting Fighter

The Su-27 gained attention in 1986, even before it made its debut in the west. During the Cold War both sides had an interest in using new combat aircraft to set flight records to demonstrate its abilities to the other side. These record attempts were observed by the *Fédération Aéronautique Internationale* (FAI – world governing body for air sports) and then documented and confirmed.

Having concluded its flight trials for the T-10S project, the T-10-15 was employed as a record-setting aircraft and designated P-42. This number was chosen as a reference to the Battle of Stalingrad, which had marked a turning point in the Second World War. The P-42 was stripped down, which was not necessary for the record flights themselves. The weapons system with the radar and IRST were removed and the radome was replaced by a light metal cone. The Krueger flaps were fixed (the operating mechanisms being partly removed), the vertical tail caps and the radio antennas beneath them were removed, the tail "stinger" was shortened, eliminating the braking parachute, and the ventral fins were also removed. Also eliminated were the speed brake on the tail "stinger," all of the paint was stripped from the outer surface of the airframe, and the combined flaps/ailerons were replaced by a fixed structure. The cannon and ammunition box were removed, as were all the weapons rails and nosewheel mudguard. Fuel was limited to a quantity suitable for each record flight. The P-42's takeoff weight was just 31,085 pounds. As engine thrust had been increased from 28,100 to 30,575 pounds, the P-42 had a thrust-to-weight ratio of almost two to one. To optimize takeoff, a type

JSC Sukhoi

of catapult takeoff was planned. The P-42 was chained to a tank with steel cables, so that it could bring its engines to full afterburning power without moving. Without this measure the P-42 would have slid, for with its reduced weight and more powerful engines, the brakes simply would not have been able to keep the aircraft in place. The tank had a deflector shield that deflected the engine exhaust gases. When the engines had reached full power, the steel cables were released electrically from the P-42's cockpit and the aircraft could accelerate fully.

The P-42 set twenty-seven world records in a variety of categories, mainly in the time to climb field. In 1993, Viktor Pugachev reached a ceiling of 73,819 feet carrying a 2,200-pound payload. The engineer responsible for the P-42 was Rollam Martirozov, while the record-setting pilots—Viktor Pugachev, Nikolai Sadovnikov, Evgeni Frolov, and Oleg Tsoi—all came from Sukhoi.

Chapter 2: Overview of Prototypes

Su-27P of the Russian Air Force. The vertical tails still have the green dielectric panels for the radio systems, typical for the Su-27 in Soviet times. The radome is white. *Dimitri Yuriev*

Another Su-27P in an unusual blue camouflage scheme. The main undercarriage locking fixture can be seen on the engine air intake. *Dimitri Yuriev*

In Russian Skies

The Su-27 entered quantity production in 1982, and in 1985, the first units began receiving the aircraft. The Soviet air force with its fighter-bombers and fighters consisted of the air forces (VVS) and the air defense forces (PVO). Whereas in the past a certain aircraft type was introduced into service in one of the two forces, from the beginning the Su-27 was to serve with both. The Soviet air defense force included the air defense radars, the missile troops (air defense), the actual fighter units, and the anti-ballistic missile defense units. The air forces were made up of the bomber, transport, frontal, reconnaissance, and close-support units. Originally, the Su-27S (unofficial designation) was the only version to enter service, and in addition to its primary role as an interceptor and patrol fighter this type also had a limited ground attack capability. The aircraft was incapable, however, of employing guided air-to-surface weapons, only free-fall bombs, cluster

bombs, and unguided rockets of various calibers. Units with the Su-27S did not train in ground attacks at their home bases, instead this was carried out at the training and conversion center at Lipetsk, where the Su-27 conversion training unit was based. It was one of the first to receive the Su-27, so that it could commence training pilots to fly the new fighter.

The PVO had a similar center at Savasleyka. When the first machines reached the units, the ground personnel in particular were overwhelmed by the size of the fighter, for they had always dealt with smaller aircraft (with the exception of the equally large MiG-25). Now they could not reach internal components without a ladder or something similar. More serious, however, was the fact that the Su-27 could not fit into the aircraft shelters built for its predecessors (Su-15, MiG-23), and initially the Su-27s had to be parked in the

Flight line at Kilp Yavr in the Murmansk Region on the Kola Peninsula. *Andrey Zinchuk*

open. Working on aircraft out of doors in subzero temperatures was of course a serious burden for the ground personnel, especially in the far north. Suitable structures providing protection for the Su-27 were later built. While the initial impression on the ground personnel was somewhat negative, the aircraft's pilots were highly enthusiastic. There was the aircraft's tremendous thrust-to-weight ratio, its great fuel capacity with resulting long range, a capable weapons system with heavy missile armament, and especially its agility, unlike that of any aircraft they had flown before. One could say that at last the pilots had an aircraft that combined everything that one could expect of a fighter aircraft. The Su-27P (also an unofficial designation) began appearing in 1987. It was designed solely for air combat with no provision for ground attacks. Negotiations to limit conventional weapons may have contributed to this, for an aircraft with ground attack capability fell into the category of an offensive weapon, the subject of these negotiations.

The Su-27 was needed, particularly in the high north and the Far East. The USSR had large and strategically-important naval bases in both regions (Murmansk, Arkhangelsk, and the Kola Peninsula in the high north; Vladivostok and Petropavlovsk-Kamchatka in the Far East) which also housed submarines armed with intercontinental missiles. These locations were favored objects for Western spies and in the event of an attack would be prime targets; but because of climactic conditions good infrastructure was lacking. Far from their bases, in the event of an armed confrontation the new combat aircraft would have to get by on their own. The

A Su-27P of the unit from Khotilovo (between Moscow and St. Petersburg) taxiing away from the last-chance position. *Andrey Zinchuk*

dated Su-15, MiG-23, and MiG-25 were not capable of successfully fighting a future war, but the Su-27 and MiG-31 absolutely were. These aircraft had long-range radars and weaponry and could cover a significantly greater area of airspace than their predecessors. They were also capable of escorting bombers.

The first units equipped with the Su-27 were therefore assigned to bases in the high north and the Far East. Later they also appeared in the western and southern areas of the Soviet Union. In addition to the threat of American bombers attacking from over the Arctic, the US Navy also had significant fleet units present in the far north, the Pacific, the Mediterranean, and in the Persian Gulf. Carrier battle groups in particular caused the Soviets serious headaches, for their

Removing snow from a Su-27P at Kilp-Yavr. *Andrey Zinchuk*

carrier-based aircraft were capable of striking deep into enemy territory. In addition to naval units, the US Air Force had bases in Norway and Great Britain, which could also launch attacks from a northerly direction. The Su-27 therefore also had to be made available in these areas. The introduction of the Su-27 into service with units of the PVO is noteworthy because in some cases the type even replaced the elderly Su-9 (but in most cases the Su-15, MiG-23, and Tu-128). In unit service the Su-27 increasingly began encountering Western spy flights close to even these sensitive sites.

The first incident made public occurred over the Barents Sea in 1987. The Soviet Navy was conducting an exercise in neutral waters of the Barents Sea. It was shadowed by a Norwegian Air Force P-3, also flying in neutral airspace. The Orion approached a Su-27 of the 941st Fighter Regiment from Kilp-Yavr, to force it out of its patrol area and continue shadowing the Soviet naval unit. During various maneuvers the Sukhoi flew beneath the Orion. The P-3's pilot abruptly reduced power, reckoning that the Su-27 would be too fast to stay with the Orion. The pilot of the Su-27, Capt. Vasily Tzimbal, did the same, whereupon the Orion pilot lost sight of

The shark mouth marking on the air intake suggests that this is an aircraft from the Lipetsk testing center, photographed while visiting Kilp-Yavr.

the Soviet aircraft and did not bargain on the Su-27's low-speed capabilities. As a result the two aircraft came into contact. One of the Orion's propellers struck the Su-27, damaging the tip of one of its vertical tails. Pieces of the propeller pierced the P-3's cabin, resulting in a loss of pressurization. The Norwegian aircraft turned away and reached its base, as did the Su-27. What followed for Vasily Tzimbal was unavoidable. He had caused an international incident and was promptly ejected from the party. Soon afterward he was readmitted and not long after that he even received a decoration, the Order of the Red Star. Nevertheless, he was transferred. Rumors circulated in the Western press, including one that Vasily Tzimbal had been accused of lack of discipline with respect to his maneuvers. However, it is absurd to believe that Tzimbal tried to drive off the Orion without instructions from a ground controller. These would have been his orders, and he succeeded. Damaging the Orion and the resulting letter of protest from Norway were certainly not desired by the Soviet Air Force, but it did show NATO that it had to take the Soviets seriously. There is always a latent risk in mutual probes and intercepts, and in some cases such actions are consciously provoked. The PVO found itself constantly confronted by spy flights on its northern and eastern borders, especially by American SR-71s, RC-135s, and P-3s (the latter flown by the Norwegian Air Force). In addition to naval bases, there was another reason to base potent long-range fighters in the far north: even though the

US Air Force had bomber bases distributed around the former Soviet Union (for example in Great Britain and Japan), the bulk of the American bomber fleet was still in the USA. The shortest route to attack the USSR with this fleet was the one over the Arctic.

In the 1980s, the Soviet Union expanded its military presence in the north, which was reflected in the stationing of large numbers of Su-27s there. NATO flew special aircraft along the Soviet territorial boundary to ascertain Soviet reaction times and intercept procedures and monitor radio traffic. To keep track of everything the Soviet Air Force was initiating, these NATO aircraft flew so close to the territorial boundary that the Soviets had to anticipate a penetration of their airspace. Interceptors took off to intercept these suspected intruders. The NATO aircraft recorded Soviet radio traffic for evaluation. The timing of the intercept was determined as was the behavior of the interceptors and air defense missile units.

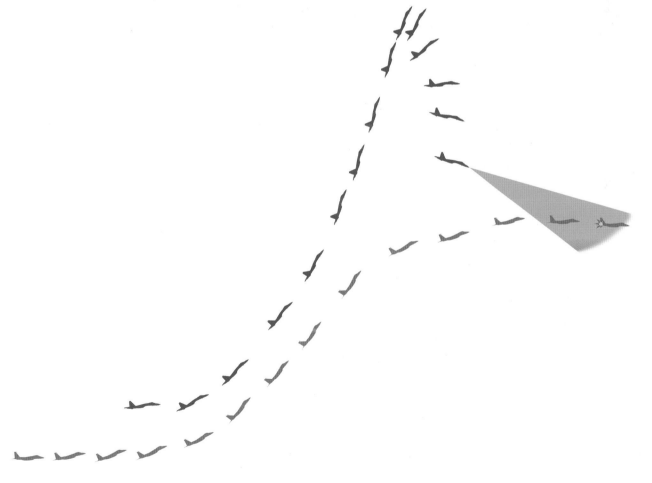

The Bell Maneuver, also called the Tailslide. *Frank Krüger*

The Cobra maneuver. *Frank Krüger*

It was not until 1989, however, that the west got to see the Su-27's true capabilities. The previous year the MiG-29 had caused a sensation at the Farnborough airshow in Britain when it demonstrated the famous "Tailslide" maneuver. The MiG-29 climbed vertically, reducing thrust until the aircraft stood motionless on its tail for a few seconds, neither gaining nor losing altitude.

In 1989, the Su-27 went one better when it performed at the Paris Airshow at Le Bourget. Viktor Pugachev, then a test pilot with the Sukhoi OKB, gave the first public demonstration of the "Cobra" maneuver. This maneuver saw the Su-27 reach an angle of attack of up to ninety degrees or more while in horizontal flight, without the aircraft becoming uncontrollable. The engines also continued to operate stably, thanks to their excellent flow characteristics and the automatic injection of oxygen under certain critical flow conditions. If one excludes aircraft with thrust vectoring, the maneuver was carried out for the first time and then regularly by only the MiG-29 and Su-27. The MiG-29 did not perform the Cobra until after the Su-27, however. The MiG was famous for its tailslide maneuver. The evolution of the Cobra began in 1987, when intensive investigations were carried out into the Su-27's behavior in a flat spin and at high angles of attack. Pilot Igor Volk played a decisive role. He spent time on space station Salut 7 as a research scientist and later worked as a test pilot at the LII. For a time he was one of a select group of cosmonauts chosen for a manned space flight in the Soviet Buran space glider, but the spacecraft never made a manned flight. During various trials to learn how to avoid a flat spin or get out of this dangerous condition, it was discovered that one could fly the Su-27 at angles of attack of up to 110 degrees without losing control of the aircraft. Igor Volk was the first to fly the "Cobra" maneuver.

Viktor Pugachev became world-famous when he performed the maneuver publicly for the first time at the Paris Airshow in 1989.

Opinions among the experts were divided as to whether the Tailslide and the Cobra maneuvers could actually be used in air combat or are just impressive demonstrations at airshows. But to a pilot, every new maneuvering ability by his aircraft that allowed it to move in the air in an unfamiliar way also created new tactical possibilities for initiating or avoiding an attack. Of course these maneuvers are now known around the world, and experienced pilots can anticipate them based on certain preliminary indicators. In the heat of aerial combat, however, a pilot must be able to deal with and react to anything, and the element of surprise could be on the side of the pilot who initiates a Tailslide or Cobra maneuver.

The Su-27's enormous range soon revealed a shortcoming. Lengthy, difficult missions took the single pilot to the limits of his physical and mental abilities. Recognition of this problem resulted in the two-seat MiG-31, which was developed from the single-seat MiG-25. The designers took the existing Su-27UB and from it created the Su-30. The two-man crew had the decisive advantage that the pilot could concentrate more on flying the aircraft, while the weapon systems officer in the rear cockpit could operate the weapons systems and monitor the radar. A retractable air refueling probe was fitted. It was installed on the left side in front of the cockpit, and the IRST/LR, previously in the center, was moved to the right side. The Su-30 was assigned the role of flying command post for a group of several Su-27P fighters. A display screen was installed in the rear cockpit for the fighter control officer and it was used to monitor the group's airspace and coordinate actions. The aircraft's radio equipment was changed for better communication with the ground and the

Not a Su-27UB, but one of the few Su-30s (identifiable by the refueling probe forward of the cockpit on the port side of the fuselage). The aircraft belongs to the Falcons display team from the testing center in Lipetsk. *Sergey Chaikovski*

group's aircraft in the air. The ground radio guidance system was also optimized for the new task. The Su-30 was regarded as a sort of "mini AWACS." The fly-by-wire system was also reworked. Series production was set to begin in 1991, but the collapse of the Soviet Union with all its catastrophic social and economic consequences prevented this. A few machines went to testing units, but regular use by air force units was out of the question.

Several years later the Su-30 was developed into the Su-30K/MK/MKI. At the end of the 1980s, the Su-27 was stationed at about sixteen bases, including about 140 Su-27S fighters of the frontal air forces and about 230 of the PVO in the European part of the USSR. In total the Soviet forces had between 500 and 700 Su-27s on strength. Of this number, about seventy aircraft were based in Poland as part of the 4th Air Army (part of the northern group of Soviet forces, while the MiG-29s in the German Democratic Republic were part of the 16th Air Army, part of the Western group of forces). These included the 159th Fighter Regiment based at Kluczewo (near Stargard, about twenty-five miles from the border of the GDR), and the 582nd Fighter Regiment at Chodziez (the two bases were about thirty miles apart by air). In 1992, all Su-27s were withdrawn from Poland. Interestingly, the Su-27s in Poland were the only ones based outside the Soviet Union, whereas a total of about 360 MiG-29s were based in the GDR, CSSR, and Hungary. The Su-27s were probably earmarked to provide fighter escort for the Soviet Su-24 units in Poland and East Germany in the event of war.

The presence of Su-27s in Poland and the ground forces based in East Germany, the strongest Soviet troop concentrations outside the USSR, was probably related to the fact that the Red Army regarded the NATO units of West Germany, France, and Great Britain as the most powerful in Europe. It is estimated that about 600 Su-27s and 140 Su-27UBs were built in the USSR.

During its brief service life in the days of the USSR, the Su-27 earned an excellent reputation in the units that flew it, and there were no accidents involving the type due to design or production mistakes. The collapse of the Soviet Union changed everything, however. When this happened in 1991, large land masses left the Soviet Union and formed independent states, including the Ukraine, White Russia, and Uzbekistan. There were approximately 120 Su-27s within the borders of these three former Soviet republics. As per agreements between Russia (regarded as the legal successor to the Soviet Union) and the new states (which included former Soviet republics that had no Su-27s), the aircraft were transferred to the Ukraine, White Russia, and Uzbekistan, while about 400 to 500 remained with the Russian Air Force. In addition to aircraft, the new Russia lost about half of the Soviet Union's former airfields, and the remaining aircraft had to be assigned to new bases. This in turn led to increased activity at the affected bases. However, the economic collapse that followed prevented intensive flight operations, not just for the Su-27 units, but for all of them. The country could not afford large quantities of jet fuel for the armed forces. The necessary annual flying hours for pilots fell to a fraction of what they had been, while the accident rate rose. Experienced pilots were able to draw on their experience, but more than a few of Russia's young, inexperienced pilots met tragic ends.

Su-27P of the 4th Air Army at Stargard in Poland.
Rob Schleiffert

Clearly visible here are the weapons hardpoints on and between the engine air intakes. *Sergey Chaikovski*

Another well-known incident took place in 1996, once again involving an aircraft of the 941st Fighter Regiment, and Norwegian F-16s. Russian combat aircraft were carrying out a cannon shoot in international waters near the Russian border. An Su-27P flown by Maj. Yevgeni Olejnik had the task of sealing off the area of the cannon shoot for safety reasons, to prevent any Russian or foreign aircraft from being shot down in error. Two Norwegian F-16s approached the Su-27P and carried out aggressive maneuvers to within 150 feet of the Sukhoi. This maneuver led to a regular dogfight, of course without a shot being fired. Soon afterward the F-16s broke off and flew away. The danger of such provocative actions was clear: there was no certainty that the mutual mock combat would not develop into a real combat situation. This can happen quickly if one side misinterprets a move by the other. As well, the danger of a midair collision is always present.

The poor operational conditions in the Russian armed forces did not improve until Vladimir Putin took power in 2000. Renunciation of the selling out of the country and appreciation of what the nation was capable of led to military reforms that resulted in improvements in operational readiness. Of course these included a reduction in personnel strengths and reorganization. One of the most significant was the merging of the former frontal aviation and the air defense units. Despite all the difficulties of the 1990s, exercises were held that represented uncharted territory for Russian fighter pilots.

In 1998, a unit comprising four MiG-31s, four Su-30s, and an A-50 (early warning aircraft based on the Il-76) carried out a ten-hour continuous exercise. Its purpose was to test teamwork between different fighter types during very long missions. The MiG-31s with their long-range radar flew in a line about thirty-five miles in front of the Su-30s to detect potential targets, after which the Su-30s would step in to engage if the MiG-31s were unsuccessful. Live air firing exercises were held in northern and southern Russia, with the fighters refueled in the air three times and the A-50 acting as air surveillance aircraft. Flight distances per aircraft averaged 5,300 miles. This demonstrated the ability of the MiG-31 and Su-30 to carry out long-endurance missions. It is difficult to imagine what the pilots had to endure on their hard ejection seats during those ten hours. Greater emphasis was placed on comfort in the designing of the new K-36-3.5, precisely to ease the physical discomfort of the pilots during such long missions.

Nevertheless, procurement of modern military technology, including the latest designs from the Sukhoi stable, was not feasible, at least not in large numbers. Consequently just a handful (in the truest sense of the word) of Su-35s (T-10M) reached the air force, and these were extensively tested at the air force test center. The original Su-27P and S fighters remained in service with the operational units.

Modernization Programs

While Sukhoi was prepared to provide the air force with modern versions of the Su-27, the state lacked the money to buy these aircraft. Shortly after the turn of the millennium, both the Russian and foreign air forces operated large numbers of Su-27S and Su-27SK aircraft. These machines represented the technical standard of the 1980s, and were in urgent need of modernization. Sukhoi saw a large market for this, especially as the remaining airframe times would provide suitably long operational lives. After Vladimir Putin came to power, Russia began a slow-paced modernization of its armed forces. In 1999–2000, Sukhoi produced the Su-30MKK and Su-30MK2, modernized and multi-role versions of the Su-30, and it planned a similar modernization of the single-seater. The domestic version was the Su-27SM and the export version the Su-27SKM.

In 2002, Yevgeni Frolov flew the converted single-seater, which had been a regular service aircraft, for the first time. In 2003, it was joined by a second prototype, which was fitted with an air refueling probe. Even before testing had been completed, the Russian Air Force selected this modification for the necessary modernization of its own Su-27s.

Prototype of the Su-27SM/SKM project, armed with R-27, Kh-31, R-77, and R-73 missiles. *United Aircraft Corporation*

Glass cockpit of the Su-27SM/SKM. *United Aircraft Corporation*

Su-27SM3 with S-25 rockets under the wings during live firing in Astrakhan. *Andrey Zinchuk*

The first machines arrived at Lipetsk, where training of pilots and technical personnel took place, at the end of 2003. The first of the twenty-four Su-27SM aircraft contracted were delivered to the air force base at Dzemgi. Most of the aircraft modernized were drawn from operational units and reequipped during overhaul. The single-seater differed from the Su-30MK2 in the arrangement and number of cockpit display screens. The Su-27SM had two large color displays and a third slender LCD indicator between the two display screens. Despite the display screens, the cockpit still retained a number of analogue instruments. A video recording system to record the HUD and display screens was installed to

Chapter 3: In Service

The Su-27SM/SM3 differed outwardly from the original Su-27 in that the IRST was moved from the center of the nose in front of the cockpit to the right, and the radar-warning receivers on the sides of the engine air intakes were deleted. The latter were incorporated into the leading edges of the wings. The Su-27SM had just one antenna on the fuselage spine aft of the canopy, while the Su-27SM3 had two. *Sergey Chaikovski*

evaluate training and combat missions. The SM was capable of carrying the same weaponry as the Su-30MK2. The weapons stations were left at ten launch rails.

Delivery of a further twenty-four Su-27SM3 fighters was negotiated in 2009, and the fifty updated aircraft were based at Dzemgi, Vladivostok, and in the Krasnodar area. The weapons system of the Su-27SM3 was updated to allow the aircraft to use satellite-guided bombs. The aircraft was powered by the more powerful AL-31F-M1, the airframe was beefed up and more weapons could be carried on a total of twelve hardpoints (instead of the previous ten). Maximum takeoff weight rose by 6,615 pounds (increased weapons load plus airframe strengthening). As well, the old K-36DM ejection seat was replaced by the new K-36D-3.5. For reasons that are not known, the IRST was moved from the center of the windscreen to the right, even though no refueling probe was fitted on the left. Tests were carried out successfully for integration of the new RVV-SD medium range air-to-air missile with the Su-27SM3, and adoption of the new AAM will take place in the near future. The Su-27SM3 was equipped with a complete glass cockpit with a total of four display screens.

There is no reliable information about the precise avionics suite. Elements of the Su-35S are said to have been installed, but exactly which ones remains unclear. If one examines the radome, one notices that its shape is unchanged from that of the older Su-27 and the pitot tube remains at the tip of the radome. This clue makes it seem rather unlikely that either the Bars (Panther) or Irbis radar is fitted. The radar warning system was changed and appears to be similar to that of the Su-30MK versions. This is recognizable by the deletion of the receivers on the outer forward engine air intakes, which now appear in another form on the leading edges of the wing. Some Su-27SM3s are located in White Russia, to defend the airspace of that nation and neighboring Russia. This is the result of an official request from White Russian president Lukachenko. NATO aircraft have long been operating from Poland and the Baltic States, and White Russia had placed its Su-27 fleet in storage, probably for economic reasons.

In addition to the modernization of single-seaters, Russia's two-seat Su-27s were also made into multipurpose aircraft. This happened in the Su-30M2 version, which is essentially a Su-30MK2 adapted to meet the requirements of the Russian Air Force. This type goes directly back to the Su-30KN. This was a modernization offer from Irkut, to make the two-seat Su-27 into a multi-role combat aircraft. The aircraft's radar and software were adapted to allow the use of guided air-to-surface weapons like the Kh-29. In the cockpit the single-color display was replaced by a multi-color display screen. Work began in 1999, and the aircraft, which was converted from a Su-27UB, was given the designation Su-30KN. Trials were successful, but the type did not enter service. As always in those days, the acute lack of funds for the Russian military was the reason why this did not happen.

Su-30M2 finished in a special paint scheme in honor of the founder Pavel Sukhoi. *JSC Sukhoi-KnAAZ*

A Su-34 from the first production batch, recognizable by the absence of air slots on the tail stinger for the APU.
Vladislav Perminov

The Su-34's tremendously enlarged tail stinger is particularly obvious from this angle. Sorbtsiya jamming pods are installed on the wingtips. *Sergey Chaikovski*

The brand-new Su-35S in a scheme reminiscent of the old Su-27. One of several missile warning sensors is visible on the left side of the nose in front of the IRST. The first production batch was finished with dark-gray upper surfaces. *Gilles Dennis*

When, a few years later, the air force received the Su-27SM, though not in large numbers, it seemed that there was another reason: the Russian Air Force seemed to be continuing to acquire single-seat fighters, like the Su-27SM, the Su-35S, and the T-50. Only the Su-34, a special fighter-bombers aircraft, was designed as a two-seater from the outset. Western states also pursued this philosophy of using primarily single-seat fighters, such as the Eurofighter, Rafale, F-35, F-22, and the Saab JAS 39 *Gripen* (even though there are two-seat versions of several). All are multi-role aircraft but primarily optimized for air combat. This is why a two-seat crew is required for the majority of ground-attack missions. The pilot is much more involved in the piloting aspect at low level than at high altitudes. A second crew member is required to operate the weapons systems in order to use the aircraft's weaponry most effectively. As the majority of the Su-27s acquired by the Russian Air Force were single-seaters, it seemed logical to modernize these in order to have the

largest number of updated aircraft. This is probably why, initially, the decision was made to modernize the Su-27SM instead of the Su-30KN. The idea of bringing the existing two-seaters up to the standard of the Su-27SM had ironically already been achieved with the Su-30MKK and Su-30MK2. And so elements of the Su-27SM were also integrated into the two-seaters and deliveries of the updated aircraft to the Russian Air Force began in 2009. Because of the small number, twenty-four aircraft, these aircraft were used less by regular combat units and more for training purposes.

Not until 2011, did the delivery of a larger variety of different types begin, such as up to 120 examples of the Su-34, forty to seventy Su-30SMs for the air force, and fifty for the navy (but no carrier aircraft), forty-eight Su-35Ss, and initially fourteen Su-30Ms. Russia's air force was equipped with the most modern versions to make up for a hiatus of about twenty years. The Su-30SM and the Su-35S alone represented an important step in the modernization of

Russia's air force, for in terms of avionics the Su-27S and P probably do not pose a serious threat to any Western combat aircraft. There is always a perceptible undertone in the Western media describing Russia's modernization as a threat. If one examines these acquisitions more closely, however, especially what they are supposed to replace, it becomes apparent that they are replacing technology from the late 1970s and early 1980s! Western militaries completed their comparable acquisition programs much sooner (the Rafale by France, the Eurofighter and *Gripen* by several European air forces, the F-16 Block 50-70, the F/A-18 Super Hornet, and the F-15 Silent Eagle, plus the F-22 and F-35 by the USA).

Russia had merely caught up and certainly gained a lead in some areas and thus at least achieved parity with the majority of Western air forces. But it was not just technology that was updated, but personnel as well. During the Yeltsin era, poor pay and in some cases poor living conditions in remote parts of the nation meant that there was little incentive for young men to sign up for lengthy commitments to serve in the military. As a result of this, Russia's combat pilots were older on average than their Western counterparts. Some of the air force's technical personnel also left the service, resulting in lower serviceability levels of the necessary combat aircraft.

The stationing of Su-35S fighters at the air base at Dzemgi was done primarily to keep the lines of communication between the manufacturer and the units short, as problems arise during the introduction of new aircraft which must be addressed immediately. Distances in Russia can reach intercontinental levels, therefore the first Su-35S fighters were placed in a location near the manufacturer. With the Su-35S, the Su-30SM is the most modern fighter in the Russian Air Force. The Russian government ordered sixty aircraft in the first two contracts, while another order for the delivery of sixty aircraft followed in 2016. The Su-30SM will gradually replace the MiG-29 and Su-27, more of which are nearing the end of their service lives and represent versions introduced in the 1980s. The navy will also acquire up to sixty aircraft, possibly the Su-24. The Su-30SM is a derivative of the Su-30MKI and is a version desired by the Russian Air Force.

Most of the Western avionics installed in the Su-30MKI were replaced with domestic equipment. Only the French wide-angle HUD and navigation system remain, but these are gradually being replaced by Russian components already

Su-35S fighters, again with a blue-gray camouflage scheme, seen here at Lipetsk. *Sergey Chaikovski*

installed in the Su-35S. Once again the radar is the important, decisive system. It is a much-modified Bars used in the MKI and is designated N-011R Bars-R. The new radar has an air-to-air detection range of 223 miles, compared to eighty-seven miles for the original Bars, plus 155 miles in pursuit mode (here too with the standard radar reflection area of 32.3 square feet). If one believes the generally available sources, these values surpass even those of the APG-70/-63(V)3/80/-77/-81 (F/A-18 Super Hornet/F-15/F-16, E/F-22/F-35) and the RBE2 of the Rafale and the Captor-E of the Eurofighter. One reason may be the Bars-R's larger antenna diameter of 3.3 feet, which results in higher transmitter performance. Furthermore, the conversion to an active antenna may have been achieved and this has been offered to India for the modernization of its Su-30MKIs. The radar is capable of tracking up to twenty-five aerial targets and engaging twelve simultaneously. The horizontal scanning angle is +/- 90 degrees, plus +/- 55 degrees in elevation. New weaponry includes the RVV-MD and RVV-SD air-to-air missiles (range of sixty-eight miles), the successors to the R-73 and R-77. The optical seeker present since the beginning has also undergone a fundamental modernization and the current version is the OLS-30SM. Its range is roughly similar to that of the OLS-30I. A closer examination of the Su-30SM, however, reveals the absence of any heat sensors to warn of missile attacks or laser illumination. It is unclear if these are to be fitted later or will only be fitted to the Su-35S for cost reasons, in any case such a system would always make sense. The active jamming system has been modernized and is now housed in containers on the wingtips. Externally, however, the Su-30SM is identical to the MKI.

Su-35S in the initial dark-gray paint scheme. Outwardly it is identical to the Su-30MKI. *Gilles Dennis*

The first aircraft were sent to Aktyubinsk for service trials in late 2012, the type having just made its first flight in September. In the following year the first service aircraft were again sent to Lipetsk, where the training of pilots and ground personnel takes place. Every new aircraft type is sent there to determine the best operational scenarios and optimal flight parameters for the type and develop the necessary flight maneuvers. The first operational unit was the wing at Domna, which is located in the Eastern Military District and is near the Chinese border.

It was aircraft of this wing that flew escort for Russian Air Force aircraft operating in Syria. The Su-30SM was also sent to the unit at Dzemgi, where the Su-35S was already based. The first naval unit to receive the type was the wing at Saki in the Crimea, due to tensions with the Ukraine. Kazakhstan was the first export customer for the Su-30SM and has so far

This image gives some idea of the size of the Su-30SM. Its camouflage scheme was also changed to blue-gray.
Plav C. de With

This Su-34 is stationed at Hmeimim Air Base in Syria and has mission markers on the fuselage nose. *Russian Defense Ministry/Vadim Savitsky*

Together with the Su-24 and Su-25, the Su-34 is the main aircraft in the Russian effort to support Syrian government forces against the so-called Islamic State. *Russian Defense Ministry/Vadim Savitsky*

Chapter 3: In Service

The Russian Su-30SM also provides air cover for Tu-22M3 and Tu-160 long-range bombers. The aircraft's nationality markings have intentionally been overpainted. *Russian Defense Ministry/Vadim Savitsky*

ordered ten aircraft with plans to order another fourteen. The first aircraft were delivered in 2015. White Russia and Iran have also shown interest in the aircraft. The latter wants to produce the aircraft under license like India, as the supply of spares for the MiG-29 and Su-24 has been less than satisfactory in the past. Such a program would also give the nation's industry a technological boost.

Following the Soviet war in Afghanistan from 1979 to 1989, since 2014, Russian combat aircraft have been massively involved abroad, namely in Syria. Syrian president Bashar Hafez al-Assad asked Russia for support in fighting the forces of the Islamic State, and Syrian government troops received air support for their ground operations against ISIS forces. Su-34 fighter-bombers attacked ground targets, while the Su-30SM provided fighter cover. Since the shooting down of two Su-24s by Turkey, Su-35S fighters have been dispatched to Syria to supplement the Su-30SM and Su-27SM3 aircraft in defending the fighter-bombers. Tu-22M3 and Tu-160 bombers have also been used, taking off from bases in Russia and landing there again after completing their missions, with a fighter escort of Su-30SMs.

At the beginning of October 2015, Israeli F-15s repeatedly entered Syrian airspace contrary to international law. Six Russian Su-30SM fighters scrambled from their base at Hmeimim in Syria and quickly forced the F-15s to depart Syrian airspace. The Israelis submitted a letter of protest, and the Russians responded by asking how the Israelis could explain the presence of their combat aircraft over Syrian territory. Attacks by the Russian Air Force against ISIS first

enabled Syrian government troops to make progress against ISIS on the ground and retake territory previously lost. Such a mission is of course also a welcome opportunity to test new aircraft, weapons, and tactics.

Nevertheless, this operational use of the Russian military cannot be seen from a purely technical aspect, for it is also of geopolitical importance. Even if Syria is not a direct neighbor of Russia, it is important for Russia that ISIS not gain a foothold in Syria, as its spilling over to Iran (via Iraq) and into the Caucasus Region would have fatal consequences, for this region has only just reached a relative state of calm. Iran sometimes permits the use of its airfields, Su-34 fighter-bombers at least having flown missions from there. Interestingly, both the Su-30SM and the Su-35S wear a camouflage scheme of dark grey upper surfaces and pale grey undersurfaces which is reminiscent of the one worn by the original Su-27s based in the USSR (while the Su-34, Su-35S, and Su-30SM wore the latter finish when introduced to service, this has now apparently given way to a more conventional scheme).

Anatoli Kvochur

Su-27PD of the Gromov/LII Flight Research Institute.

The Test Pilot Team

The shining hour of the LII's Test Pilot Aerobatic Group began in 1992. It was founded by no less than Anatoly Kvochur, who was an outstanding test pilot, even far outside the borders of Russia. He was known from the 1989 Aerosalon in Paris, where he crashed a MiG-29 (he was then a Mikoyan test pilot) during a low-altitude display and escaped unhurt by ejecting. Co-founder of the test pilots group was Vladimir Loginovsky. The test pilots group flew the Su-27P and Su-30. They practiced advanced aerobatic maneuvers and gave displays at a variety of events. But research and development work formed and forms a large part of the test pilots' program. Much effort was devoted to improving ergonomics in the cockpit. The group around Kvochur played a major part in the development of Russian liquid crystal displays, although of course they did not design them themselves. However, the experience and recommendations of the test pilots flowed into the operation of the displays, the menu, the contents, the arrangement in the cockpit, and other aspects. The group is still involved in aviation medicine problems, with aspects of

"super maneuverability" and in the past with air refueling and long-range flights.

For example, nonstop flights were made from Moscow to the North Pole and back with several air refuelings. A special satellite navigation system was developed to allow the tanker aircraft and those requiring fuel to find each other in the high latitudes. Several such flights were made, lasting ten to twelve hours depending on the route. These flights were made by a Su-27PD (Bort number 598), as it had a refueling probe; and as it was a single-seater, Kvochur flew alone the entire time. In 2006, a Su-30 (number 597 of the LII) made a similar flight, which was no less unusual. Once again the pilot was Anatoli Kvochur, with Sergey Korostiyev as copilot.

The purpose of the flight was to verify the experience gained in the flights over the North Pole in 1999, and if necessary improve on it. The aircraft took off from Zhukovsky and flew east over northern Russia. An Il-78 took off from Vorkuta to refuel the Su-30 several times, before finally reversing course near Sakhalin. The return flight was made

Cockpit of the Su-27 LI24-05 of the LII with sidestick
controller and multifunction display.

over the southern part of Russia. Over Tomsk the Sukhoi rendezvoused with an Il-78 from Ryazan, and the Il-78 from Vorkuta landed near Irkutsk. The flight lasted fifteen hours and covered 7,700 miles. The satellite-based navigation and communications systems performed well. The ability of the tanker and receiver to organize and carry out the rendezvous without ground support was tested during the flight. The Su-30 was shown the position of the tanker at distances of up to 480 miles. Once again the Su-30 was fully equipped with color display screens. The experience gained during this flight flowed into subsequent combat aircraft development, and existing aircraft were retrofitted with the equipment.

As previously mentioned, another aspect of the group's activities was determining the optimal cockpit ergonomics for the Su-27 and its variants. One Su-27 was fitted with a side stick controller, which was positioned on the right console. The side stick did not have the range of movement of a regular stick, as there simply was not room in the side console. As well, the range of movement of the pilot's control arm was severely restricted during aggressive maneuvers. If the pilot now wanted to increase the deflection of a control surface, the pilot simply had to push the side stick more forcefully in the desired direction. The aircraft's designation was LMK-2405, and when translated into English the LMK means Flight Simulation Complex. The machine was a

modified production aircraft operated by the LII. The aircraft was capable of transmitting flight directly to the ground station, while at the same time measurements and assessments could be made from the ground. An interesting detail is a prism cube mounted on each wingtip missile rail. These cubes serve as radar reflectors and create a more precise radar picture of the aircraft and make it possible to determine the aircraft's exact position in the air by way of receivers on the ground.

Lessons learned with the side stick flowed into the construction of the eleventh prototype of the T-10M project (designation Su-35; not to be confused with the latest version, the Su-35S), which was later given the designation Su-37. The sidestick controller was first used by the F-16. This concept appears to have proved itself and has been adopted by the Rafale, F-22, and F-35. Not all modern fighters have adopted the sidestick controller, however, not the Eurofighter, the *Gripen*, F-18 Super Hornet, F-15 Silent Eagle, MiG-35, or the Sukhoi T-50. The new Su-35S has a conventionally-mounted control stick. Another research and development field in the LII concerns thrust vectoring (see chapter on engines). The LII aircraft with the Bort number 598 was equipped with two AL-31F-M1 engines, and the thrust nozzles have resulted in bulges. These suggest that 598's AL-31F-M1 engines have been modified. The 117S by

The same aircraft as the one in the previous photo, here with radar prisms on the wingtip launch rails.

The banner of the formerly Soviet, now Russian Air Force is painted on the aircraft's vertical tail. *Olav C. de With*

The newest member of the Warriors is the Su-30SM. *Russian Defense Ministry/Vadim Savitsky*

Saturn is installed in the actual model of engine installed in the Su-35S and T-50, and the entire nozzle module pivots.

The Russian Warriors Aerobatic Squadron

The Russian Warriors is an aerobatic team that gives aerobatic displays at a variety of functions. They are based at Kubinka at the 237th Testing and Demonstration Center near Moscow. The unit's history goes back to the 1940s. Combat missions in defense of Moscow were flown from Kubinka in 1941. After the Second World War the 9th Fighter Division were stationed there, and some of that unit's aircraft actively participated in the Korean War. From 1952, the 234th Fighter Regiment was based there. The unit gave formation demonstration flights, over the years flying types from the piston-engined La-9 to the MiG-17, -19, and -21, to the MiG-29 and Su-27.

The Su-27 arrived at Kubinka in 1989, and formed the 1st Squadron of the 237th Testing and Demonstration Center. Close formation flying in the Su-27 required more work than did the smaller MiG-29; this was due to the type's larger dimensions and greater weight, its own certain sluggishness and unique fly-by-wire system. This should not give the impression that the Su-27 is not a highly agile aircraft, only that more attention is required during close formation flying. The Russian Warriors made their first appearance outside Russia in 1991, in Great Britain, where they performed with the Red Arrows. In 1993, they were in Canada and the Canadians asked them to take part in a display competition at the public airshow. The outcome was inevitable for the Canadians. Unaware of the big fighter's capabilities, they succumbed to the mighty Su-27. To this day the team has given demonstrations in Europe, Asia, and North America, and has earned an outstanding reputation worldwide. In 1995, the team was involved in an accident in Vietnam in which three aircraft with four pilots flew into a mountain with fatal results. Poor visibility caused by fog and low cloud led to the accident. Later aircraft delivered to the team were fitted with a satellite navigation system to avoid such accidents in future. It took the team some time to get over this accident, but in 1996, it returned at the Maritime Airshow on the Black Sea. Before this appearance the Russian Warriors received a new paint scheme.

In 1997, one of the team's Su-27s was put to a hard test. While landing at Bratislava, the undercarriage of one of the unit's aircraft obviously failed to lower and the pilot landed on the weapons pylons mounted under the air intakes. The aircraft was subsequently jacked up, the undercarriage was extended (it therefore probably worked) and a thorough examination of the aircraft was made. No further serious damage was found and the aircraft was flown back to Kubinka. Not only did the display team take part in public demonstrations, it also paid visits to other units, such as the Blue Angels of the US Navy.

The pilots of the Russian Warriors came from air force units and joined the team at Kubinka. There they flew both single-seat and two-seat versions of the Su-27 and carried out combat as well as aerobatic training. At home the Warriors often appeared with the Swifts (*Strizhi*, MiG-29s). The Warriors received their first Su-30SM aircraft in autumn 2016, and their demonstrations, previously limited to airshows, were completely changed.

Su-27P and Su-27UB of the Russian Warriors
air display team. Viewed from above, the large
areas of natural metal on the upper surfaces of
the engines are striking. *Gilles Dennis*

CHAPTER 4
Foreign Users

Close to 750 single- and two-seat Su-27s had been produced for the Soviet military by the time of the collapse of the USSR. All of the fighter aircraft produced for the PVO by Sukhoi—such as the Su-9, Su-11, and Su-15—had been restricted to domestic service.

With the collapse of the Soviet Union, large contracts for the domestic armed forces were no longer a possibility, for the new Russia and all other republics of the former Soviet Union and now independent states were devastated, economically and socially. Money for new military equipment was the last budget priority. If Sukhoi, like other aircraft manufacturers and their associated factories, wanted to survive, they had to seek customers outside the borders of the country. The result was the first export of the Su-27 to China in 1991. Since then roughly 1,000 additional Su-27s and developed versions have been sold on the market, including in Russia itself, but the lion's share of the 1,000 aircraft have gone abroad. This impressive figure does, however, include those aircraft built under license in China and India. Were it not for these exports, surely no T-50 or Su-35S would be flying, for one can say with a high degree of certainty that the sales to these most populous nations on Earth guaranteed Sukhoi's survival. Mikoyan, the company's eternal rival, is in much worse shape, having failed to achieve such major sales and earn the associated capital with which to design and build fifth-generation combat aircraft.

Sukhoi, meanwhile, has undeniably risen to become the leading manufacturer of combat aircraft in Russia. For the sake of completeness, the three main factories producing the Su-27 are named here. These are parts of the major company UAC—United Aircraft Corporation—with each factory also developing and marketing its own versions, making them competitors! The factory in Irkutsk, the Irkutsk Corporation,

was and is responsible for production of the Su-27UBK and Su-30K (-MKI/ -A/ -M, and -SM), while the factory in Novosibirsk, the Shkalov Novosibirsk Aircraft Plant, builds the Su-34. Sukhoi itself is the main developer and is linked to the factory in Komsomolsk on the Amur River, the KnAAZ (formerly KnAAPO). The Su-27S and -P are or were built there, as well as the Su-27SK, -SKM, -SM, the Su-33, Su-30MK versions, the Su-30MKK, and the Su-30MK2. Production of the Su-35S also continues there.

Algeria

Since gaining its independence in the early 1960s, this North African nation has operated Soviet combat aircraft, from the MiG-15 and Su-7, to the MiG-25 and MiG-29 (from the Ukraine and White Russia after the fall of the Soviet Union), and the Su-24. Many of the aircraft came from Egypt, to which, in its day, the Soviet Union delivered aircraft with downgraded avionics, provided the type was still in service with the Soviet military. And thus Algeria, too, received aircraft with downgraded avionics. This changed in 2006, when that country signed an agreement with Russia for delivery of thirty-four MiG-29SMT and twenty-eight Su-30MKA fighters. The contract for the Su-30MKA was valued at approximately 2.5 billion US dollars and was concluded at the end of 2009.

Sukhoi itself trained the Algerian pilots at Zhukovsky. In 2009, Algeria negotiated delivery of a second batch of Su-30MKA aircraft after returning the MiG-29SMTs it had received from Russia. It was said in official Algerian circles that quality defects had been discovered in some of the aircraft delivered by RAC MiG. This may have been partly true, for several managers, mainly from subcontractors, were sentenced to prison sentences in Russia for having sold used parts as new ones. Whether the possibility had existed that RAC MiG could have addressed the complaints in a predetermined time and paid a penalty, may be a matter of opinion. If it had, the SMTs would have remained with the Algerian Air Force and nothing would have stood in the way of their use. Of course accusations of such shortcomings shook the buyer's confidence, although even to this day the scale of the defects is not known. It might have been possible for the SMTs to remain, but there were two opposing camps in the Algerian Air Force command, one pro-Russian and one pro-west. Apparently the pro-western one succeeded in getting its way, at least as far as returning the MiG-29SMT was concerned. The fact that Algeria procured sixteen Su-30MKA fighters in their place would argue against this, however.

The second batch of Su-30MKAs was delivered in 2014, increasing the total number of Su-30MKAs in service to forty-four. An Il-78 tanker was also procured. Some of the MKAs wear a two-color, gray and pale turquoise camouflage scheme, while others are finished in a dark gray finish overall. From the technical point of view, the MKA is based more on the MKI than the MKM, even though the Israeli components were completely replaced by French and Russian avionics. Instead of the Israeli HUD and targeting pod (Litening by Rafael), a French HUD and Damocles targeting pod are used, while the electronic warfare package is completely Russian. The missile warning system is a Russian product (MAW-300), the laser warning system comes from SAAB Avitronics, and the communications system is in part from Germany. As the Yak-130 advanced trainer was also procured by Algeria, the Irkut Corporation made provisions for the Su-30MKA and Yak-130 to exchange information by data link. The Su-30MKAs are stationed at the Oum El Bouaghi air base in the northeast part of the country near the Tunisian border on the Mediterranean.

A final delivery of aircraft took place in 2015, when Algeria purchased another fourteen Su-30MKA fighters. This brought the number of these Su-27 derivatives in service with the Algerian Air Force to fifty-eight aircraft. At the end of 2015, a contract was signed between Algeria and Russia for delivery of twelve Su-34 fighter-bombers, making Algeria the first export customer for the Su-34. After several adjustments to the agreement, delivery took place in 2017.

Angola

Since achieving its independence from Portugal in 1975, Angola had to endure a lengthy civil war that finally ended in the 2000s. While there were no direct tensions with the country's neighbors, Angola's oil wealth made it possible for the country to shop for new defense technology on the world market. Thus in 2000, Angola became the second African country after Ethiopia to procure the Su-27, obtaining eight aircraft from White Russia, where pilot training was also carried out. Technical support was provided by Ukrainian companies, which also conducted initial flying operations. To what degree Angola used the Su-27 for air combat operations cannot be said with certainty, as the Angolan aircraft were finished in earth colors. As these make the aircraft easy to see at a great distance, it appears that the Su-27s are primarily used in a ground support role.

In 2013, Angola signed an armaments contract with Russia with a total value of approximately one billion US dollars which included delivery of fifty overhauled Su-30K fighters. It is well-known that Russia took back the first Su-30Ks delivered to India in exchange for the more modern Su-30MKI and sent them to White Russia. There they were overhauled by the 558th Maintenance and Repair Plant before then being sold by Russia to Angola. During overhaul it was discovered that the airframes had been badly overstressed, the result of flight operations by the Indians. Reinforcements were required to return airframe strength to original levels. As well, the aircraft's radar was modified so that it could engage two targets simultaneously instead of just a single target as per the original N-001. Ground mapping was now possible, which made possible the use of guided air-to-surface weapons. Russian color displays were added to the cockpit. Avionics were to be provided by the White Russian company, which appeared to make possible a similar level during modernization of White Russian aircraft and later Su-27s from Kazakhstan. This made it possible for the Angolan Air Force to engage air and ground targets with guided weapons, which would represent a significant increase in capability compared to the older Su-27.

With this type Angola was in a position to respond to South African *Gripen* fighters, in particular, should foreign intervention into Angola's internal affairs take place once again. One Su-27 was allegedly shot down by a handheld surface-to-air missile during the Angolan civil war in 2000.

Ethiopia

The first African nation to operate the Su-27 was Ethiopia. At the end of the 1990s, the main combat aircraft in use there were the MiG-21, MiG-23, and MiG-27. It was clear to air force commanders that new military technology was needed to deal with any eventuality arising from the simmering tensions with neighboring Eritrea and Somalia. Territorial claims by these countries ultimately led to war between Eritrea and Ethiopia in 1998-2000. Their origins went back to Eritrea's split from Ethiopia and its achievement of independence from that country in 1993. It found a source of equipment in Russia, which, as the Soviet Union, had previously supplied the nation with arms.

In 1998, eight used Russian service aircraft from the Krasnodar region (near the Sea of Azov) were brought up a standard equivalent to the Chinese Su-27SK at the repair facility there. The aircraft were disassembled and transported to Ethiopia in an An-22 transport aircraft. Russia supplied additional technicians, instructors, and in particular pilots, both for training and initial flight operations. The pilots were not active members of the Russian Air Force, rather pilots who had only recently left active flying service. A former air force general commanded the first Su-27s. Despite this, one Su-27 was lost during its acceptance flight. The Russian pilot ejected and Russia quickly replaced the aircraft. It was not long before a second Su-27 was lost during a night training mission.

In combat, however, luck was with the Ethiopian Su-27s, no further crashes taking place. Then in 1999, the unusual situation arose when Eritrean MiG-29s and Ethiopian Su-27s met in combat. The Su-27s made flights along the border region with Eritrea, making it clear that Eritrean units could only successfully conduct ground support missions if Ethiopian Su-27s were prevented from securing the airspace. The Sukhois would have to be driven off or destroyed. Four MiG-29s were sent to intercept two patrolling Su-27s flying in the frontline area around Badme. As this is a direct border region, it is difficult to say whether or not the Sukhois violated Eritrean airspace. Whatever the case, the MiGs attacked the Sukhois, firing several R-27 missiles, all of which missed. One of the MiGs was ultimately shot down in close combat. Just one day later a MiG-29UB was another victim of a Sukhoi, which was noteworthy because, according to unconfirmed sources, the aircraft was piloted by a woman, Aster Tolossa. This is contradicted by unconfirmed statements that A. Tolossa did not qualify on the Su-27 until years later.

In the period that followed there were further engagements between MiG-29s and the Su-27s, in which several more MiG-29s were claimed shot down. Just two MiG-29s were confirmed shot down in 1999-2000. Why none of the R-27s struck their targets in these engagements is the subject of speculation. It was possibly due to the inexperience of the pilots or insufficient training on these weapons. There are rumors that Russian mercenary pilots flew the Ethiopian Su-27s in the first engagements against Eritrean MiG-29s, but this too has been denied. This does not explain the R-27's poor performance, however. If the R-27 was in fact that ineffective, it would be difficult to understand why the Russian and other air forces continue to employ this missile family.

Somalia is another combat area for the Ethiopian Su-27s, attacking bases of the Shabiha militia, which several times has attacked troops involved in the UN peace mission there.

China

For decades China procured military equipment from the Soviet Union and in the present from Russia. At the end of the 1980s/beginning of the 1990s, the Chinese Air Force's equipment, mainly copies of Soviet combat aircraft, in part derived from the MiG-21, was largely obsolete. China's traditional opponents, India and Japan, were modernizing their air forces, India obtaining the Mirage 2000 in the 1980s, and Japan building the F-15 under license. A proposed collaboration with American companies came to nothing after the USA imposed sanctions on China after the well-known incidents at Tiananmen Square. The USA wanted to prevent China from obtaining advanced technologies, then copying and further developing them. The Soviet Union had stopped delivering military equipment to China in the 1960s. The reason was high tensions between the two countries in the late 1960s, over differing views on Communism and dealings with the west (Khrushchev sought to reduce tensions with the west, which displeased Mao Tse Tung, who saw it as a betrayal of communism). Chinese territorial claims against the Soviet Union further strained relations (there were even border clashes, for example on the Usuri River).

Not until after the collapse of the Soviet Union did the Russians see China as a potential customer for modern Russian military technology. In 1991, a contract was signed and China received twenty single-seat Su-27SK fighters from the manufacturer KnAAPO (now KnAAZ) and four two-seat

Su-27UBK from the factory in Irkutsk (Irkut Corporation). China thus became the first user of the Su-27 outside the CIS. The first aircraft were delivered the following year. In 1995, a second delivery of sixteen Su-27Ks and six Su-27UBKs was negotiated and the two contracts together had a value of 1.7 billion US dollars. This total of course included the delivery of ground equipment, spares, armament, and training of pilots and technical personnel. The aircraft were stationed with the 3rd Air Division at the base at Wuhu. In 1996, a storm in the province of Fujiang destroyed many of the aircraft; however, the manufacturer KnAAPO was able to repair them.

The Su-27SK/-UBK had a slightly modified radar and IFF system and a less capable N-001E radar (initially able to engage just a single target), but after delivery of the second batch the Sorbtsiya jamming pod could also be carried. The R-27 AAMs delivered to the Chinese were limited to those with semi-active radar seeker heads, and R-60MK and R-73 short-range AAMs were also delivered. While initially the Su-27SK had a maximum gross weight of 61,729 pounds, the Chinese requested that the Russians make the aircraft operable with maximum weapons load and fuel weight. Weapons load rose to a total of 17,637 pounds and maximum gross weight to 72,752 pounds. This required strengthening of the airframe and undercarriage, but the aircraft could still only be flown with a full weapons load and reduced fuel or vice versa. The two factors together were first realized in the Su-30MKK. Russia foresaw the prospect of additional lucrative contracts to bring modern production methods to its combat aircraft industry, but the Chinese insisted on producing the aircraft under license in their own country. This caused considerable disgruntlement in government circles in Russia, for they feared that the Chinese could sell license-built aircraft to third-party countries below the market price, leaving Sukhoi to come away empty-handed. The two countries reached an agreement that a license would only be issued if China was contractually obligated not to sell any of the Su-27s built under license.

The third contract, worth 2.5 billion US dollars, was signed in 1996, and covered the production of 200 aircraft. In 1997, the Shenyang Aircraft Corporation (SAC) received, the complete documentation required to build the Su-27SK and a year later the first machine, designated the J-11, took to the air. Production gained pace rapidly, and the need to train sufficient pilots resulted in the procurement of an additional twenty-eight Su-27UBK trainers, which were delivered by 2002. License production included the delivery of kits, which were then assembled in China. Later, China produced most components domestically, with the exception of engines, the radar, and weapons, which continued to be supplied by Russia. Within three years of production beginning, quality issues began affecting the Chinese aircraft. The Chinese first had to meet the increased requirements of precise quantity production with very fine tolerances. These problems were supposed to have been overcome in 2002.

It is known that China copied foreign systems, in order to then develop their own components from them. The contract therefore contained a clause obligating China to first receive approval from Sukhoi before modernizing the aircraft with its own resources. In the end it is not surprising that China in the foreseeable future developed its own systems to advance its own armaments industry and reduce its dependence on Russia. One weakness in this regard proved to be the Chinese engine industry. For a long time the Chinese industry was incapable of producing reliable and powerful engines for the J-11 in quantity, even though examples of the WS-10, the counterpart to the AL-31F, ran satisfactorily at test facilities.

By 2004, KnAAPO had delivered 105 kits to China. The aircraft assembled from kits were designated J-11 and those completely manufactured in China bore the designation J-11A. Even though the designation J-11A suggests that the Chinese continued production of the Su-27K after all of the kits received from Russia had been assembled, this seems questionable based on various Western media reports, which stated that license production of the J-11 ended after the 105 kits delivered by the Russians had been assembled.

Since 2000, the Chinese Air Force had the modern and multirole-capable Su-30MKK in its inventory, and continued production of the J-11, with its late 1970s/early 1980s era technology, would not have enabled it to keep pace with Japan or India. China was convinced that procurement of the Su-27SK was just the first step in gaining familiarity with fourth generation combat aircraft and their capabilities. It was logical to request a much updated version of the Su-27, which in addition to improved air-to-air weaponry could carry out precision ground strikes. The acquisition by India of the Su-30MK and MKI multi-role aircraft may have been the deciding factor in obtaining a similar aircraft.

The result was the Su-30MKK. Like the Indians, the Chinese also saw a two-seat multi-role aircraft as the best

Su-30MK/MKK prototype, armed with R-77, Kh-59M, Kh-31, and R-73 missiles. The APK-9E guidance pod is located under the port engine air intake. *United Aircraft Corporation*

choice. The Su-30MKK therefore has a pilot and a weapons system operator. Externally, the vertical tail surfaces are reminiscent of those of the Su-35, which are larger with horizontal tips. Additional fuel is also housed there. For increased range a retractable refueling probe is housed in the left fuselage nose. Canards on the LERX were not adopted. The main requirement was for the aircraft to be able to fly with maximum weapons (17,637 lb) and fuel (20,944 lb), which resulted in a maximum gross weight of 85,540 pounds. The necessary reinforcements were installed and there are now ten hardpoints available, allowing the requirement to be met. In addition, a nose gear with twin wheels was necessary to better handle the increased weight. The aircraft's radar had to be upgraded to permit the use of modern air-to-air missiles and precision air-to-ground weapons. The N-001 was replaced by the N-001VE, which retains the former's twist cassegrain antenna. A new Baget computer was added that greatly enhanced both air-to-air and air-to-ground radar modes. The N-001VE can now detect

targets in the air (thirty-two to fifty-four square feet of reflective surface) at ranges up to sixty-six miles, and two targets can now be engaged with AAMs at one time instead of the previous one.

Also new is use of the R-77 AAM. Low-flying or hovering helicopters can now also be detected and engaged. The radar can now produce radar maps of the Earth's surface when in ground mode. Tank groupings can be detected from distances of thirty to fifty miles and cruiser/aircraft carrier class ships at up to 155/215 miles. The optical targeting system is the OLS-30, which is also installed in the Su-30MKI and MKM. Maximum target acquisition range in pursuit mode with the target in afterburner is fifty-five miles and up to twenty-five miles for a target on a reciprocal heading. The laser rangefinder now measures the distance to ground and air targets at up to six miles instead of the previous 3.5. The improved Sura-K helmet-mounted sight works in conjunction with the OLS-30. The improvements in the radar and IRST make it possible for the aircraft to use television-guided weapons like the Kh-29T, Kh-59M, and Kab-500Kr/-1500Kr. Use of the Kh-59M requires carriage of the APK-9E guidance pod to transmit guidance signals that may become necessary during the flight to the target. The Kh-31P is carried to engage enemy radar and air defense complexes. It receives its target coordinates from its own SUV-P weapons complex and the L-150 radar warning device. Thanks to the N-001VE's increased radar detection range, the extended range versions of the R-27 can now be used. A satellite navigation system has been added to the navigation equipment and it can process both GPS and GLONASS signals, the latter being a Russian counterpart to the American NAVSTAR (GPS) system. By way of a data link system, up to sixteen aircraft can network and exchange their sensor data. The cockpit has also undergone a thorough redesign. Many of the analogue instruments and operating consoles have disappeared, their place taken by two large 8″x6″ color monitors made by the Russian company RPKB in Ramenskoye. The avionics system computer has been replaced by a more modern one. The fly-by-wire system has been adapted for use with the changed aerodynamics (tail surfaces) and higher maximum weights.

The first prototype with the Bort number 501 flew for the first time in 1999, with Vyacheslav Averyanov at the controls. This prototype was itself converted from the Su-30 (T-10PU-5). That same year a contract for a total of seventy-six Su-30MKK aircraft was concluded, valued at about 3.3 billion US dollars. Delivery of the first ten aircraft took place in 2000. Delivery of the seventy-six Su-30MKKs was concluded three years later.

In the three years in which the Chinese gained important operational experience with the Su-30MKK, the navy's desire to also receive an effective combat aircraft also grew. In particular, the aircraft appeared capable of engaging shipping. And so KnAAPO modified the N-001VE radar of the Su-30MKK into the N-001VEP, resulting in a change in the aircraft's designation to Su-30MK2. It was now possible for Chinese combat aircraft to employ the Kh-31A air-to-surface missile against shipping and engage two targets simultaneously. The number of aerial targets that could be engaged simultaneously was also increased from two to four.

Otherwise the Su-30MK2 was similar to the Su-30MKK. The Su-30MK2 is used by the 4th Naval Air Division and because of the situation in the waters off China's east coast it is probably viewed as a counter to Japanese and South Korean warships. A contract for twenty-four aircraft was signed in 2003, and all were delivered to China the following year. That China did not procure the Su-30MKI version may have been due to the early availability of the Su-30MKK. For the ultimate, most modern equipment state of the Su-30MKI appeared after the MKK entered Chinese service. Meanwhile, the Chinese have also upgraded the Su-30MKK and MK2 using their own resources, installing Chinese weapons and avionics.

It is also clear that the country would like to produce as much of its own military equipment domestically as possible, equipment that can be exported. The updated Su-30MKK bears the designation J-16 and has Chinese WS-10A engines and is supposed to have an active phased-array radar. With this new radar and a targeting pod possibly made in China, the aircraft can use the most modern domestically produced guided weapons (PL-10, PL-12, and guided bombs with various types of guidance). An additional display screen has been added to the cockpit. An electronic warfare variant, the J-16D, is currently being tested. The cannon and IRST have been removed to make room for the necessary jamming avionics. The Sorbtsiya jamming pods on the wingtips have been replaced by Chinese ones, about which no information is available. In 2016, a J-16 conducted firing trials with the PL-21, a new Chinese long-range air-to-air missile. It resembles the European Meteor and is said to have an active seeker head and a ramjet engine. Claimed range is ninety miles. Both the J-16 and the J-11D would be capable of carrying the PL-21.

J-11B

Even before China decided in 2004, to cease production of the original variants of the license-built J-11, consideration began as to how China could update the J-11 with domestically made systems, and the resulting aircraft was designated J-11B. The first clues appeared in 2000, when SAC presented its own model. A J-11 later appeared carrying weapons that were clearly of Chinese origin. Use of these weapons was not possible with the original N-001VE, therefore either the Chinese had cracked the radar's coding, which had previously permitted the use of Russian weapons only, or a Chinese radar had been installed. Logically they would also want to use their own weapons with a Chinese-built radar. The radar is capable of tracking up to eight targets and simultaneously engaging four. Detection of cruiser-size vessels is said to be possible at up to 210 miles. The radar uses a flat slot antenna.

Front cockpit of the Su-30MKK with Russian-made color multifunction displays.

The aircraft carries PL-8 infrared-guided short-range air-to-air missiles and the PL-12 active radar medium-range air-to-air missile. The PL-8 is a license-produced version of the Israeli Python short-range air-to-air missile and is gradually being replaced by the newly developed PL-10. It is also an infrared-guided dogfighting missile and will be in the same class as the AIM-9X, ASRAAM, or IRIS-T. It has a 90-degree seeker head and a range of about 1.2 miles. The PL-12 is a weapon similar to the AMRAAM or the R-77. The Chinese have borrowed the seeker head from the latter. Precision-guided weapons like laser- and GPS-guided bombs (LT-2 or LS-6) can now also be used by the J-11B. The Chinese are now copying the Russian Kh-31P anti-radar missile as the YJ-91.

The aircraft's power plants are now also supposed to be Chinese. In this area China long lagged behind prominent manufacturers, both Eastern and Western. The WS-10, a copied and modified Russian engine, first flew in 2002. Problems continue to plague the engine. Engine thrust and maintenance intervals in particular are below requirements for a replacement for the AL-31F.

In the spirit of the times, the cockpit was equipped with several color displays and a wide-angle HUD, and the HOTAS concept was adopted successfully. The fly-by-wire system was updated and the navigation system was expanded through the addition of a satellite receiver. Even a radar warning device based on UV sensors was installed in the tail

Su-30MKK with S-13 rocket pods, each containing five 122 mm rockets. *Sergey Chaikovski*

stinger, but it only provides coverage for the J-11B's rear hemisphere. Installation of a 360-degree system must, therefore, be causing major difficulties. The OLS-27 IRST is now also being produced in China. Copying of the AL-31F and the OLS-27, to say nothing of the J-11B itself, must have taken place without the approval of the Russian manufacturers.

Another innovation in Chinese aircraft construction is the installation of an integral oxygen producer. The J-11B was delivered to the Chinese Air Force in 2007, and the Naval Air Arm (no carrier aircraft however) in 2010. Meanwhile, the percentage of carbon fiber materials has been greatly increased to reduce weight and radar signature.

J-11D

The J-11D falls somewhere between the J-11B and the J-20 stealth type. An active fixed antenna radar is said to be installed, but there is conflicting information. Allegedly the Chinese still have no production radar of this kind and it

therefore seems more likely that the Chinese have installed a passive fixed antenna radar or a test radar. As the Chinese do not have the research or production experience of the Russians or Americans, who have been building fixed antenna radars for the B-1B and MiG-31 since the late 1970s and early 1980s, this would suggest that a Chinese active fixed antenna radar is still some way off.

Through the intensive use of composite materials, the aircraft's empty weight has been reduced by 1,540 pounds compared to the original Su-27SK. There is information that the air intakes have been redesigned to reduce the aircraft's radar signature and that radar absorbing materials have been used, resulting in the J-11D having a radar reflective area of less than 32.3 square feet instead of the 161 square feet of the Su-27SK. For increased range, a refueling probe has been fitted on the left side of the nose next to the IRST. First flight by a J-11D took place in April 2015, and the aircraft is involved in service trials.

J-11B, recognizable by the missile warning sensors on the vertical tails and the fuselage aft of the cockpit.

J-15

China has been for a long time seeking retired aircraft carriers, in order to acquire them and after gaining the required knowhow to build its own carriers. The procurement of the carrier *Varyag* makes an interesting story. When the Soviet Union collapsed, the vessel, a sister ship to the later *Admiral Kuznetsov*, was in the Ukrainian shipyard in Nikolayev and seventy percent complete. After several attempts, in 1998, the Chinese finally obtained the *Varyag* for a laughable twenty million US dollars. The price not only included the ship but also all of the design materials. Whether this in fact was a distress sale in order to save the shipyard in the chaotic conditions that prevailed after the Soviet Union, or whether the deal was corrupt in nature, is unclear.

Ironically, India, which has a great rivalry with China, purchased the aircraft carrier *Admiral Gorshkov* from Russia in 1995. In a process lasting many years, the vessel was converted into the *Vikramaditja*, an aircraft carrier very similar to the *Admiral Kuznetsov*. Thus two potential adversaries had very similar carriers that might face each other in a conflict.

The *Admiral Gorshkov* was originally sold to the Indians for 750 million US dollars, although the cost of converting the ship from a *Kiev* class carrier into one similar to the *Admiral Kuznetsov* ultimately doubled the price. The enormous price difference is more than clear. Back to the *Varyag*. An investor from Macao (actually a member of a Chinese firm) finally turned up as buyer, intending to convert the carrier into a casino and recreation center. The contract forbade the purchaser from in any way using the ship for military purposes. In the Ukraine all systems that might have a military purpose were removed, including the electronic systems. Transport from the shipyard on the Black Sea also proved more problematic than thought. In 1999, the ship left Nikolayev under tow and prepared to enter the Dardanelles; however, Turkey refused passage through the Dardanelles Strait for the powerless carrier and its tugs. Allegedly they feared that the *Varyag*, which was incapable of maneuvering, might come adrift and damage other ships or installations on the waterway. The *Varyag* was forced to tie up and remained there for three years. Not until the Chinese government raised an official protest and promised a security deposit of one million US dollars to cover possible damage, were the *Varyag* and its tugs able to put to sea in 2002. They arrived at the Chinese shipyard in Dalian in March the same year. When the *Varyag* was handed over to the People's Liberation Navy at the latest, did it become obvious that it had never been planned to turn the *Varyag* into an entertainment center. Restoration was completed in 2006, and work began to install the ship's propulsion system and other systems. Removal of the launchers for the Granit anti-shipping guided weapons systems, in particular, created space for a significant number of carrier aircraft. The island was redesigned, its most obvious feature being the installation of a different radar. Whereas the *Admiral Kuznetsov* has visibly flat antennas on all four sides of the island, those of the Chinese carrier are slightly curved. The aircraft carrier remains conventionally powered. In mid-2011, the government officially announced that China was working on a used carrier it had acquired and that it was going to be used for research, training, and test purposes.

That same year the carrier, which was not yet fully equipped, put to sea for the first time and was christened the *Liaoning*. While the *Liaoning* was being converted, a similar installation was created ashore, the Wuhan Naval Research Installation, similar to the NITKA complex in the Crimea. The training of future Chinese carrier pilots took place there. The *Liaoning* serves as a training and testing ship for future carrier and carrier aircraft crews. The principal objective is to gain fundamental experience. The J-15 is the interim carrier aircraft, but the J-20 (Chinese stealth fighter) and FC-31 (equivalent to the F-35) could also be based on the *Liaoning* for test purposes, in preparation for future basing on a first, purely Chinese aircraft carrier.

Of course the Chinese had no suitable carrier aircraft with which to equip the *Liaoning*; consequently they had to look elsewhere. They wanted to save time and money, and for this reason they initially decided against developing their own aircraft. It made more sense to try to obtain a Su-33 or MiG-29K from Russia or the Ukraine, for the former *Varyag* had been designed precisely for these aircraft. The Chinese were unable to conclude a contract with either Mikoyan or Sukhoi. The Chinese allegedly procured two prototypes from the T-10 series from the Ukraine, which the Shenyang Aircraft Factory then began examining intensively.

Technologically, the J-15 is a mixture of the Su-33 and the J-11B. As much of the structure as possible was taken from the Su-33, while the weapons system and radar in particular were adopted from the J-11B. AL-31F engines were initially chosen to power the aircraft, but redesigned WS-10 engines will probably replace them in the future. With color displays, the cockpit layout is similar to that of the J-11B. After extensive trials using the onshore deck landing system, the J-15 made its first carrier landing and takeoff during the *Laioning*'s first cruise in late 2012. The first operational J-15s appeared on the *Laioning* two years later and these were used for trials and training. The carrier is certainly not just a training ship, but instead serves to demonstrate the will and growing capabilities of the Chinese Navy in the waters around the country.

Finally, a word about China's information policy. Official Chinese sources continue to be very guarded when it comes to information about new military technology and it is thus difficult to obtain reliable statements. This is particularly true when they involve products that are intended primarily for Chinese forces. For export of the J-11 and J-16 would never be kept secret from Russia, and this armaments exporter surely has no desire to alienate China in the near future, as long as it has not caught up technologically in this field. The sale of twenty-four Su-35S fighters (worth two billion US dollars) by Russia to China at the end of 2015, therefore strengthens the assumption that the Middle Kingdom has not yet caught up with the Russian aircraft makers. Whether they are now particularly interested in the 117S propulsion system, the aircraft's radar, or both, is speculative.

China has not only become a world power economically, but in military affairs it must be included geopolitically. Even if the People's Liberation Army does not carry out any large international missions like Western armies, because of its size and steadily growing modernity it is a factor to be taken seriously, especially in the Far East. A significant aspect is of course the political and regional rivalry with India. For China's neighbor is also continually modernizing its forces, and the two states regard each other with mistrust, which is another story.

Operations

Great demands are placed on the Chinese Air Force for it to counter the strong presence of American and Japanese warships. Long-range anti-shipping operations are therefore of vital importance to make China's territorial claims clear to other neighboring states. The South China Sea is believed to contain major deposits of various raw materials, which awakens the greed of neighboring countries. With its Asian fleets, the US Navy underlines its claim to superiority in this part of the world. China is thus confronted by forces that can only be countered with modern means.

The latest variants of the J-11, the J-15, and the J-16 are all capable of this. The fifth generation of combat aircraft, machines like the J-20 and J-31, must first complete flight testing and service trials before they become available to the military in sufficient numbers. Thus the main burden falls on the shoulders of the current service types, the J-11 and J-16. These regularly intercept American maritime reconnaissance types, the EP-3E and P-8 Poseidon. RC-135 SIGINT (signals intelligence) reconnaissance aircraft are also among the types that frequently approach Chinese border areas without, however, violating the nation's airspace. "Enemy" reconnaissance aircraft also shadow naval units during maneuvers. The Chinese try to prevent this by launching interceptors to drive off the unwelcome observers (something also done by Western fleets).

Most recently, in May 2016, it was reported that two J-11s drove off an American EP-3E over the South China Sea. The J-11s are said to have flown so close to the EP-3E that it was allegedly forced to descend immediately to avoid a collision. The fact that the EP-3E had approached the Hainan Islands, on which is located the headquarters of the Chinese offensive submarine fleet, was however swept under the carpet by the American side. There is probably no air force that would not try to prevent a potential enemy from snooping about such a sensitive site.

In 2014, a J-11 passed inverted right in front of the nose of a P-8 Poseidon, showing its weaponry. It is doubtful that it would have used its weapons, and another aggressive maneuver would have been sufficient. An incident in 2001 showed, however, that such maneuvers are anything but innocuous: a Chinese J-8 collided in midair with an EP-3. The J-8's pilot was killed and the EP-3E made a forced landing on Hainan. The Japanese island of Okinawa, home to a base for American strategic bombers, must also be an area in which the J-11 and its derivatives must routinely fly missions.

Eritrea

After a civil war in Ethiopia lasting twenty-nine years, in 1993, Eritrea announced its independence from that country, resulting in Ethiopia losing some of its northern territories. Eritrea found itself in the situation of requiring a military to defend its independence, one that could stand up to that of Ethiopia. Technically it had the same defensive equipment as the former motherland. As Ethiopia could possibly have some of its MiG-21s and MiG-23s updated by Israel, Russia approved the sale of eight used MiG-29s and two MiG-29 UBs, to Eritrea that were delivered in 1998. For subsequent maintenance of its MiG-29s, however, Eritrea turned to the Ukraine. This was almost certainly because that country had promised more favorable terms.

At about the same time Russia delivered eight Su-27s to Ethiopia, also providing maintenance help and pilot training. The inevitable finally happened: combat between MiG-29s and Su-27s. Between 1999 and 2000, Ethiopian Su-27s shot down several Eritrean MiG-29s without loss. In the period that followed, the Ethiopian Su-27s hampered Eritrean ground operations, as the Su-27s either attacked ground targets themselves or provided fighter cover for fighter-bombers. Eritrea finally decided to procure its own Su-27s, and in 2009, ten Russian aircraft were purchased. With this purchase Eritrea hoped to achieve parity with Ethiopia in the air war.

India

India has operated Soviet-Russian defense technology, including various types of combat aircraft, for decades. Following the collapse of the Soviet Union, Russian aircraft producers sought customers for their products abroad, as there was uncertainty as to when Russia's armed forces would be in a position to purchase new equipment. In 1993, Sukhoi came up with the idea of developing the Su-30 into a multi-role aircraft, which would be capable of attacking ground targets with guided weapons. The Su-30 was given a new paint scheme and was demonstrated at the Le Bourget airshow in 1993. The weapons mockups carried by the aircraft were intended to show what the future type would be capable of, for at that time it had no suitable weapons system. India was impressed by the type and showed strong interest in procurement.

The vertical tails of the Su-30MKK are similar to those of the Su-27M, with horizontal tips. *Sergey Chaikovski*

A contract with Russia was finally concluded in 1996, this initially covering the purchase of forty Su-30K and MK aircraft by 2001. India also requested approval for license production of the type in India. The Russians had mixed feelings about this, for it would open the door for India to sell Sukhois itself. On the other hand, it was feared that if they refused India license production rights (in its agreement to build the Su-27SK under license, China was contractually forbidden to sell the aircraft it built), the country might decide not to buy the Su-30K at all.

Following the collapse of the USSR, until the late 2000s, the Russian builder of combat aircraft was hanging by a slender thread where its survival in the armaments sector was concerned. In the end the Russians agreed to allow the aircraft to be built under license in India. Initially, however, several areas of avionics and engine technology were not passed on to the Indians. Russia insisted on the construction and sale of domestic elements to India, which it accepted. The contract

called for Russia to deliver eighteen Su-30Ks in two batches, with the first eight to be delivered in 1997, and ten more in 1999. The future Indian instructor pilots and the first ground personnel were trained at Zhukovsky in 1997, with Viktor Pugachev acting as pilot instructor. When the contract was signed in 1996, development work was complete on neither the multi-role Su-30MK nor the ultimate Su-30MKI, therefore the first aircraft to be delivered would be Su-30Ks.

Subsequent deliveries would be the ground-attack-capable Su-30MK. In the final stage, the Su-30Ks and Su-30-MKs would be upgraded to MKI standard. The Su-30K is an export variant of the Su-30 with slight modifications to the IFF, navigation, and communications equipment, and India purchased eighteen of this variant. The Su-30MK was to be the first Sukhoi fighter capable of using precision-guided air-to-surface weapons. All previous variants of the Su-27, including the Su-27S, could only use unguided air-to-surface weapons. The Su-30M was envisaged for the Russian Air

**Pre-production Su-30MKI wearing a
special paint scheme.** *Irkut Corporation*

Force, but this service showed no interest in the aircraft, primarily due to lack of money in the 1990s. Sukhoi therefore decided to build the Su-30K (K indicating export), and India purchased thirty-two Su-30MKs.

The first prototype of a Su-30MKI was converted from a Su-30 and was flown for the first time in 1997, by Vyacheslav Averyanov. The aircraft's Bort number was 01. This aircraft featured all of the latest aerodynamic improvements, including canards and thrust vectoring engine nozzles for the AL-31FP power plants. Through a special arrangement (see chapter on engines), the engine nozzles could be vectored horizontally as well as vertically. A twin-wheel nosewheel member was provided to deal with the type's increased weight. The second prototype of the MKI flew in 1996, and was assigned the Bort number 06. It was created from a Su-27UB and retained the single nosewheel. Aircraft 01 gave its first foreign demonstration at Aero-India in 1998, while 06 performed at the Paris Air Salon in 1999. During a practice flight during the airshow, Averyanov initiated a loop too soon and did not have sufficient altitude to complete the maneuver. The inevitable followed, and the MKI's tail struck the runway, breaking fuel lines and the exhaust tube of the starboard engine. The aircraft caught fire and entered a 90-degree climb, ultimately becoming uncontrollable. Averyanov and Shendrik (in the rear cockpit) ejected from the doomed aircraft and landed unhurt by parachute. Apart from the MKI, there was no damage to persons or equipment. The crash had been due to pilot error. The airshow organizers had forced Averyanov to shorten his routine by several minutes, but he wanted to give the most spectacular display possible and probably began a final loop for this reason. The crash left just a single MKI prototype and this hampered program development considerably, placing the entire burden on a single aircraft.

Despite the accident, the Sukhoi leadership had great faith in Averyanov's abilities, and his performance at the MAKS 99 airshow in Moscow confirmed this. His demonstration was something entirely new for a production combat aircraft and was the high point of the airshow. Finally, a third prototype with the Bort number 05 joined the test program, and it was equipped with the complete avionics package. Averyanov demonstrated the prototype at Aero-India in 2001, with great success. The Indian air marshal flew in the rear seat and even took the controls for a time. He was extremely impressed by the performance of the MKI.

India received the first ten Su-30MKI aircraft in 2002, followed by twelve more the following year, and the last ten in 2004. All of these aircraft were fully assembled and ready to fly, and actual series production in India did not begin until later. Another eighteen MKIs were delivered between 2008 and 2009. The first batch of Su-30Ks was returned to Russia, and India received these aircraft in return. The Su-30MKIs of the 2002–2004 batch were equipped to different standards and were designated MK1, MK2, and MK3 by the Indians, with the MK3 representing the latest and ultimate standard described in the contract with Russia. The MK1 and MK2 standards did not include all Bars radar operating modes, which limited the types of Russian guided weapons that could be used. An agreement was finally reached with the Russians to bring the MKI and MK2 up to MK3 standard and this was done. The value of the MKIs delivered by Russia was approximately 1.7 billion US dollars.

In 2004, the first Indian-built Su-30MKI was handed over to the air force. The Indian company HAL (Hindustan Aeronautics Ltd.) was responsible for license production. This extended from the assembly of simple components to very complex structures and finally to the complete aircraft. India did receive some prebuilt parts and assemblies, which HAL installed on the production line, but it also produced an increasing number of components itself.

For India, the Su-30MKI was a combat aircraft that had a significantly greater range than any of its previous aircraft. In case of war this made it possible for it to counter hostile Pakistan or its regional adversary China and also to attack Chinese territory. Operating the MKI was not without problems. Since 2009, there have been seven crashes with one pilot lost.

The first crash was caused when the pilot inadvertently switched off the aircraft control system. In the Indian media it was reported that he had mistakenly operated the switch in question, which was located behind the seat. Placing such an important switch in such a place was called a design error by the Indians. But the question remained: how does a pilot reach behind his seat when he is flying? The pilot of the MKI (or all other two-seaters) generally sits in the front cockpit. Therefore, could this crash have been caused by the ESO inadvertently turning off this switch? The latter lost his life in the crash in question. Some light, however, is shed by the fact that this toggle switch is in fact located on the left console, in front of the throttle lever under a cover. Did the pilot strike it with his left hand? He would, however, have had to open the cover and then simultaneously operate the switch. The second loss was due to an engine failure caused by ingestion of a foreign object. The resulting fire spread so quickly that it could not be extinguished and led to the crash. The third crash drew attention to the fly-by-wire system. During a flight after a 400-hour inspection, flight oscillations began. The pilot spent twenty minutes trying to fly the aircraft, but when he realized that it was becoming uncontrollable he and his WSO ejected. Sukhoi investigated the accident on the spot and undertook changes in the fly-by-wire system. In 2013, a Su-30MKI caught fire during an exercise and the crew ejected safely. The aircraft released flares during the exercise and the aircraft launched a guided missile. Immediately afterward it caught fire and broke up in the air. That same year another MKI was lost because of a problem with the fly-by-wire system. Russian accident investigators blamed the incident on human error.

An otherwise so reliable system as the ejection seat also caused a considerable uproar at times. In 2008, an Indian pilot was killed on the ground when a seat allegedly fired uncommanded. In 2014, a pilot and WSO were taxiing for takeoff, when both seats unexpectedly fired. Both men survived. The same year another crew experienced an uncommanded ejection while on approach to land. Both survived unhurt. Both the Indians and Zvezda, the makers of the ejection seats, conducted investigations and officially no problems were found with the seats. The fact that no sort of abnormalities were found in any other aircraft suggests that the seats were not to blame.

Since 2012, the Indian Air Force has registered above-average engine problems in the form of significantly shorter maintenance intervals. HAL in particular has criticized bearing wear, which leads to contamination of the lubricating oil. Increased vibration has also been reported, which could also be due to the bearing problem. Lubricating oil pressure, which in some cases is too low, is another fact that reduced engine reliability. The manufacturer Saturn modified the lubricating oil system and the shaft bearings, and better-quality oil is also now being used. Fuel contamination has also been responsible for engine problems. More than a few AL-31FP engines required major overhaul after 500 hours instead of the initially designated period of 1,000 operating hours. HAL itself carried out modifications developed by Saturn. Saturn declared that the required interval between overhauls was now 900 hours

instead of 500. This in fact was probably a purely Indian problem, for neither the Chinese nor the Russians, nor other operators of the Su-27, reported similar problems, even though in part this information was intentionally suppressed. For one, the MKI differed from all other versions in having the thrust-vector versions instead of the AL-31F. It seems unusual that it was the MKI that reported increased engine problems. Use of the thrust-vector nozzles may have resulted in loads when they were pivoted, and pressure variations may possibly have placed excessive stress on the shaft bearings. Another factor that must be considered is whether the transfer of production of the Su-30MKI and its power plants to India resulted in a deterioration of quality.

There were also times when the operational readiness of the Su-30 was criticized. In some cases this fell well below sixty percent, the required value. The main reason was the initial poor supply of spares, which the Indians found to be insufficient. Some on the Indian side complained that while it was true that those in Russia paid great attention to the production of aircraft, important ground equipment for maintaining or repairing them was in used condition when delivered or even unusable. If this was true, it could be blamed on the general conditions that prevailed in Russia after the collapse of the USSR. The Indian contract was concluded just two years later, when many companies were on their knees or no longer existed. It is all the more amazing that Sukhoi and all of its subcontractors ultimately succeeded in achieving high-quality series production of the Su-30 and Su-30MKI, albeit with some delays. The integration of Western avionics in the Sukhois also proved more problematic than first thought, and here too there were always new problems. During training, the Indians often carried out long-range missions lasting up to ten hours, and it was obvious that this would result in greater and faster wear than on comparable Western or Russian types. With no other fighter aircraft anywhere in the world were such long missions reported as routine. If one adds that the Su-30 and MKI, by now far more than 200 aircraft, have been in service since the end of the 1990s or early 2000s, and that just seven aircraft have been lost in crashes, it is difficult to speak about serious problems with the Sukhoi. This is a very low loss rate and it is definitely no higher than that of comparable aircraft. The wear associated with long-range missions and the sometimes poor spare parts supply leads to a poorer serviceability rate for the Su-30 family in India.

**Indian Su-30MKIs with Litening
targeting pod under the starboard
engine air intakes.** *Irkut Corporation/
Katsuhiko Tokunaga*

In addition to technical factors, the human aspect must also be considered. India (not just the air force) trains for a two-front war (against Pakistan and China) and in this the Su-30MKI plays a decisive role. This type can deliver weapons over a long range against targets far from the MKI's home bases. It is thus predetermined that in case of war it will strike either China or Pakistan. At the least, long-range patrols are possible, which the Indians practice intensively. The Indians train to fly missions up to ten hours long, which in a cramped cockpit also surpasses the limits of the crew's performance. This would be another shortcoming that cannot be underestimated. While Indian flight crews are very well trained, their technical personnel are less so. Incidents involving ground personnel are common, and India has acknowledged that a high-technology aircraft like the MKI also requires highly qualified technical staff.

Even though India has a large inventory of aircraft, the majority of them are obsolete. These aircraft must be retired and replaced by new equipment. Strength reductions inevitably take place more quickly than the procurement of replacements. Thus India does not have enough modern aircraft available and those that it does have must fly more missions. This of course increases wear on men and materiel. The aircraft do not receive all of the necessary maintenance work, which can later have negative consequences. Even though one hears that the serviceability of the Indian Mirage 2000 fleet is higher than that of the MKI, it must not be forgotten that the Mirage has been in service significantly longer than the MKI. It would not be surprising if types with thrust-vectoring power plants are exposed to loads that have not previously been considered. The transfer of production from the mother manufacturer to India may also have been responsible for problems in the initial phase. This phase can cover years, for we are speaking here of technology of a Generation 4+ aircraft. It is also true that the Indian Mirage 2000 fleet has a higher crash rate than other Mirage operators, and the same can be said of the Sea Harrier.

License production originally consisted of HAL or contracted companies assembling parts and subassemblies made in the Sukhoi factory in Irkutsk into completed Su-30MKI fighters. This procedure was followed strictly in the beginning, but over the course of years an increasing number of parts were made and installed in India. India is working very hard on developing and manufacturing computer technology in particular, including equipment associated with the radar and communications systems, parts of the EloKa system, color display screens, and the IFF system. Even though the Bars radar and the AL-31FP are not produced from domestically made parts, the complete assembly of these components takes place at HAL and associated companies. This also ensures that an enhanced transfer of technology to Indian industry takes place. The maker of the AL-31FP is delivering a total of 920 kits for final assembly in India. The license production contract is valued at about 3.5 billion US dollars.

Further delivery contracts for the delivery of sub-assemblies for assembly in India were signed in 2007 and 2012, the two contracts covering eighty-two MKIs valued at approximately three billion US dollars. As a possible indication of shortcomings in Indian production, one can mention the complicated processing of titanium. Titanium blanks were supplied by Russia, which were then so wastefully processed in India that on average just 1/30 of the titanium blank remained. A representative of the Indian company HAL stated that the unit price of a Su-30MKI produced in India was 22.5 million US dollars, while one made in Russia cost 37.5 million, but these prices have not remained stable. 270 Su-30MKIs are now in service with the Indian Air Force and represent the largest contingent of modern Sukhoi aircraft worldwide. One can also say that it was the money earned from the MKI contracts that enabled Sukhoi to develop and perfect more modern versions, from the MKI to the Su-34 and Su-35S to the T-50.

Computer technology produced in India is of a very high standard, while Russia is pursuing the development of advanced technologies. Since 2015, India has strived to update the MKI to the latest technological standard and put together a corresponding modernization package. The mission computer, display screens, a missile warning system, improved radar warning system, and the navigation and communications systems can be replaced with modern Indian systems. Concerning the radar, there is no confirmed contract with NIIP, but it has offered updated software in conjunction with a new computer or the complete conversion from the passive to an active antenna. Integration of the BrahMos could also be concluded, allowing the Su-30MKI to finally employ this weapon.

The Indian Air Force Su-30MKIs are distributed among at least seven bases, most of them in the country's northern periphery. There the country borders India's archenemy Pakistan and its regional adversary China. In the event of war,

The leading-edge root extensions had to be adapted to accept canard surfaces, as can be seen here. *United Aircraft Corporation/Katsuhiko Tokunaga*

from its northern bases the Su-30MKI can reach all of Pakistan and the Tibetan part of China. Neither Pakistan nor India possesses long-range bombers. China does possess such weapons systems, however, and thus poses a threat to India. While the MKI is not capable of flying bombing missions in the grand style, with the necessary stand-off weapons it can launch more than tactical strikes against Chinese targets and thus represents a certain threat to China. The fact that all three nations now possess nuclear weapons has resulted in a similar situation to the Cold War between the USA and the Soviet Union, but less acute. Each party realizes that if it uses atomic weapons it will automatically be struck in return. Even if the outcome is that one nation is defeated in a nuclear war,

the neighboring "victor" would receive so much nuclear fallout that the result could scarcely be called a victory. It is unlikely that the Su-30MKI's presence and capabilities are enough to deter a nuclear war, much less a conventional one. It does, however, make an important contribution to the modernization of the Indian military. The MKI is based at Tezpur and Guwahati/Chabua (Tibet Region), Bareilly, Haryana and Halwara (northern India, Kashmir region), and at Lohegaon and Bhuj (west coast). Further bases are to follow in the future, specifically where obsolescent MiG-21s and MiG-27s are still based. Because of the tensions, border incidents are inevitable.

Chapter 4: Foreign Users

Su-30MKIs of the Indian Air Force during an exercise at Nellis Air Force Base in the USA. *Irkut Corporation/Katsuhiko Tokunaga*

In 2012, several Su-30MKIs flew a routine mission in the Arunchal Pradesh region, which borders Chinese territory (Tibet). The MKIs stayed in Indian airspace but flew toward the Chinese border and were picked up by Chinese ground radar near Lhasa. Two Chinese Su-27Ks were immediately scrambled and flew toward the Indian Su-30MKIs. Indian ground radar then detected the Su-27SKs and the situation became more serious. Ultimately one Indian and two Chinese squadrons, several dozen aircraft, were placed on full alert. In the end, neither country's airspace was violated. The incident did show, however, how sensitively one side reacts to military actions by the other and how tense the foreign policy of both states is. These are both nuclear powers and direct neighbors.

In recent years India has taken part in a growing number of joint exercises with Western air forces, including those of the USA, Great Britain, and France. Reports on the results varied considerably, especially concerning the air battles against F-15s during exercise Ex Cope India 2004, and against British Eurofighters in 2007 and 2015, during the

Indra Dhanush exercises. The Indian media reported that the Indians had won ninety percent of the engagements against F-15Cs. Whether this number is accurate cannot be said with certainty, but immediately after the exercise in Alaska had been completed it was used as proof of how urgently the F-22 was needed and that consideration should be given to increasing the number procured for the air force. It is highly unlikely, however, that the Americans lost so badly on purpose in order to get more F-22s. The fact is, however, that once again they so underestimated an opponent and Russian military technology that they had to receive a bloody nose.

The last time the Americans had such an experience was in 2003, when they faced the MiG-29 and it was still equipped with technology of the 1970s and early 1980s. And they knew that the Su-30K (and MKI) would hardly be less effective, even if it had first flown almost thirty years earlier. But the Indian pilots also displayed a high skill level and were completely underestimated. They showed a high degree of adaptability and flexible thinking, which is vital in a constantly changing air battle. While the Americans impose certain limitations on their "opponents" during exercises in order to practice certain things, the Indians train against each other without limitations and its pilots are thus forced to constantly adapt and therefore appear more variable. Four F-15Cs flew against twelve Indian aircraft, which included MiG-21 Bison (also called the MiG-21 UPG, with equipment from the MiG-29) and MiG-27 fighter-bombers.

On the other hand the F-15Cs flew in the so-called aggressor group, which was allowed fewer means to achieve its mission than the group around the Su-30Ks. This would explain the Sukhois' high victory rate. Even higher victory rates were reported against the Eurofighters. The Indian Air Force made no official statements to this effect and the media relied on unofficial sources, which in part were interpreted. The British did, however, attest to the Sukhoi's outstanding maneuverability in close-in combat when it used its thrust vectoring capabilities. The Americans used the F-15C, an older version of the sir superiority fighter, which did, however, have an upgraded APG-63V2 radar, while the Eurofighter has entirely up-to-date equipment. The French, who exercised against the Su-30K and MKI, were very impressed by how maneuverable and powerful the big Sukhoi fighter is in close-in combat. If the Sukhoi did not gain a victory in the first attempt, there was no second. In long-range combat (BVR – Beyond Visual Range) the Mirage 2000-5 with its more modern radar was superior to the Su-30K, but things would be different against the Su-30MKI with its Bars radar.

Indonesia

Indonesia found itself in a similar situation to Venezuela, which needed replacements for older machines. It, too, had received first-generation F-16s in the 1980s, which were overhauled by American companies. Logically, the supply of spares also came direct from the USA. When, in 1999, East Timor held a referendum and seemed to succeed in breaking away and achieving independence (East Timor had never belonged to Indonesia territorially), Indonesian troops marched in. The UN raised the issue and Indonesia was boycotted by the west, including the USA. More important for the west, however, may have been the fact that Indonesia is the most populous Islamic nation in the world. No necessary overhauls of F-16s were provided by American companies,

and badly needed spare parts also failed to reach the air force. And so the even older F-5 Tiger shouldered Indonesia's air defense. The Indonesians were forced to find another armaments supplier.

In 2003, Indonesia and Russia concluded an agreement for the delivery of two Su-27SK and two Su-30MK (identical to the Su-30MKK) aircraft, which were delivered the same year. The Su-27SK was equipped to a similar standard as the Chinese aircraft. Initially there were operational problems with the Sukhois, the cause being the incompatibility of Indonesia radio equipment, which was addressed. Another contract was signed in 2007, and by 2010, three updated Su-27SKM and three Su-30MK2 fighters were delivered (the former is equivalent to the Su-27SM and is also an export designation). A third delivery increased the number of Su-30MK2s to nine. All of the Sukhois are operated by the 11th Fighter Squadron based at the Sultan Hasanuddin airport near the city of Madagascar. In 2012, a joint exercise was held in Australia involving its air force, the US Marine Corps, and the air forces of Singapore, New Zealand, Thailand, and of course Indonesia with its Su-27SKM and Su-30MK2. The exercise was dubbed Pitch Black 12.

Since the appearance of the Su-35S Indonesia had shown great interest in the most modern Su-27 type, and in 2016, there were successful negotiations to procure the type. The Indonesia Air Force thus became the second foreign air force to operate the Su-35S. There is already agreement about the purchase of the Su-35S, but like India with the Su-30MKI, this nation would also like to receive a transfer of technology from Russia, but to what extent is at present uncertain. Sukhoi was able to win out against the Rafale and the Eurofighter with the type, in which the Su-35S's great range may have been a deciding factor. Indonesia had a total area of 770,000 square miles and extends approximately 3,170 miles east to west and about 1,180 miles north to south. Another factor is that the net of airfields is not so dense that aircraft can be based at many locations in the country. A long-range fighter is thus more advantageous, as is the ability to operate from less well-equipped airfields.

The Indonesian Su-35S is the most modern combat aircraft in the Asia-Pacific region, but technologically it must share this title with the Australian F-35. In some areas, especially stealth technology, the F-35 may even be superior, but in air combat, whether long or short range, the Su-35S will still hold the scepter.

Kazakhstan

When Kazakhstan was still a Soviet Republican, no fourth generation combat aircraft were based there. It was instead home to strategic weapons like the Tu-95 bomber and SS-18 and SS-20 intercontinental and medium-range ballistic missiles. After Kazakhstan achieved its independence in 1991, the country came into possession of these weapons, but it was interested neither politically nor militarily in having nuclear weapons or their carriers. As the legal successor state to the USSR, Russia wanted to obtain the Tu-95 bombers (and the intercontinental missiles, even though some had been disassembled because of disarmament agreements) and in exchange offered Kazakhstan MiG-29, Su-25, and Su-27 aircraft as well as L-39 Albatros trainers. Kazakhstan agreed, and beginning in 1996, received twenty-two Su-27s and four Su-27UB two-seat trainers. The Sukhois were based at Taldikorgan, in the border region (by Kazakh standards) with Kirghizia and China, as well as at Aktau on the Caspian Sea.

During operation of the aircraft the need arose for necessary overhauls, which could not be carried out in the country. The Kazakhs first turned to the Ukraine but decided in favor of Aircraft Repair Park No.558 in Baranovichi in White Russia. There, several aircraft, both single- and two-seaters, were updated to the Su-27M-2 and Su-27UBM-2 standard. These are similar to the White Russian Su-27UBM-1 variant and have a satellite navigation system and are capable of carrying the Litening targeting pod made by the Israeli company Rafael. The aircraft are capable of using laser- and TV-guided weapons of Russian origin, requiring modification of the N-001 radar. The update also included an increase in detection range for fighter-size targets (assumed radar reflective area of 32.3 square feet) to 118 miles. A jamming pod developed and offered by the White Russians, bears the name Satellite (see chapter White Russia). Kazakhstan is supposed to have received additional Su-27s from Russia as compensation of debts, raising the total number of aircraft to about forty single-seaters and eight two-seaters.

A data transmission system enables target data to be transmitted to accompanying aircraft or ground receivers. About eighteen aircraft were updated to Su-27UBM-2 standard, but even if the aircraft are modernized and overhauled, the end of their airframe lives is foreseeable and Kazakhstan is looking for a new type. Through the sale of oil and natural gas, the country has the resources with which to buy modern combat aircraft, and its initial acquisition was four Su-30SM fighters at the same price offered to the Russian Air Force. Thus Kazakhstan became the first export customer for the Su-30SM. Additional aircraft of this type are on the Kazakh Air Force's shopping list. In addition to the Su-30SM, the country has received the Yak-130 trainer and light combat aircraft.

Malaysia

Malaysia was in the market for a modern combat aircraft to replace the F-5E and augment the MiG-29 and F-18D. In 2003, Sukhoi and Malaysia concluded an agreement worth approximately 900 million US dollars for eighteen Su-30MKM fighters, winning out against the F-18 E/F Super Hornet. Two MKI prototypes were equipped with the avionics of the MKM and flew for the first time in May and June 2006, with Vyacheslav and Yevgeni Averyanov and Sergey Kostin at the controls. The bulk of the testing was carried out at the LII and the State Flight Testing Center in Aktyubinsk.

The first aircraft were delivered to Malaysia by An-124 and were assigned to the 11th Wing of the Royal Malaysian Air Force. The nineteen remaining aircraft were delivered in 2009. This unit is based at the Gong-Kedak Air Force Base in Kelantan Province. Both the pilots and ground personnel were trained by Russian personnel in Malaysia, with Sukhoi test pilots Yevgeny Frolov, Sergey Bogdan, and Sergey Kostin acting as instructors. The Su-30MKM is essentially a Su-30MKI with several modifications. Aerodynamically both variants are identical, with the main differences in avionics. The percentage of Russian avionics in the Su-30MKM is higher than that of the MKI. The MKM has a French IFF system, recognizable by the stub antennas forward of the cockpit glazing. The wide-angle HUD is also French and replaces the Israeli device. The display screens are also of French origin, with three available to the pilot and four to the WSO. The Israeli Litening targeting pod has been replaced by a French Damocles pod. This enables the use of air-to-ground guided weapons and also has a channel for identifying laser-illuminated targets, but it can also mark targets with a laser and guide laser-guided weapons onto them. Range measurement is also accomplished by laser. The pod has an infrared channel for bad visibility or bad weather conditions (FLIR – Forward Looking Infra Red). This image is either shown on the HUD or on one of the display screens. Clearly recognizable ground structures can be displayed at up to six miles at a resolution of 20x20 m (65x65 ft), and if the resolution is lowered to 100x100 meters (330x330 feet), range for usable recognition

An Indonesian Su-27SKM, identifiable by the position of its IRST, which has been moved to the left, and the radar warning receivers in the leading edges of the wing instead of the engine air intakes. *Resa Wahu Giang*

Indonesian Su-30MK2s and Su-27SKMs during Exercise Pitch Black 12, with an Australian F/A-18. *RA.AZ/flic.kr/p/ecAJg8*

Former Russian Su-27Ps now in service with Kazakhstan's air force finished in a locally applied camouflage scheme.

Hugh Dodsun

of ground targets is thirty miles. The pod weighs approximately 584 pounds and it is usually carried on a rack under the engine air intakes. The radar warning and chaff/flare (approx. one hundred rounds) systems are purely Russian. Jamming pods are now also carried on the wingtips and they too come from Russia. Elements of the radar warning receivers are now mounted on the wing leading edge and no longer on the sides of the forward engine air intakes.

The N-011M Bars radar, the OLS 30I, the Sura helmet-mounted sight, the K-36D-3.5 ejection seat and the thrust-vectoring AL-31FP were adopted unchanged from the MKI and the total airframe life is also 6,000 hours. All Russian weapons can be carried, from the Kh-29 (TV- and laser-guided) to the Kh-31, Kh-38, and Kh-59 models, as well as all guided bombs from the Kab-500 to the Kab-1500 (TV- and laser-guided). The MKM is also capable of carrying an arsenal of air-to-air missiles of the R-27 family, including the R-73 and R-77. Malaysia may

In the foreground, another Su-27P from a production batch prior to 1987, recognizable by its very cylindrical tail stinger and somewhat different arrangement of flares and chaff. *Talgat Ashimov*

also desire a modification for the use of satellite-guided weapons. Whether the use of the Yakhont missile is planned cannot be said, but it is technically feasible.

While the MKI still has a considerable number of Indian-made computers, on the MKM these have all been replaced by Russian systems. The missile and laser warning system is all new. This addresses what had previously been a major concern, but now it is integrated into the Russian combat aircraft. Talk is of the South-African company Avitronic, a subsidiary of the Swedish SAAB Group. The missile warning system is mounted beneath the cockpit and on the fuselage spine aft of the speed brake and thus monitors the airspace above and below the aircraft. This system detects both infrared and UV missile signatures. Laser warning sensors are also mounted beneath the nose facing forward, with two more on the sides of the engine air intakes facing aft, to warn of laser illumination by the enemy laser rangefinders.

Another novelty in Russian combat aircraft design is the installation of an onboard oxygen-generating system, which was developed and built by Zvezda. (The K-36 ejection seat is produced by the same company.) With this, system operations are not limited by the amount of oxygen carried. It is also used by the Su-35 and MiG-29K. The navigation system consists of a distance measuring system (TACAN), an inertial system with laser gyros, and a satellite system (Glonass/GPS). Formation lights are mounted on the sides of the airframe for safe and precise formation flying. The Malaysian Air Force of course also takes advantage of opportunities to fly its modern Su-30MKM against other air forces. Like the Indians, this took place against the Americans, who sent F-15s and F-22s to take part. The mutual objective was not to indicate each other's limitations. On the contrary, an effort was made to learn the other side's operational methods so that joint combat operations might be carried out efficiently.

The Kazakh Su-30SM also wears the dark-gray camouflage on its upper surfaces. *Hugh Dodsun*

Uganda

Negotiations for the procurement of the Su-30MK2 took place in 2010, and the following year a deal was reached for the delivery of six aircraft. These are based at Entebbe, the former capital of Uganda, on the shores of Lake Victoria. Totally unexpected problems arose during early operations, the reason being the pilots. Of the handful of qualified pilots, several left the Ugandan Air Force to fly commercially. The reason was probably the much higher pay rates. Unconfirmed reports state that the Ugandan Su-30MK2s took part in African UN missions against the Somali Al-Shabaab militias or could do so if required. Neighboring South Sudan and Congo, with their unstable internal political situations and the various hostile groupings, are cause for Uganda to defend its borders with the Su-30MK2, with its ground-attack capabilities.

Whether Uganda has acquired modern guided weapons from Russia, and more importantly can use them, is questionable, as these are cost-intensive weapons. And whether the Ugandan pilots are capable of employing these professionally would be another questionable point, for this requires training on the munitions, which would again be a costly burden for the Ugandan Air Force.

Ukraine

When the Ukraine declared itself independent in 1991, after the collapse of the USSR, it inherited such a considerable share of the former Soviet state's armory that numerically its air force became the strongest in Europe. It was clear, however, that with the coming economic problems the country could not and did not want to maintain this size. The result was a drastic reduction in combat aircraft, leaving just the Su-24 and Su-25, plus the MiG-29 and Su-27 to serve long-term. The latter type had been based in the Ukrainian Soviet Republic, with about seventy aircraft at the base in Mirgorod and at the Ukrainian Flight Test Center at Kirovskoye.

The Soviet Red Star emblem gave way to yellow and blue roundels on the upper and lower surfaces of the wings. Either a triangle or a stylized diving bird of prey, depending on which

Chapter 4: Foreign Users

interpretation one chooses to believe, was painted on the vertical tail surfaces. From 1996 on, Su-27s were also based at the base in Belbek, and later all Su-27s of the Ukrainian Air Force were based at Mirgorod. Like Russia, after the fall of the Soviet Union the Ukraine also had to struggle with a drop in flying hours, which unlike in Russia continues to the present day. Ukrainian pilots fly an average of forty hours per year, less than an hour a week! This means that neither flight safety nor operational efficiency can be guaranteed. As well there is the general technical condition of the aircraft, as no money is available for necessary major overhauls to say nothing of modernization. Although the majority of all necessary work on the airframes, engines, and avionics is carried out by Ukrainian companies (many come from the Soviet times and developed many necessary systems), the Ukraine simply lacks the necessary finances.

While some MiG-29s and Su-25s have been updated, the Su-27 fleet is clearly lagging behind. Of the roughly seventy aircraft initially on hand, only about forty remain (Ukraine having sold a number of its used Su-27s), and of these only about twenty are serviceable. These receive necessary maintenance, and a new camouflage scheme is being used. Since the mid-1990s, one Su-27 has had a camouflage scheme of various shades of blue and gray, with zigzag borders between colors, similar to the scheme formerly worn by the service's Su-27Ms. Some Su-27s now wear a digital scheme similar to that of Slovakian MiG-29s, but instead of all gray shades it continues to use shades of blue and gray. Other aircraft are painted in the same colors, but not in the digital scheme. Shortly before the Crimea joined Russia, the Ukraine evacuated its non-flying MiG-29s stored at Belbek, and Russia then installed Su-27SM and Su-30SM fighters there.

Su-30MKM prototype, identifiable by the missile-warning sensors on the underside of the forward fuselage.
United Aircraft Corporation

SUKHOI SU-27

The antennas of the non-Russian IFF system are clearly visible in front of the cockpit. *Gilles Dennis*

The installation of the missile-warning sensors under the fuselage nose and spine is clearly visible on these two aircraft.
Gilles Dennis

Since 2016, a handful of Su-27s of West Ukraine (the author's unofficial name for the pro-western Ukraine) has made a handful of Su-27s NATO compatible, primarily with respect to radio and IFF systems. The aircraft's combat capabilities have also been upgraded, the work carried out by a Ukrainian company called MiGRemont and located in Zaporozh. The radar system's old computers were replaced, resulting in the N-001's detection range increasing to about eighty miles. The radar also delivers a better tactical overview with improved resolution and it is more resistant to electronic countermeasures. The radar's failure intervals have also been improved. The navigation system is based on a satellite system that is compatible both with GPS and GLONASS. It is possible to program up to twenty route segments, each with a maximum of thirty waypoints. A new digitized ÄKRAN (see

technical description) has been installed, and the HUD indications are now video-recorded and can be played back for evaluation. The state of the equipment is now also digitally monitored and can also be evaluated. Approximately twenty aircraft are believed to have received this upgrade.

From the point of view of the aviation world, a catastrophe recently struck the Ukrainian Air Force. During an airshow at Lviv, a Ukrainian pilot initiated a roll in his Su-27UB from too low an altitude and crashed into spectators on the ground. More than eighty people were killed and another 500 injured, some of them seriously, mainly from burning aviation fuel. This was the worst disaster at an airshow anywhere in the world. The pilot and copilot ejected when the aircraft struck the ground and escaped with minor injuries. Both were later given several years in prison.

In 2009, the Ukraine sold two Su-27s to the American Department of Defense for evaluation. The same thing happened in 1997, when the USA obtained more than twenty MiG-29s from Moldavia for a laughable price. By purchasing the Su-27, for the second time the USA obtained an example of a fourth-generation Russian fighter for evaluation and analysis (even though the aircraft had nothing in common with the latest Russian variants).

Uzbekistan

Exactly like White Russia and the Ukraine, after the dissolution of the Soviet Union there were former Soviet Su-27s on Uzbek soil. These belonged to the Soviet Air Defense (PVO) and twenty-five single-seat and six two-seat aircraft were located at the base in Andijan in Uzbekistan. The base was situated in the extreme east of Uzbekistan near the border with Kirghizstan, but China, Kazakhstan, Pakistan, and Afghanistan were also within the operational radius of the Su-27. During the initial period of Uzbek independence the aircraft were operated and serviced mainly by Russian air and ground personnel, and Russia also looked after the airfields. In order to ultimately have an independently operated air force of their own, the Uzbeks created an academy to train their own people. At the time of writing, approximately twenty-five Su-27s are said to be in active service with the Uzbekistan Air Force.

Venezuela

At the turn of the millennium, the Venezuelan Air Force's fleet of combat aircraft included F-16s received in the 1980s, and various Mirage types like the Mirage III/V and Mirage 50. At the beginning of the new century it was clear that the Mirages, despite the possibility of modernization, would not be up to the requirements of a modern air war. The same was not true of the F-16, for which the type's maker offered the most modern update packages. However, the election of Hugo Chavez as the country's leader also changed the politics of the nation. Because of oil wealth and the changes to the exploitation of natural resources in Venezuela's favor, the USA turned away from the country and imposed various economic and military boycotts. Maintenance and modernization of the country's F-16s thus became impossible and the number of serviceable aircraft dropped steadily, as necessary repairs by American companies were impossible because of the boycott.

Venezuela had to turn to another provider to maintain an adequate number of operational combat aircraft. Western countries were out of the question and ultimately Venezuela turned to Russia. In the past there was often talk of the country procuring MiG-29s, but this did not happen. Instead the Venezuelans decided on the Su-30MK2 and in 2006, a contract was signed for twenty-four aircraft, to be delivered by 2008. The value of the contract was set at approximately 1.5 billion US dollars, and the additional procurement of several dozen Mil helicopters (Mi-17, Mi-35M) was valued at an additional two billion US dollars. Russia had thus gained a foot in the door of the Latin-American market. An aircraft maintenance center was also created in the country. Training of the first pilots and technicians took place in Russia. The aircraft of the 131st and 132nd Squadrons are based near the city of Barcelona on the coast of the Caribbean. As the Su-30MK2 is a variant capable of anti-shipping strikes, the base is not a coincidence. In addition to the Su-30MK2, there have been rumors that Venezuela is also interested in the Su-35S, but as yet no contracts have been signed.

Vietnam

After the Vietnam War, the country received Soviet aircraft technology and by the turn of the millennium the air force's equipment was totally obsolete. The Vietnam War had left the country devastated, and repairing the infrastructure was the top priority. Thus there were no funds available for the procurement of new aircraft in the 1970s, 1980s, and 1990s. Despite the former war, however, the country opened itself to the west and was able to establish itself as a regional economic power. Consequently the procurement of new combat aircraft became thinkable if not urgently necessary.

This resulted in the delivery of the first Sukhoi fighters in 1995, Su-27SKs and UBKs similar to the aircraft delivered to China. By 1997, Vietnam had received seven single-seat and five two-seat aircraft. During delivery, an An-124 crashed with two two-seat Su-27s on board. These were later replaced. However, the Vietnamese also wanted a multi-role aircraft and had realized that the Su-27K would not meet their future needs. They therefore decided to procure the Su-30MK2, thirty-six of which were delivered in the period from 2004 to 2016.

The first batch of aircraft was finished in a blue-gray camouflage scheme, which was optimized for aerial combat

This Ukrainian Su-27P is wearing a unique camouflage scheme introduced after Ukraine split from the USSR. The stylized archer of the former Sukhoi Design Bureau can be seen on the vertical tail surface. *Chris Lofting*

and low-level operations over water, while the second and third had green-brown camouflage on their upper surfaces. Vietnam received the Kh-59MK for anti-shipping strikes with the Su-30MK2, which enabled the country to defend its territorial waters, at least from the air. The 3M-54AE was offered for use with the Su-30, however this would have required a not unsubstantial reinforcement of the airframe, as the weapons racks between the engine nacelles were not designed to carry such heavy weapons. The Su-30MK2 can, however, carry six Kh-59NK missiles without any modifications. The different camouflage on the last two batches suggested that they were intended for operations over land, for the green-brown camouflage made them easier to spot them from above when flying over water. The Sukhois are operated by the 923rd and 935th Fighter Regiments, one

base in the south near Ho Chi Min City (formerly Saigon) and the other in the north near Hanoi.

White Russia

During Soviet times, Su-27s were based at Baranovichi in the White Russian Soviet Republic. When in 1991, White Russia declared itself an independent state, it came into possession of the twenty-four Su-27s and Su-27UBs on its territory. The Red Star of the Soviet Union was retained as a nationality emblem until 2009, which then gave way to White Russia's white flag. The Su-27s continued to operate from Baranovichi, which was also home to MiG-29s. Also located there is Aircraft Repair Works No.558, where necessary overhauls and modernization work are carried out. The MiG-29BM and

Su-27UBM-1 projects were developed there in cooperation with Russian companies (between 2004 and 2005).

The Su-27UBM-1's N-001 radar was updated with new software and hardware, giving the Su-27 new capabilities, particularly against ground targets. Maximum detection range against fighter-size targets was increased to 118 miles and six aerial and four ground targets could now be engaged at the same time. Helicopters could be detected at ranges up to forty-three miles and ground vehicles with a radar reflection area of 323 square feet at up to twenty-five miles. Large warships could be detected to a maximum range of 217 miles. In ground mode the radar was now capable of producing ground maps of the earth's surface with different resolutions, which permitted the use of laser- and television-guided versions of the Kh-29 and Kab-500. The modifications made

to the N-001 enabled the use of the R-77 AAM and Kh-32A/P ASM. The radar could be equipped with a passive phased array antenna with the designation Pero, which was offered by developer NIIP (with the Ryazan State Instrument Works responsible for production). The old cassegrain antenna was replaced by the Pero, with required modifications to the software and other radar modules. A data-link system was capable of transmitting target data to ground stations or other aircraft and thus improved cooperation with these elements.

The navigation system was significantly improved, making it possible to input up to ninety-nine waypoints and/or eight complete routes. During flight the navigation system can be operated automatically or the pilot can manually override the system's programming. Prior to this modernization, just six waypoints and two routes were programmable. Among other

A formation of Su-27P fighters with full missile armament. The aircraft in the center has a fake cockpit painted under the nose, and the rear one wears a digital camouflage scheme. *Chris Lofting*

The latest in camouflage schemes, a digital design, also worn by other Ukrainian combat aircraft, albeit in shades of gray. *Chris Lofting.*

The first Su-30MK2 delivered to Venezuela with special paint scheme. *Jose Ramirez*

things, this makes possible the use of the satellite system, which is accurate to +/- fifteen feet. In addition to the weapons systems, cockpit ergonomics were also slightly improved. The old single-color indicator screen was replaced by a multicolor operating screen, which provides a much more efficient display for navigation and weapons use. A video system is installed for flight and combat evaluation, which displays the front of the aircraft and the HUD picture. The Satellit radar jamming system, developed by the White Russian company, is integrated for self-defense. It is contained in two pods, each located between the wing itself and a weapons rack, which allows it to continue to carry weapons. The system radiates in an angle from 60° from the horizontal and 45° in elevation and produces several false radar images of the carrier aircraft, making it more difficult for incoming missiles to determine the real one. The jamming transmitters are effective to the front and rear. The Satellit system weighs just 110 pounds.

White Russia apparently consciously chose to develop the two-seat Su-27 into a multi-role aircraft, having decided that a two-man crew could more effectively conduct attacks on ground targets. As the White Russian fleet included only small numbers of the Su-27UB, the overwhelming part continued in the pure intercept role. The Su-25 close-support aircraft was also available for use against ground targets. Like the Scandinavians, White Russian pilots train to operate from selected sections of highway, in case runways should be knocked out during wartime.

White Russia is not a particularly pro-western state, which makes it a NATO target. With the exception of its border with Russia, the country is surrounded by NATO members. As these nations, led by the Baltic States and especially Poland, pursue an aggressive-provocative policy toward Russia and White Russia, President Lukachenko saw the need to ask Russia for support in guarding their common airspace. The situation was complicated by the fact that the White Russia Air Force retired all of its Su-27s in 2012-13. The reason was the age of the aircraft and the fact that a modernization of the entire Su-27 fleet seemed financially impossible. Fuel consumption also played a decisive role.

According to the commander-in-chief of the White Russian Air Force, for example, aircraft were flown to intercept airborne objects near the border or for pure training purposes. The aircraft subsequently had to remain in the air for a certain amount of time to burn off enough fuel to reach landing weight. This made the Su-27 expensive for the White Russians to operate. This, however, contradicted what appeared in the White Russian press, that a modernization of the Su-27 was under consideration in early 2016. From this one could surmise that the Su-27s were in storage and were available for further use.

The end of the Su-27 in White Russia thus appears to have been put on ice. Whether White Russia might be better off with smaller and cheaper aircraft such as the MiG-35, especially as fewer of the much more expensive Sukhois could be bought, depends on several factors. A larger aircraft

A Vietnamese Su-30MK2. In the background are open aircraft shelters that have no plant growth for better camouflage.

Nguyen Phuong

Vietnamese Su-27SK with typical four-digit Bort number, like those previously used during the Vietnam War. *Nguyen Phuong*

The large area of protective skinning around the cannon in the starboard LERX is very noticeable on this White Russian Su-27UB. It is somewhat narrower on single-seat aircraft. *Wojciech Kowalski*

can carry a larger radar, providing greater detection range. Its great fuel capacity also provides superior range to that of smaller types, and in this the Su-27 is unsurpassed. However, the MiG-35 is equipped with an active radar, which is expected to provide a significant increase in range in the future. This diminishes but does not eliminate the big Sukhoi's advantages over the MiG-35.

To guard the joint airspace of White Russia and Russia, in 2013, Russia sent a number of Su-27SM3 aircraft to Baranovichi, from where they operated with the remaining White Russian MiG-29s, watching over the country's airspace and sending a clear signal to outsiders.

In the future up to twenty-four Russian Su-27SM3s are to operate from the White Russian base at Bobruisk to patrol joint-use airspace over White Russia. Since the Su-30SM entered service in Russia, White Russia has expressed great

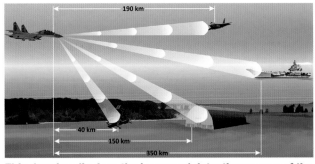

This drawing displays the increased detection ranges of the Su-27UBM. *JSC 558 Aircraft Repair Plant*

interest in this type, but according to reports it could not expect delivery before 2020 at the earliest, as Russia must first complete deliveries to the Russian Air Force as well as to Kazakhstan and China.

Cockpit of a Su-27UBM-1. The numbers in blue squares identify the changes made to the cockpit. *JSC 558 Aircraft Repair Plant*

There have been reports in the press that Indian Su-30Ks, which are being returned to Russia in exchange for new Su-30MKIs, are to be overhauled and updated to Su-27UBM-2 standard at Aircraft Repair Works No.558 in White Russia. Russia subsequently plans to sell the aircraft to White Russia. That country has refused to buy the Su-30K because of disagreements with Russia over the price of natural gas. Another aspect of the non-procurement of the returned Su-30Ks could be their condition. Deformations of structurally important airframe components have allegedly been found on the Indian Su-30Ks, the result of excessive structural loads during service with the Indians. The necessary technology exists in Baranovichi to address these problems, but the state coffers do not allow it. In 2009, an Su-27UBM-1 was involved in a tragic crash at an airshow in Radom, Poland in which both crewmembers were killed.

The Satellit jamming pod is located between the wing and the launch rail for the R-73. *JSC 558 Aircraft Repair Plant*

CHAPTER 5
Variants in Detail

This section describes variants that have either entered frontline service (both in the Soviet/Russian and foreign air forces), or represent significant technological advances.

Su-27UB (T-10U)

Since the first Soviet jet fighter, the MiG-9, two-seat training versions of most tactical combat aircraft were developed in parallel with the standard fighters (Su-7U, Su-17UM, Su-15UT/UM, Su-25UB, MiG-9UTI, MiG-15UTI, MiG-21U, MiG-23U, MiG-25U, and MiG-29UB). Soviet fourth-generation combat aircraft were distinguished by highly-developed avionics and armaments and high performances, which previously had not been combined in one aircraft. Demands on their pilots rose considerably if they were to best exploit the enormous performance and modern weapons system. It was therefore decided to design a two-seat version of the Su-27 for training of future pilots. Development of the two-seat Su-27 began even before the first prototype of the single-seat aircraft took to the air. It was to be as similar as possible to the single-seater, both to make training as realistic as possible but also to keep down costs and development time. As it was assumed from the beginning that the entire weapons system of the single-seat version would be installed, and from the initial stages of the program, consideration was given to carrying out full-value combat missions, especially long-range missions, with the type. A traditional tandem two-seat cockpit was chosen, which required less-comprehensive design work than a side-by-side configuration. The rear seat of the aircraft, by then designated the Su-27UB (project name T-10U), would be occupied by the flight instructor and he had all necessary control and weapons operating elements. Also

there were systems for simulating certain conditions for the student in the front cockpit, for example systems failures. A sort of curtain was installed in the student cockpit for instrument flight, which could be closed. The rear seat was raised to provide the flight instructor with the best possible view forward.

These rather modest modifications seem to have been chosen because the aircraft was to retain the complete avionics suite of the single-seater, and these components could not be located elsewhere without having to make major changes. The height of the double cockpit grew, which made an increase in the size of the vertical tail surfaces unavoidable in order to maintain directional stability. For simplification the canopy was designed as a one-piece structure, which also saved time during ejection. The fuselage spine and parts of the wing were adapted to provide the required maneuverability and stability, and the speed brake was also enlarged. The total empty weight of the Su-27UB rose by about 3,300 pounds compared to the single-seater, in part because of the beefing up of airframe load-bearing components. In addition to the complete operational avionics system, the single-seater's full fuel capacity was retained, and not surprisingly the two-seat version's greater weight and drag reduced range by about a quarter. The first aircraft was completed in 1985, and made its maiden flight later that year with Nikolai Sadovnikov at the controls. It entered service with the Soviet military one year later.

The rear seat of the Su-27UB is mounted somewhat higher, to provide a relatively good view forward. This aircraft belongs to the Falcons display team of the testing center in Lipetsk. *Gilles Dennis*

Su-27M (T-10M/Su-35)

By the early 1980s, Sukhoi was already considering transforming their pure air superiority fighter into a multi-role aircraft, which in addition to even greater air combat capabilities would also be able to attack ground targets with guided weapons. The aircraft's radar, in particular, had to be improved. A slot radar antenna had originally been planned for the Su-27, with electronic scanning at altitude. There were problems, however, readying this in time for the Su-27, which was entering production. And so the Su-27's N-001 used a cassegrain antenna.

The Soviets looked continuously to the USA, as the F-15A was seen as a serious threat in a tactical air war. The Eagle's APG-63 radar in particular had a great influence on Soviet thinking. In the Soviet Union it was expected that the radar with a flat slot antenna and electronic scanning would be superior to the APG-63. As the Americans had by then installed the APG-70 radar in the F-15E, and later also in the F-15C, it was time for Sukhoi to proceed with further development of the Su-27. Aerodynamically they wanted to build a more perfect fighter than the Su-27 already was,

which resulted in the Su-27M. The LERX area was redesigned and canards were installed there. At high angles of attack beyond ninety degrees they improved lift by delaying flow separation on the upper surface of the wings and tailerons. The aerodynamic loads on the wing roots at high angles of attack were also minimized, and the canards also provided an advantage when aligning the aircraft's longitudinal axis on the target. Even if the future Su-27M was not designed primarily for extreme low-level flight, the canards diminished gust loads. Wing loading in close combat also fell, as a result of which it was possible to fly the Su-27M at a maximum of 10 g without the need for structural reinforcements, which produced a further weight saving.

To enable the pilot to endure these g loads, the K-36DM ejection seat was installed tilted back at an angle of thirty degrees. These additional control surfaces were logically integrated into the fly-by-wire system, which was also heavily redesigned, and canard deflection took place within a range of +10/-50 degrees. In addition to controlling the aircraft, the canards can also be used as speed brakes during landing, which, combined with the braking parachute, further shortens

The Su-27UB's IRST is mounted directly in front of the windscreen. Those of the Su-30 variants have been moved to the right because of the air-refueling probe installed on the left side of the nose. *Chris Lofting*

The canard surfaces, the relocated IRST, the horizontal tips of the vertical tail surfaces, the absence of the pitot tube on the tip of the radome, the twin nosewheels, and the Bort number 709 reveal that this is the ninth prototype of the Su-27M (Su-35). The cupola of the rocket-warning system is on the fuselage spine aft of the cockpit. *Rob Schleiffert*

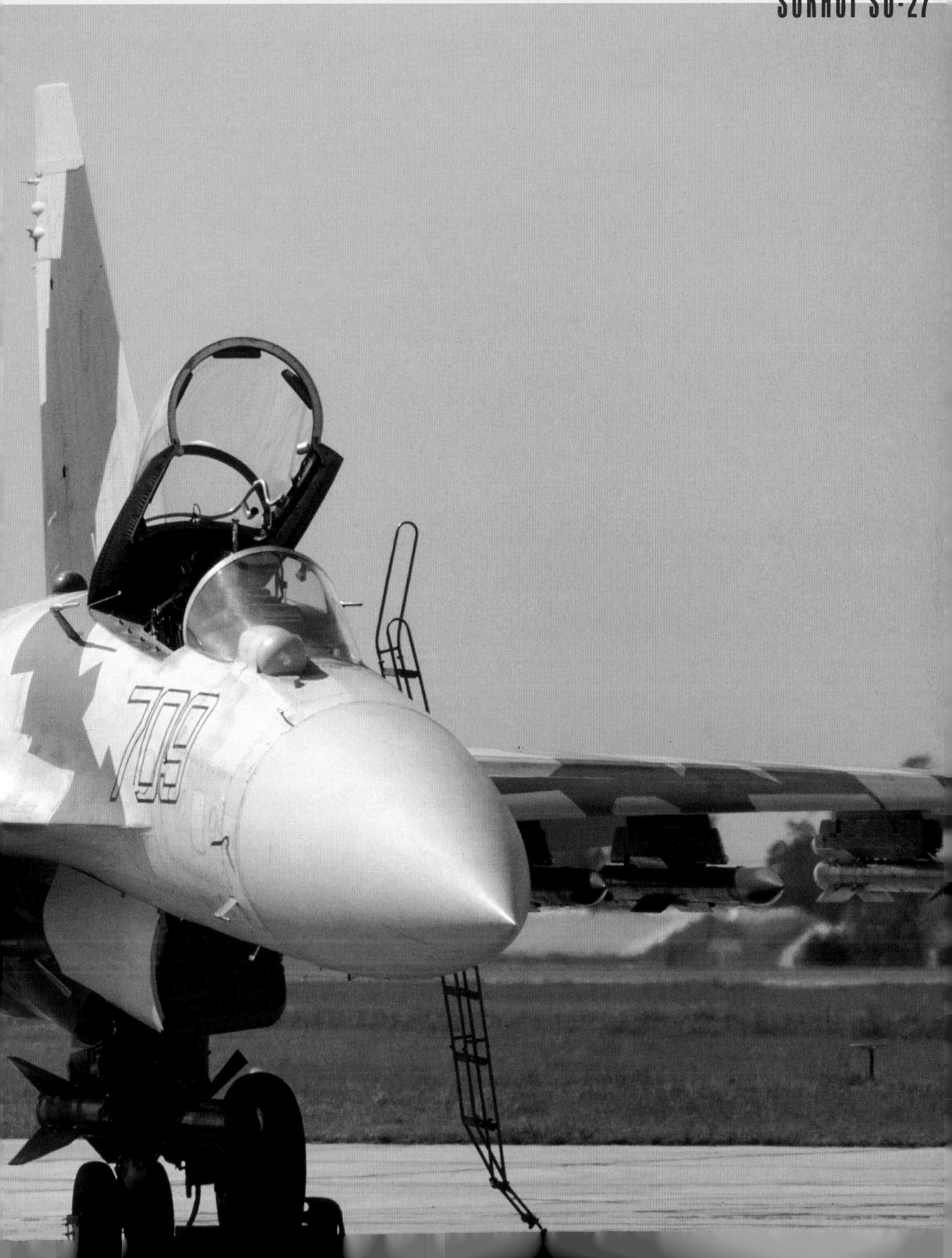
709

the landing distance. The fly-by-wire system is now completely digital and not only includes control about the lateral axis, but also about the longitudinal and vertical axes. Mechanical control rods are no longer present. The resulting increase in agility is a significant improvement, even over the performance of the original Su-27.

Foreign observers were forced to acknowledge this at numerous airshows, and they were certainly shaken when they realized that the previously unsurpassed maneuverability of the Su-27 had been further improved on by the Su-35. The cobra maneuver and the tail slide were even easier to fly with the Su-35 and automatic systems prevented a spin or recovered from it. The Su-35 had an anti-spin cartridge in the last section of the tail boom, which in a spin could be ignited against the direction of the spin. Another visible change was the larger vertical tails, now made of carbon fiber, with horizontal tips. This increase in size was made necessary by the increase in gross weight, in order to maintain longitudinal stability. Fuel tanks are now also integrated into the vertical tails, and together with the larger internal wing tanks fuel capacity was increased by 1,874 pounds to 22,600 pounds. The Su-27's range was already quite long for such a heavy and agile fighter, but the designers wanted to further improve this. Thought was given to external long-range tanks, but in the end an air refueling probe was fitted. It is retractable and is located on the left side of the fuselage forward of the cockpit glazing. The resulting range and duration required an increase in the onboard oxygen supply. Containers for food and drink were created for the pilots, to counter physical deterioration during lengthy missions.

Even though the Su-27M carried more internal fuel than the Su-27, because of its higher weight, range was somewhat less. The most important changes, however, were made inside the Su-27M, with the aircraft's radar being the key point. Finally, as Sukhoi and then radar developer NIIP had originally intended for the T-10, an antenna with electronic scanning was integrated into the fighter. Designated the N-011, the radar had a flat slot antenna, with electronic vertical scanning and mechanical lateral scanning. Maximum scanning angle in all areas is +/- 90 degrees. The radar can track up to fifteen air targets and simultaneously engage a maximum of six, although initially it was expected that a maximum of twenty targets could be tracked and eight engaged. Maximum detection range for air targets with an acceptable radar reflection area of 32.3 square feet is up to

eighty-seven miles on a reciprocal course and forty miles in pursuit mode. Large air targets can be detected at up to a range of 240 miles, while correspondingly large ground targets can be located at up to 120 miles.

A new feature was the radar's ground attack capability, which made the Su-27M into a true multi-role aircraft like its rival the F-15E. The N-011 is capable of detecting and attacking moving ground targets, producing radar maps of the earth's surface for navigation in ground mode, and acting as a ground pursuit radar in low-level flight. While the N-011 had a clearly superior performance, it weighed much more than the N-001. The nosewheel undercarriage had to be strengthened and fitted with a second wheel. The radome was given a more aerodynamic shape and the pitot tube installed there on almost all Soviet combat aircraft disappeared. Something completely new in fighter design was the installation of a self-defense radar, the N-012, in the aircraft's tail. This was of course much smaller and was used to monitor the airspace behind the aircraft. Despite this, it had a range of up to thirty miles for an accepted radar reflective area of 32.3 square feet for an enemy fighter and up to sixty miles for larger aircraft. The scanning angle was up to sixty degrees to each side and vertically, and it operated in the decimeter wave band.

The Kopyo-F and Pharaon-M were also considered as self-defense radars. Both are active phased array radars and have a detection range of up to forty-six miles for closing targets and eighteen miles in pursuit mode. Up to twenty targets can be tracked simultaneously and four engaged should rearward-firing missiles become available. Both radars also have different ground operating modes. While the Kopyo-F weighs about 165 pounds, the Pharaon-M weighs just one hundred pounds. Interestingly, during demonstrations of the Su-35 in the 1990s (the Su-27M designation was then changed to Su-35, but is not to be confused with the present-day Su-35S), it was said that the Russians were considering employing rearward-firing air-to-air missiles. This would have brought about a complete rethinking of close combat tactics, for in a dogfight a pursuer would have to expect a missile, which could be fired at any time, even though he was behind the enemy. However, no installation was ever seen on the Su-35 to suggest the use of rearward-firing missiles. There is also no visible self-defense radar on the Su-35S. The N-012 was installed in the tail "stinger" of the tail boom, and can be recognized by a small radome there. Whether a self-defense radar is actually installed there or a radome is only suggested cannot be said with certainty. The Su-35 has the improved OLS-30 IRST for optical search and tracking. Enemy aircraft can be detected at ranges up to fifty-five miles in pursuit mode. Scanning angle is sixty degrees to each side and -15°/+60° in elevation. With its more powerful radar, the Su-35 required new and accurate weapons to demonstrate its full combat capabilities. The R-27T and R-27R, which were already in service, were modified into the R-27TE and R-27ER with significantly greater range.

The aircraft was also capable of using guided air-to-surface weapons, including the Kh-29T/L and Kh-31A/P plus the Kab-500 and Kab-1500 TV- and laser-guided bombs. The heavy television-guided Kh-59M with APK-9 data link pod can also be employed by the Su-35. Thus the new Sukhoi fighter could strike ground targets accurately from a safe distance, and if it was engaged in air combat its chances of emerging victorious would be very high. Developed in parallel, the Su-35 and the MiG-29M gave the Soviet Union true multi-role combat aircraft which need not fear any opponent. The number of weapons hardpoints was increased by two to twelve and weapons load was increased to 17,637 pounds. Gross weight rose to 74,957 pounds.

More powerful engines were vital if the designers wanted to achieve the maximum possible increase in maneuverability, therefore experimental AL-31FM power plants producing 28,100 pounds of thrust were installed. As the Su-35 was now a multi-role combat aircraft, it was also inevitable that the pilot's workload rose. The concept of the glass cockpit was adopted to ease his workload. A large number of analogue indicators and instruments were removed and three to four multifunction color displays were fitted in the cockpit (depending on the prototype's equipment state). These simplified the pilot's tasks of operating and monitoring many systems, which had a positive effect, especially during ground attacks or aerial combat. Whereas previously the pilot had to operate many weapons system switches during combat while still flying the aircraft, with the help of the displays and automation of the weapons system, significantly fewer hand movements were required during hectic combat situations.

In addition to the fully active location system, great importance was placed on the expansion of warning systems. The Su-35 therefore had a system to warn of incoming missiles. This sensor was located on the fuselage spine immediately in front of the speed brake and was hemispherical

in shape. The radar warning system was made more reliable and ensured all-round monitoring. For defense against infrared- and radar-guided missiles, like the Su-27, the Su-35 carried a large number of chaff and flare cartridges. To prevent an attack from taking place at all, the Su-35 can carry a Sorbtsiya ECM pod on the outer wing stations to jam enemy radars. The advantage of carrying two pods, as far apart as possible, is very good 360° coverage. This is achieved by installing both forward and aft facing antennas in the pods. With two pods it is also possible to search for enemy radars while jamming others. The pods are effective against both air- and ground-based radars. As the Soviets were already using radar-absorbing paint and materials on the MiG-29M, which first flew in 1986, similar measures may also have been used by the Su-35.

The Su-35 never entered production, but twelve prototypes (the Su-37 is included in the Su-35 family here) were produced with a wide range of equipment. Their Bort numbers were 701 to 712, with 701 being the first and 712 the last prototypes. 701 was a converted Su-27S and it first flew on June 28, 1988, with Sukhoi's then chief test pilot Oleg Tsoi at the controls. As a result, 701 did not have the Su-35's vertical tails, retained the single nosewheel, and had ten instead of twelve weapons hardpoints. The new weapons system with the N-011 radar was likewise not yet installed. Of note was the coarse facetted camouflage scheme with large areas painted in ever darker shades of gray. The aircraft was photographed from the air and ground, to see how the different shades of gray caused the machine to blend into its surroundings. On the wing upper surfaces there were sensor cords that were attached with sealing compound and used to measure load forces. This method of affixing sensors was originally developed in the Soviet Union.

702 flew for the first time in January 1989, and it was also converted from a Su-27S. Aircraft 703 was the first true Su-35 and first flew in April 1992. 701, 702, and 704 to 707 were converted Su-27S fighters and had the standard vertical tails and single nosewheel. 703 and 708 to 710 were built as Su-35s and had that version's typical features. 706 and 707 were displayed to various military leaders of the CIS in the early 1990s, but as far as is known there was no procurement. Aircraft 701, 706, and 707 were extensively tested by Russian Air Force pilots at the state research institute at Aktyubinsk, while 703, 709, and 710 underwent testing at Sukhoi by company pilots.

The larger vertical tails of the Su-27M are quite marked. Smoke generators have been mounted on the outer launch rails for an impressive flight demonstration. *Rob Schleiffert*

In the 1990s and 2000s, 703 and 709 received individual three-color camouflage schemes (703 shades of brown and green, 709 shades of blue). The aircraft were demonstrated at many airshows and caused a considerable stir in the camps of Western aircraft manufacturers, but the type was not exported and did not enter service with the Russian Air Force. After the collapse of the Soviet Union, Russia lacked the financial resources with which to procure such modern and expensive aircraft as the Su-35 (it lacked the funds to procure even less expensive combat aircraft). A handful of Su-35s were given to the air force, and these remained in Aktyubinsk for testing, while several flew with the *Russkie Vityazi* (Russian Knights).

Outside the CIS there was more interest in two-seat types like the Su-30MKI, as a number of air forces had reached the opinion that only a two-man crew was up to the demands of modern air combat. Not until 2011, did the Russian Air Force receive the redesigned Su-35S, but more on that in the

chapter on that type. From 2004, the Su-35 prototype 710 was used to test the power plant for the new Su-35S or T-50, Product 117, which was a much modified AL-31FP.

The apex of the Su-35 is represented by the Su-37 Terminator, which is supposed to overshadow its sister. The Su-27 and Su-35 were capable of performing impressive cobra, tailslide, and hook maneuvers; however, these took place in an area where the aircraft's speed fell to zero mph. Control with the aerodynamic control surfaces was impossible there and the attitude change achieved by the Sukhoi was too brief for the aircraft to aim and shoot a missile at the enemy. To extend this targeting phase, the aircraft simply had to remain controllable, which was only possible with thrust vectoring.

At the request of Sukhoi, SibNIA had begun basic research in 1983, running simulations. In 1986, Lyulka-Saturn began designing a swiveling nozzle for the AL-31F. In 1989, this was ready and was installed on one engine of a Su-27UB (see chapter on engines). It demonstrated clearly the superiority of an aircraft equipped with thrust vectoring compared to a conventionally-powered fighter. There was a desire to make the Su-35 more agile and logically this was achieved with thrust vectoring power plants. These were AL-31FU engines with 28,101 pounds of thrust and a round nozzle that was completely adjustable, though only in elevation.

In 1988, even before the start of practical testing of the thrust-vector nozzle, Sukhoi began work to install this system in the likewise brand-new Su-35. The eleventh Su-35 prototype with the Bort number 711 was used. Now designated Su-37, the aircraft carried out maneuvers that, until then, had been thought impossible and that one could only imagine if one saw them oneself. The machine was capable of turning about individual aircraft axes in flight, which took place on the spot and no longer had a turn radius (unless one calls a loop with a diameter of approximately one hundred feet a turning radius). There are virtually no limits to the flight movements of a thrust-vectoring aircraft, apart from of course a certain flying altitude. Thrust vectoring control is particularly capable of demonstrating its advantages at speeds near the zero mark, but it also offers enormous advantages at high speeds. KNAAPO had the Su-37 airframe ready in 1995, but the AL-31FU was still undergoing testing and so the AL-31FU was fitted with the vectoring nozzles of the AL-31FP. Because of the less powerful engines, this resulted in some loss of flight performance, but Sukhoi was able to begin ground testing.

In order to fully exploit the advantages of thrust vectoring, control of the engine nozzles had to be integrated into the fly-by-wire system, which was now designed to be fully digital for all axes. This system was programmed so that over control was scarcely possible as the system kept the aircraft in the controllable region in all flying states and overrode the pilot's impulse to over control. To counteract the increased agility and associated physical loads, a sidestick controller was fitted in the Su-37's cockpit in place of the usual joystick. The Su-37 thus became the second type worldwide after the F-16 to have a sidestick controller. This was extensively tested at the LII in a converted Su-27 (see chapter on operational use). The throttle lever was also redesigned and it is no longer movable, reacting instead to the pilot's hand pressure without moving. The greater the hand pressure, the higher the thrust. The Su-37 has a true glass cockpit with four color display screens made by the French manufacturer Sextant Avionique and a wide-angle HUD, which further

reduces pilot workload. Even though the N-011 radar of the Su-35 is far superior to that of the Su-27, during flight testing it became clear that in the long term only a fixed-antenna radar (passive/active) would have a future. The developer NIIP was able to draw on its experience in building the first fixed antenna radar for a fighter aircraft anywhere in the world, the Zaslon, which entered production for the MiG-31 in the early 1980s. A fixed antenna was developed and the N-011 was redesigned to use such an antenna. The result was the N-011M Bars, which was then used in the Su-30MKI/MKM and MKA. The electronic warning and jamming equipment was further improved and a satellite communications system was also added.

Sukhoi test pilot Yevgeni Frolov made the first flight in the aircraft on April 2, 1996. At the Farnborough Airshow in September 1996, a Russian fighter aircraft with thrust vectoring was finally able to demonstrate the future of air combat. It was flown so impressively by Yevgeni Frolov that a maneuver was even named after him. Called the "Frolov chakra," it represented an exaggerated cobra. This means that the cobra can be continued beyond 120 degrees until the nose is pointing in the initial direction of flight. There is no loss of altitude and it is actually a loop with no significant diameter. Tailslide maneuvers are also carried out in which the aircraft tips to the side over one wingtip at the apex of the maneuver. While the fly-by-wire system controls the thrust vector nozzles, the pilot must press a button to activate them.

Testing of the Su-37 concluded in 2000. The aircraft was given the name Terminator because of its unique flight maneuvers and was demonstrated to potential customers at many airshows. But no one ordered the Su-37. This had nothing to do with its equipment and abilities, which were undeniable, but the Indian contract in 1996 had made it clear that countries that could afford such an aircraft would insist on a two-man crew. The Su-35/Su-37 project was thus ended and all attention was directed to preparing the Su-30MKI.

The Su-37 clearly showed the path that future fighter aircraft would have to follow if they were to survive the air battles expected in the future. It was often claimed that long-range radars and missiles made dogfighting a thing of the past for fighters of the fourth and fifth generations. But with the expanding use of stealth technology by the USA and the possible existence of a plasma generator in Russia, which would completely screen an aircraft carrying the device from enemy radars, such an opponent could suddenly initiate a close-in combat, requiring the maximum degree of maneuverability. Thrust-vector technology is in use not only in Russia but also in the USA on the F-22 and it is proposed for the Eurofighter. This shows that it is too soon to announce the end of close aerial combat.

Su-27K (Su-33/T-10K) and Su-27KUB (Su-33KUB/T-10-KU)

During the Second World War the Soviets recognized the means of power represented by the aircraft carrier. After the war the Soviet naval command wanted to build a carrier fleet. Before he died, Stalin could not decide to give the green light to this ambitious but costly program. The damage his nation had suffered in the war was too great and the cost of putting the Soviet Union back on its feet was enormously high. And so the Soviet command considered which priorities to set and came to the conclusion that, for the navy, the development of nuclear submarines should receive the greatest attention. For the time being there was no room in their plans for expensive aircraft carriers; however, the construction of ships capable of accommodating aircraft was not completely ignored. The result was the *Moskva* Class.

These were helicopter carriers specially designed to hunt submarines, especially American ballistic-missile-carrying submarines. Two of these vessels joined the Soviet fleet in the 1960s. The 1970s saw the appearance of the *Kiev* Class, which carried Yak-38 VTOL aircraft and Ka-25 and Ka-27 helicopters. The Yak-38 lacked the range and payload to be used in an offensive role and its maneuverability was less than satisfactory. Its weaponry was largely restricted to unguided weapons, and its only guided weapon, the Kh-66, had such limited range that the Yak-38 was more likely to be shot down before it could guide its semi-active guided weapon to its target.

At the same time that the *Kiev* was joining the fleet, the Su-27 and MiG-29 were far along in their development and a new, true aircraft carrier was proposed for these types. Shipbuilders had already begun working on this new generation of aircraft carrier and had presented their design to the minister responsible. However, Defense Minister Greshkov died and with him Fleet Adm. Gorshkov lost his supporter of the new carrier generation. The new defense minister Ustinov rejected the large and expensive aircraft carriers, instead proposing a redesign of the *Kiev* Class.

The proposed carrier aircraft were the MiG-23, Su-25, and Yak-41, but this class of vessel was too small to accommodate a sufficient number of aircraft. Ustinov saw this for himself when he went aboard the *Kiev* during a naval exercise. This visit caused him to increase the displacement of the new carrier by 11,000 tons. The ship, now designated Project 1143.5, lacked steam catapults as they were simply not available in the Soviet Union. Another way had to be found to get the aircraft into the air. A twenty-foot-high ramp was built on the bow with an incline of 14°, similar to those of the British Invincible Class carriers. On the rear section of the deck there were four arrestor cables plus detents and jet blast deflectors to secure the aircraft until they were released for takeoff at full afterburning power. Should a landing aircraft miss all four arrestor cables and be unable to go around, a net would be deployed and stop the aircraft. There were two different takeoff positions, one with a length of about 640 feet and the other 344 feet. This flight deck runs straight over the bow and is not angled like those of other aircraft carriers. Maximum width of the flight deck is 236 feet.

On the starboard side there is an island with radar antennas and electronic systems. The air defense radar was a new type with fixed antennas and it was used on the *Baku*, the fourth and last *Kiev* Class carrier. The ship's heavy armament was typical for a Soviet aircraft-carrying vessel. In the central part of the foredeck are twelve vertical shafts for P-700 *Granit* anti-ship cruise missiles (NATO designation SS-N-19 Shipwreck). Air defense consisted of about 200 missiles in a Kinzhal complex (a naval version of the land-based Thor), which was housed in a revolver-like drum frame. For close-in defense the ship had six Gatling guns (AK-360; six-barrel automatic cannon) and eight Kortik-type systems, each system combining two 30 mm revolver cannons and eight surface-to-air missiles. The Project 1143.5 had a conventional, non-nuclear power plant.

At the beginning of the 1980s, it was realized that the new carrier would have to be equipped with the MiG-29 and Su-27 if it was to stand up to the US Navy. The Yak-41 then in development was envisaged as a replacement for the *Kiev* Class's Yak-38s. Finally, in 1982, the first and ultimately last carrier of Project 1143.5 was laid down in Nikolayev and was given the name *Riga*. The name changes several times, from *Riga* to *Brezhnev* (1982) to *Tbilisi* (1987) and finally to *Admiral Kuznetsov* (1990). Construction took three years and the ship was launched in December 1985. Immediately after this the

Brezhnev's sister ship, also called the Riga, was laid down. It was launched in 1988, and by 1991, was about seventy percent complete. The Ulyanovsk, the first Soviet nuclear-powered aircraft carrier, was laid down in 1988. It was about twenty percent complete in 1991, but in the chaotic conditions following the collapse of the Soviet Union, Russia could not have begun to complete both ships. Negotiations were begun with the Ukraine to purchase both vessels, but the price asked exceeded Russian resources. And so both ships remained in the Ukraine until China bought the Varyag in 1998. The Ulyanovsk was scrapped in 1992.

In the early 1970s, a ground installation was created in Saki to provide realistic deck-landing training. This applied only to the Yak-38 VTOL aircraft, which was envisaged for the Kiev Class. However, when in the early 1980s, the MiG-29 and Su-27 were selected as possible future carrier-borne aircraft and the Yak-41, successor to the Yak-38, ran into difficulties and would not become available in the foreseeable future, the NITK complex (later renamed NITKA) was

converted so that it would be available for the MiG-29 and Su-27 by 1982. This complex had a recreation of the complete "ski-jump" and arrestor system from the carrier. The ski-jump was dubbed Trampolin T-1 and was about 360 feet long, 180 feet wide, and thirty feet high. A MiG-29KWP made the very first takeoff from the T-1; a few days later the Su-27 followed with the prototype of the first version, the T-10-3. It had a takeoff weight of 40,124 pounds and required 755 feet to become airborne at 143 mph. Tests with the Trampolin T-1, which took place in 1982–83, confirmed that the ski-jump was capable of launching both the MiG and Sukhoi fighters. During trials the front part of the T-1 was redesigned and received a bulged fairing resulting in the designation T-2. After the successful completion of ski-jump trials, the next task was to test the arrestor cable system. A MiG-27 was fitted with an arrestor hook for the very first arrested landing trials, only afterward were arrestor hook experiments carried out with the MiG-29KWP and the T-10-3 in 1983.

Su-27K prototype T-10K-1 without wing-folding mechanism. *JSC Sukhoi*

In 1984, in the Soviet Union, it was decided to use the T-10K (the K stood for *Korabl*, "ship" in Russian) variant as a carrier-based fighter and the MiG-29K as a carrier-based ground attack and anti-shipping aircraft, with both types serving on a carrier at the same time. This was obviously inspired by the US Navy, which then operated the F-14 and F-18, then the most capable carrier-based aircraft, from the same carrier. As Sukhoi recognized the enormous potential of the redesigned T-10S, an example of this type, the T-10-25, was also used in navy trials. It was fitted with an arrestor hook, strengthened undercarriage, larger flaperons, and a more reclined ejection seat. Flight tests on the redesigned Trampolin T-2 began at the NITKA complex in 1984. These included not just the actual takeoffs and landings but the associated systems as well, such as an optical approach system, close-in navigation and landing radar, and an approach navigation system. In 1984, while flying to Aktyubinsk, the T-10-25's rudder hydraulic system failed and pilot Nikolai Sadovnikov was forced to eject. The T-10-24 entered the NITKA trials stage in 1986. Sukhoi had been working with canards even before the T-10's maiden flight in 1977, but it was not until 1985, that the T-10S version of the T-10-24 was fitted with canards and completed its first flight that same year. The aircraft's leading edge root extensions were redesigned, as that is precisely where the canards were mounted. Flight trials showed that this arrangement yielded benefits that were advantageous for a carrier aircraft. The resulting lower approach speed had a positive impact on braking and the actual stopping distance. This prototype also had a short life, however, crashing after just six flights at the NITKA complex. The pilot escaped by ejecting. The second

prototype of the Su-27UB was used to fill the gap and allow trials to continue. The Su-27 appeared to resist being conceived as a carrier-based aircraft, for this machine was also lost in a crash.

Work on the actual T-10K series (official designation Su-27K) had been going on since 1984, and the first of its type, the T-10K-1, flew in 1987, with Viktor Pugachev at the controls. The T-10K-2 followed at the end of 1987, flown by Nikolai Sadovnikov. Fate did not favor Sadovnikov. During a flight in the T-10K-1 the aircraft's hydraulic system failed, rendering the aircraft uncontrollable. He ejected, but a resulting spinal injury ended his flying career. It was suggested that a flat spin had been responsible for the crash, which Sadovnikov could not confirm or deny. The remaining T-10K-2 completed about another 300 test flights including tests on the carrier itself. In 1988, while trials at NITKA were still going on, standard Su-27s made simulated approaches to the *Baku*, the fourth carrier of the *Kiev* Class. Incidentally, the MiG-29K did not begin testing until 1988, a year after the Su-27K, and this was later to play a decisive role.

When the *Tbilisi* (the aircraft carrier's then ultimate name) finally put to sea in October 1989, deck overflights at ever-decreasing heights began, leading up to touch-and-goes. Both the carrier and the Su-27Ks and their test pilots were ready for the first ever carrier landing by a non-VTOL Soviet aircraft. On November 1, 1989, Viktor Pugachev successfully landed the T-10K-2 on the deck of the *Tbilisi* and rang in carrier service in the Russian fleet. The next day the T-10K-2 was supposed to carry out the first deck launch. The aircraft was moved to takeoff position, the detents were engaged, the water-cooled jet blast deflector was raised, and Pugachev engaged afterburner. After six seconds the wheel detents were supposed to lower and release the aircraft, but the restraints stayed up and the engine badly damaged the jet blast deflector. The takeoff had to be abandoned and the carrier sailed back to the shipyard for repairs. As the T-10K-2 itself had suffered no damage, it was decided to take off without the detents and jet blast deflector. A longer takeoff roll was selected and the takeoff succeeded without aids. The first stage of testing had been completed successfully and all the assembled data was analyzed.

On November 21, of the same year, Pugachev made the first night landing in the T-10K-2, thus completing basic testing. Before the year ended, Sukhoi announced that it was ready for quantity production of the Su-27K. Nevertheless, a pre-

The T-10-3 prototype during a launch from the Trampolin T-1. *JSC Sukhoi*

T-10-3 during an arrested landing at the NITKA complex at Saki in the Crimea. *JSC Sukhoi*

production batch was built, a total of seven aircraft (not counting the T-10K-2). Further carrier trials were carried out in 1990, but this did not happen immediately. The reason for this was that, in addition to the Su-27K, the MiG-29K and Su-25UTG were also on board, carrying out test programs. The Su-27K was unable to carry out joint operational practice flights or conduct rocket firing. In addition to MiG and Sukhoi pilots, military pilots also took part in the carrier trials. Some of these pilots came from the State Testing and Research Institute of the Air Force (naval aviation section) on the Crimea. Even they had to receive approval from the NITKA complex before they could finally make deck landings and takeoffs in their MiG-29Ks and Su-27Ks. In addition to testing the Su-27K in the military role, this group of qualified carrier pilots was also responsible for developing flight tactics for the aircraft.

Factory trials were completed from spring to autumn 1990, despite the catastrophic political and economic conditions in the Soviet Union. After the end of trials the carrier was renamed for the final time, becoming the *Admiral Kuznetsov*. The previous name, *Tbilisi*, was the name of a city in the Georgian Soviet Republic, but the unrest there and efforts to break away led the Soviet command to bring about this change of name. The pre-production aircraft began flight trials in spring 1991. The carrier pilots suffered the loss of one of their aircraft. Due to an error in the T-10K-8's fly-by-wire system, Timur Apakidze was forced to abandon the aircraft in flight. But the year 1991 had something unusual to offer, when Viktor Pugachev made the first fully automatic landing at the NITKA complex. The collapse of the Soviet Union in December 1991, created an uncomfortable situation for ship construction in Nikolayev. This city with its shipyard, the only one in the Soviet Union capable of building aircraft carriers, was now in the Ukraine, which was an independent state and no longer part of Russia.

In December 1991, the *Admiral Kuznetsov* moved to Severomorsk, where it joined the Russian Northern Fleet. The decision to transfer the aircraft carrier had been made before the Soviet collapse, in order to protect the USSR's northern flank against carriers and landing forces of the US Navy. On board was the 100th Shipborne Fighter Aviation Regiment with its first fifteen military pilots, under the command of Colonel Timur Apakidze. The unit was formed in 1986, in order to have operational pilots when the carrier was commissioned. It officially entered service with the Russian Navy in January 1992; the Su-27L entered production and was later given the designation Su-33.

In design terms, the most obvious change introduced by the Su-33 is the installation of canards. These were first used on the T-10-24 prototype and were originally intended for investigating the flight characteristics of an improved Su-27 variant (the later Su-27M). As the results also turned out to be advantageous for the Su-27K, the canards were adopted for the carrier version. The folding mechanism for the wings and stabilators were not installed, as they were not yet ready. This mechanism was then installed in the second prototype, the T-10K-2, which first flew a year later.

Other changes affected the airframe structure, which had to be strengthened due to the increased loads associated with carrier takeoffs and landings. Corrosion protection also had to be provided. The aircraft's higher gross weight resulted in a twin-wheel nose gear (smaller wheels) with a longer oleo. The main undercarriage was also reinforced with higher tire pressure. Shackles were installed for tying the aircraft down to the flying deck. For improved taxiing on the flight deck, the nosewheel castor angle was increased to +/- 70°. The number of hardpoints was raised to twelve; however, weapons load rose by just 1,100 pounds to 14,330 pounds. In order to accommodate the Su-27K below deck, the vertical tail surfaces had to be shortened. The tail stinger was also shortened to enable the aircraft to operate from the carrier at higher angles of attack without scraping the deck. This reduction in length meant that the chaff and flare dispensers could no longer be accommodated there. They were therefore moved forward to a position abeam the engine compressors, but as before they were mounted centrally. The arrestor hook is located directly beneath the fuselage. As the braking parachute had become superfluous, it was completely removed and the radar warning receivers, previously on the side of the air intakes, were mounted in the tail stinger. The

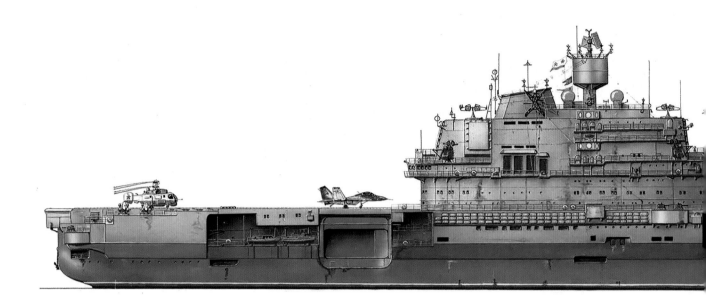

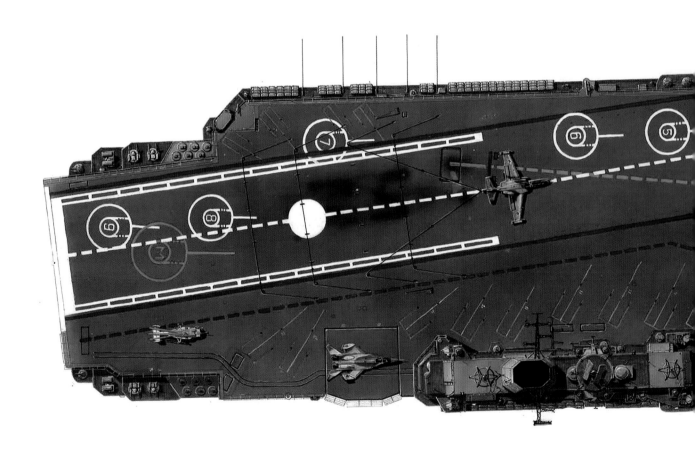

The aircraft carrier *Tbilisi* during deck trials with the Su-27K and MiG-29K. The broken yellow lines mark the different takeoff routes, the white circle at the stern the optimal touchdown point during an arrested landing. *Manfred Meyer*

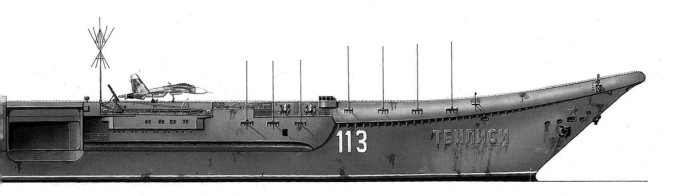

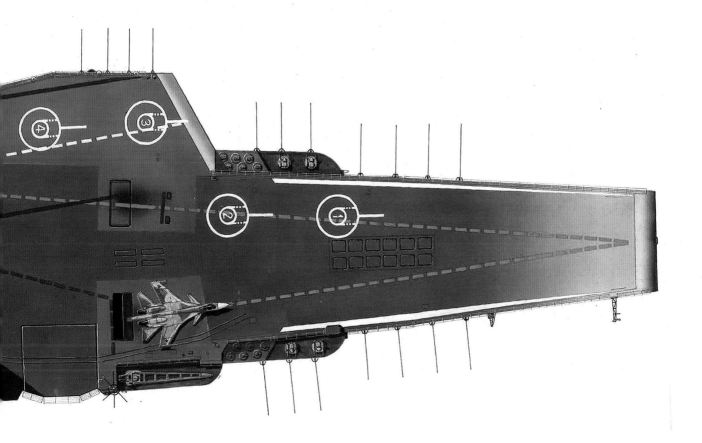

SUKHOI SU-27

In addition to the wings, the tailerons also fold. This aircraft is carrying an unusual and extremely unfavorable ground attack armament. Because of their limited range, the unguided S-8 rockets (80 mm) would force the Su-27K to fly dangerously close to its target.

The flaps and auxiliary air intakes on the undersides of the forward air intakes are clearly visible in this image. *Chris Lofting*

wings also underwent design changes. Wing area was increased from 667 to 732 square feet without changing the wingspan. High-lift devices were fitted to the Su-27K to counter the short takeoff distance available from the carrier's deck and improve lift. Whereas the land version of the Su-27 had a continuous flaperon on each wing (without taking up the entire trailing edge of the wing), the Su-27K had double slotted flaps on the inner and central parts of the wing trailing edge and smaller flaperons outboard. The Krueger flaps were also increased in size. These changes resulted in fifty percent more lift compared to the land version. This enabled the aircraft to leave the ski-jump safely at the low takeoff speed of 111 to 124 miles per hour. The addition of the canards and high-lift devices meant that the fly-by-wire and hydraulic systems had to be redesigned. The wings were of course made foldable to save space inside the carrier (folded span of 27.4 feet), but the tips of the stabilators also fold upwards.

Not only can the Su-27K's wingspan be reduced, but its length as well. This is provided by folding the tip of the tail "stinger" and folding up the pitot tube on the tip of the radome, which results in external dimensions rivaling those of the MiG-29K. Though of suitably stable design, the folding mechanisms for the wings and stabilators are responsible for a reduction in maximum allowable airframe loads. These are now 8 g rather than the usual 9 g of the Su-27; however, the MiG-29K also had to pay a similar price for the wing fold mechanism.

To test stowage of the Su-27K, a wooden model and a non-flyable aircraft were converted into a full-scale mockup (T-10-20KTM). It included the folding mechanisms and allowed stowage experiments to begin on the *Admiral Kuznetsov*. Another negative aspect of the mechanism is a somewhat lower internal fuel capacity; however, for the maritime role the T-10K was given a refueling probe. It is fitted on the left side of the fuselage in front of the cockpit, and for space reasons the IRST was moved to the right. With a corresponding tanker, the probe provides a flow rate of 290 to 528 gallons per minute. To enable refueling in the dark, two searchlights are deployed. They are situated on the side of the nose and direct their beams in the direction of the refueling hose. The Su-27K can be fitted with a UPAZ refueling pod in order to serve as a tanker itself. The maximum refueling rate is 608 gallons per minute. The more powerful AL-31F Series 3 engines were installed and have a maximum thrust of 28,100 pounds. This maximum thrust represents a short-term special regime and it is primarily intended for use in the event of a failed approach to the carrier deck with no possibility of landing successfully. The increase in power is achieved by raising engine inlet temperature by 75K and is not meant for continuous use, as it reduces engine life to 700 operating hours. In addition to the external changes, the aircraft's inner life was also partially changed.

A Su-27K taxis forward to the forward launch position's raised takeoff blocks (visible beneath the wings) on the deck of the Admiral Kuznetsov. *JSC Sukhoi/KnAAZ* **Right: the aircraft normally take off with full afterburning power.** *JSC Sukhoi/KnAAZ*

The main feature is a precise navigation system for use over water. As no ground-based navigation aids are available during a sea cruise, the carrier must provide navigational guidance and the Su-27K must be able to receive it. An autopilot system was integrated so that preprogrammed routes can be flown. During flight the navigation data can be corrected by the carrier's long-range navigation system or by satellite (the latter option was not added to the carrier until later). An automatic return flight mode to the carrier even permits an automatic approach until the undercarriage makes contact with the carrier deck. Logically, this operating mode is based on interaction with the associated systems aboard the carrier. An auto-throttle system is integrated into this system (automatic thrust regulation). It is rather questionable if this automatic landing system is used routinely. For in daily operations the standard landing serves as training, and should the automatic system become unserviceable, the pilot can call upon experience to make a routine landing. For this landing approach there is a light on the nosewheel leg, which transmits signals to the landing approach coordinator. The latter can then immediately determine if the approach is within the allowable parameters and can advise the pilot of this. Also located on the nose gear is a radio transmitter, which gives the ship a better radar image of the approaching aircraft. For at times the carrier's entire radio system is subject to powerful interference, which can interfere with or complicate the landing approach. In order to make the acceleration forces on the pilot bearable during takeoff over the ski jump, the K-36 ejection seat is installed at an angle of thirty degrees.

No major changes were made to the weapons systems. The OLS-27K IRST received new programming and can now detect targets at up to fifty-five miles in pursuit mode. The N-001 radar's look-down capabilities for detecting targets against the background of the sea were improved. It was also made capable of cooperating with the carrier's shipboard air defense radar, which can guide the Su-27K to its targets without the aircraft having to turn on its own radar. The interference caused when the radars of the Su-27K and the carrier overlap also had to be eliminated. The modified radar enabled the Su-27K to carry the large, supersonic Kh-41 Moskit anti-shipping missile. Because of its size and weight (about 8,800 pounds), just one of these missiles can be carried between the engine nacelles. The Su-27K has a data link system so as to be able to receive information from other aircraft of the carrier group and transmit information to them. Active *Sorbtsiya* jamming pods are carried on the wingtips for self-defense and these are considered very effective as they cover a broad spectrum.

The reason why the MiG-29 was ultimately not chosen for the carrier is probably due to the fact that Mikoyan appeared to place more value on testing the aircraft's advanced weapons system. With respect to attacks on ground and sea targets, this was in fact clearly superior to that of the Su-27K, but it was not ready in time for the MiG-29K's state acceptance trials. Too much time was spent on avionics testing and the MiG-29K with its modern equipment did not enter trials until a year after the Su-27K. One of the two prototypes was then damaged in a landing accident, which delayed testing significantly. Because of its superior range, greater numbers of hardpoints, and thrust-to-weight ratio, the air force command saw the Su-27K as the better choice. To what degree Simonov still knew how to use effective contacts from his time as deputy minister of the aviation industry, in order to have the Su-27K alone chosen for the new carrier, is questionable but is worth considering.

Originally both the Su-27K and the MiG-29K were supposed to be used together on the carrier. In the end, a total of twenty-four Su-33s were built and since mid-1994, they have served on the *Admiral Kuznetsov*, whose air unit was renamed the 279th Shipborne Fighter Aviation Regiment. The division of territory resulted in the loss of the NITKA complex, and the Russian Navy was unable to train additional carrier pilots there. For a time, the entire burden of conversion training fell on the Su-25UTG, which was used to train new carrier pilots. Not until 1994, after political negotiations and a basic renovation of the complex, was the Russian Navy again able to train there, making it possible for the service to guarantee an adequate number of trained carrier pilots. This finally happened twelve years after the first and only Russian aircraft carrier was laid down.

According to a leasing agreement reached in 1997, to use the facilities at Paki, Russia had to pay about 500,000 US dollars per year. After Viktor Yushchenko, with his anti-Russian stance, took office in the Ukraine, for a time Russia was again unable to use the complex. A new lease agreement was signed in 2007, and now Russia had to pay two million US dollars per year. With Russian military intervention in the

South Ossetian conflict with Georgia in 2008, and the division of the Ukraine in 2013, Russian carrier pilots were again unable to train at the NITKA complex. Not until the Crimea joined Russia did they again have unhindered access to the complex. But the absence of unhindered access to the NITKA complex was not the only thing that hampered and delayed the training of sufficient numbers of carrier pilots. As all flying units of the Russian military learned to their discomfort, in the 1990s, in particular there was almost no money available for fuel for military aircraft. This resulted in pilots not logging sufficient aircraft to remain current, which was reflected in a higher crash rate.

Carrier Operations

The *Admiral Kuznetsov* carried out its first long-range mission in 1995. The carrier left the Barents Sea, passed through the Atlantic into the Mediterranean, and paid a fleet visit to Syria. On board were six Su-27K production aircraft and one prototype. The pilots included members of the carrier wing and test pilots from Sukhoi and military testing establishments. As in Soviet times, the Russian fleet unit was shadowed by vessels of the US 6th Fleet, but unlike in previous times, a delegation from the Russian fleet was invited aboard the American carrier USS *America*. Wing commander Timur Apakidze subsequently flew in an A-6 Intruder. While the Russians did not allow any Americans on board the *Admiral Kuznetsov*, they did demonstrate the Su-27K impressively. During the cruise the carrier developed serious propulsion problems, sometimes having to sail at half power to avoid

further damage. The carrier's air defense radar was also not fully operational, as vital parts for it were made in the Ukraine and could no longer be delivered. The collapse of the economy not only took place in Russia as successor state to the USSR, but in all former Soviet republics that had become independent states. Many companies in the Ukraine were forced to close. The Su-33's radar and radar warning systems revealed serious shortcomings.

This was first demonstrated during a flight by an Su-33 as part of a fleet exercise in the Mediterranean in 1996, when suddenly and without warning by the radar warning system the aircraft was intercepted by two Israeli fighters that tried to force it to land in Israel. Thanks to the skill of the pilot and the capabilities of the Su-33, the aircraft was able to break away and return safely to the carrier. The carrier finally began its return to the Northern Fleet. They would soon be confronted with other problems, however.

Many important suppliers of military equipment closed after the collapse of the Soviet Union, and there was soon such an acute shortage of new tires for the Su-33 that flight operations had to be curtailed drastically. The fact that the air force now had to buy its jet fuel led to another reduction in flying hours, which had a negative effect on the carrier wing's operational readiness. In 1997, a handful of carrier pilots carried out air refueling experiments with the LII in Zhukovsky. These included trials with the UPAZ refueling pod, which enabled one Su-33 to refuel from another. That same year an exercise was held in the Barents Sea in which the pilots of the carrier wing conducted live missile firing. Then in 1999, the first night carrier landings above the Arctic Circle took place

The aircraft are taxied from the parking positions to the launch positions, ready to fly. *JSC Sukhoi/KnAAZ*

The deck elevator is such a tight fit for the Su-27 that the aircraft's main undercarriage touches the outer edge of the elevator. *JSC Sukhoi/KnAAZ*

Su-27KUB, here with double-swept canards.

in poor weather conditions on the *Admiral Kuznetsov*. The pilots—Maj. Gen. Timur Apakidze and Cols. Igor Kozhin and Pevel Kretov—were members of the carrier wing.

Predictably, because of Russia's difficult economic situation in the 1990s and early 2000s, the navy found itself facing a growing shortage of pilots. At times there were more cosmonauts than operational carrier pilots in Russia. This is also reflected in their average age of forty-three. In 2007, a Russian fleet unit, with the *Admiral Kuznetsov* as flagship, again made a cruise to the Mediterranean. An old acquaintance of the Russian Navy, or the former Soviet one, was the US Navy with its 6th Fleet in the Mediterranean. A *Ticonderoga* Class guided missile destroyer appeared and shadowed the fleet unit for a short time. For the carrier group, part of the exercise was of course to fly air sorties. These included Su-27Ks from the *Admiral Kuznetsov* escorting two Tu-160 long-range bombers carrying out simulated attacks in the Atlantic. There was criticism because no night flights were made during this cruise. The reason was that the Russians simply had not carried out enough night flights in the past to justify it. While the Su-27K was a dedicated carrier aircraft, it conducted much of its service from land

A Su-27K at the Severomorsk-3 land base. *Sergey Chaikovski*

(Severomorsk-3), because from a financial point of view Russia simply could not afford to operate the carrier and its Su-27Ks year round.

Another shortcoming that came to light was the language abilities of its pilots. Soviet and Russian pilots normally did not learn aviation English, resulting in communication difficulties, should, for example, an aircraft have to land at a foreign airfield in an emergency during the Mediterranean cruise. Six Su-33s had been lost since entering service, some were storage in depots, thus on average ten were based on the *Admiral Kuznetsov*. The latest crash occurred in early

December 2016, during operations in the Mediterranean Sea against ISIS. During an attempt to land, an arrestor cable again broke and the Su-33 crashed into the sea. The pilot ejected successfully. A MiG-29K had crashed in November 2016, also because of an arrestor cable failure during landing. The Russians never stated whether the condition of the system, construction, or the approach was responsible for the cable failure.

The fact that Russian carrier pilots could not regularly go to the NITKA complex for training and certification, and the fact that only the Su-25UTG was available for prospective pilots to train on the *Admiral Kuznetsov*, resulted in ever louder calls for a training aircraft. A naval version of the Su-27UB was considered; however, this was rejected because the view from the rear cockpit would have been inadequate, especially during the stressful landing phase. Sukhoi had begun looking into this problem in the late 1980s, and in this case a solution was not found until 1991.

Not until the 1990s, when carrier pilots openly complained about the lack of flight time and resulting lack of practice on the *Admiral Kuznetsov*, was the idea revived. The type was given the designation Su-27KUB. Sukhoi did not simply want to build a trainer, however. A variety of different versions should be able to be derived from it, or it should be a multi-role aircraft. A striking feature of the KUB is its double cockpit, with the seats arranged side by side like those of the Su-34, but with a round, conical radome. Access to the cockpit is not by way of a canopy, rather up a ladder and through an access hatch in the nosewheel bay as on the Su-34. The canards, vertical tail surfaces (slightly shortened), and stabilators are larger than those of the Su-33, and wingspan and wing area have also been increased (from forty-eight to 52.5 feet and from 730 to 753 square feet). The leading edge of the wing has a flexible sealing lip so that when the Krueger flaps are extended the airflow in this area encounters less drag. The fly-by-wire system was updated and adapted to the new aerodynamics, which together with the altered wing geometry results in better agility and increased range. The lift-drag ratio was improved by ten percent. The folding mechanism was moved outboard by about five feet on the wings and removed from the stabilators. These changes reduce the number of aircraft that can be accommodated on the carrier. The wings only fold to a vertical position, not to a position close to the vertical tails as on the Su-33. The KUB was converted from

the T-10K-4 and greater use was made of composite materials to avoid a significant increase in weight as a result of its increased dimensions.

Viktor Pugachev made the first flight in the Su-27KUB in April 1999, and that summer tests began at the NITKA complex to prepare the aircraft for carrier trials. These took place aboard the *Admiral Kuznetsov* in autumn 1999. The KUB was involved in a serious in-flight incident in 2000, and had it not been for the precise observations of Igor Votinzyev (then a Sukhoi test pilot) in an accompanying aircraft and the piloting skill of Viktor Pugachev, the aircraft would probably have been lost. As it was, he successfully flew the KUB back to Zhukovsky. In addition to testing the aircraft itself, the Su-27KUB was also used to test its onboard systems. It tested the Zhuk-MS/-MSE and MSFE radars made by Phazotron-NIIR. The MS and MSE had an electronically scanned slotted planar array and were superior to the N-001 in all respects; the MS matched the performance of the Bars installed in the MKI, while the MSFE (passive fixed antenna) surpassed the latter even though it was about two-and-a-half times lighter than the Bars radar of the Su-30MKI, at least according to information provided by the manufacturer. In 2003, the KUB was fitted with AL-31FP thrust-vector power plants and in 2004, began making flights from the *Admiral Kuznetsov*. The leading edges of the canards were modified to double delta planform.

Two prototypes were built, but consideration for procurement by the Russian military did not take place, for to this day none have been purchased or ordered. The navy must simply have lacked the money to procure the KUB and has repeatedly postponed the necessary modernization of the carrier and even the Su-33. For some years Russia has been developing and building a completely new carrier, which will take some years. The Sukhoi T-50 might be a possible carrier aircraft, for without updating, the Su-33 will have a difficult time coping with the F/A-18E/F, the Rafale, and the F-35.

Consequently, one should not expect to see the KUB enter service, at least with the Russian Navy. It is unlikely that China is interested in the KUB, as it is trying to build its own designs. A comprehensive update of the Su-33 seems long overdue, and this could be based on elements of the Su-30SM or even the Su-35S. For its aircraft carriers the USA has developed the F-35, which is smaller than the F-22, allowing more aircraft to be accommodated shipboard. As the new Russian carrier will surely not become available for some time, modernization of

Su-27KUB landing on the arrestor hook installation at Saki. *Alexey Micheyev*

the Su-33 will become vital if Russia does not want to fall too far behind Western aircraft carriers and their aircraft.

In autumn 2016, the *Admiral Kuznetsov* carrier group made its way to the Syrian coast, where Su-33s flew combat missions against ISIS forces in Syria. This was only made possible by installation of the new SVP-24 bomb-aiming system, which made it possible for the Su-33 to use unguided bombs against stationary targets with a level of precision approaching that of guided weapons. The system is supported by the GLONASS satellite system in order to accurately compare the position of the aircraft relative to the target. First, however, it analyzes flight data, such as airspeed, altitude, and attitude. An advantage of this system compared to the American JDAM, in which a guidance package is fitted to unguided bombs, is that the SVP-24 is permanently installed in the aircraft and only has to be purchased once. It can also be installed in all existing combat aircraft. This system represents a long overdue update of the Su-33, although it can only be seen as a beginning. The original radar warning system has been replaced by a more modern one

(Pastel), and more powerful AL-31FM-1 engines with a longer operating life have been installed, illustrating the need to update the Su-33 until it is replaced by a new type.

Su-30MK/-MKI (T-10PMK)

Sukhoi's goal for the Su-30MK was to create an aircraft that could operate, not just in the role of air combat fighter, but also as against ground targets using guided air-to-surface weapons. The aircraft's weapons system had to be significantly upgraded to use such weapons. The radar was upgraded and, although it could still track just ten air targets, it was now capable of engaging two simultaneously. Detection range for a target with a radar reflective area of 10.75 square feet (one square meter) was sixty miles, and the radar's guidance range for the R-27R air-to-air missile was up to forty miles. The updated radar also made it possible to use the equally new R-77 AAM. The available versions of the R-27 were retained in the Su-30MK's armament spectrum.

Chapter 5: Variants in Detail

A new generation of Soviet guided weapons, the television- and laser-guided Kh-29, was first used in the Soviet war in Afghanistan. This weapon made it possible to accurately strike pinpoint targets, albeit at ranges of only up to six miles. The Su-30MK had available a developed version of this weapon, the Kh-59ME, with a television seeker head. Also added to the arsenal were the Kh-29L and T (laser-/TV-guided versions), the Kh-31P and A (anti-radar/-ship), the S-25L (laser-guided large-caliber rocket), the Kh-25ML (laser-guided), and the Kab-500Kr/Kab-500L and Kab-1500L television- and laser-guided bombs. The Su-27S's weapons load was initially increased from 8,818 to 17,636 pounds and the number of hardpoints from ten to twelve.

Additional avionics had to be added to enable the aircraft to use television- and laser-guided weapons; however, there was no room in the airframe of the Su-30MK unless the designers were willing to undertake an expensive redesign. The necessary avionics were therefore housed in pods that could be mounted on one of the hardpoints if required. The proven GSh-301 cannon with 150 rounds of ammunition was mounted in the starboard wing root. To protect the airframe from powder gases, a large area of protective skinning was placed in front of the muzzle. The standard of the ultimate version delivered to India was the Su-30MKI (I stands for India). External features of the MKI are the canards mounted on the leading edge root extensions (LERX) and its two-seat cockpit. The former improve airflow over the fuselage, especially at high angles of attack.

The first production version to use these canards was the Su-27K. In addition to these aerodynamic improvements, thrust-vector control was incorporated into a production combat aircraft for the first time. The selected power plants are the AL-31FP, which represent a further development of the AL-31FU from the Su-37. In contrast to those of the Su-37, the engine nozzles can now be deflected fifteen degrees vertically as well as horizontally, which further drastically increases the palette of flight maneuvers. If the pilot wishes to use thrust-vector control, he must simply flip a switch to integrate it into the flight control system. Thrust-vector control was adapted into the fly-by-wire system, and this automatically controls the thrust-vector nozzles in combination with the control surfaces to achieve the optimal interaction between them. The fly-by-wire system was expanded about all flight axes and is designed with quadruple redundancy.

A Su-30MKI from the pre-production series with brown sensor cords on the upper wing surfaces. *Irkut Corporation*

Litening targeting pod from the Israeli manufacturer Rafael.

The Su-27 had just one such channel for the pitch axis. The main focus of the MKI, however, is its increased combat capabilities. Foremost is its N-011M Bars radar developed by NIIP, a passive phased-array radar. Instead of the original ten targets, fifteen can now be tracked simultaneously, while up to four can be engaged at the same time. Detection range is up to eighty-five miles, thirty-six miles from the rear in air-to-air mode. Search angle is 70° in azimuth and +/- 40° in elevation (up to 40° in azimuth with electronic scanning, while 70° is achieved with mechanical scanning).

Tank formations can be detected at up to thirty miles, ships of destroyer size or greater at up to 150 miles (while with a radar resolution of sixty-five feet, marine targets can be detected at up to 240 miles), and bridges at up to seventy-five miles. The Bars (Leopard) can be used in ground tracking and mapping modes, and resolution can vary from 980 to ten feet depending on purpose. The ability to track ground targets while simultaneously engaging aerial targets is offered as an example of the Bars' versatility. The developer gave the Bars the ability to count the compressor blades of approaching aircraft (provided they are not concealed by parts of the airframe) and to identify the type of aircraft based its radar reflection. This is roughly comparable to sonar detection of submarines, which for a long time could be identified by their sound signatures. The Bars-M transmits target data to the navigation system, allowing the pilot to set course toward the target. The radar then temporarily turns itself off to avoid detection for as long as possible as the aircraft approaches its target.

India insisted on a multinational collection of avionics, while the radar and IRST remained Russian. The head-up-display and electronic defense system came from Israel and the helmet-mounted sight from the Ukraine. The IRST is the much improved OLS-301. It is capable of detecting targets

{"cx":0.70,"cy":0.21,"w":0.42,"h":0.25}

up to fifty-five miles away if they were moving away (hot exhaust gases from the jet exhaust facing the OLS). Approaching targets could be located at up to thirty miles, scanning area is sixty degrees in azimuth and -15 to plus sixty degrees in elevation. The cockpit underwent a thorough redesign, with three color displays in the front cockpit and four installed in the rear cockpit. These and the navigation system (with laser gyros and GPS) came from France.

The Rafael Litening targeting pod was also of Israeli design and was envisaged for the use of guided weapons at any time of day and in all weather conditions. The pod houses an infrared imaging sensor, a digital television channel, and a laser target illuminator and rangefinder. It is capable of engaging moving and stationary targets. The targeting pod is used by many air forces and has been used successfully in many combat situations. Also updated was the radar warning system, in which the receivers disappeared from the outsides of the engine air intakes and were integrated in revised form in the leading edges of the wings. This arrangement was adopted by all newly developed or updated versions of the Su-27. The Su-30MKI's aircraft system computers are produced in India.

A new feature of the Su-30MKI is the K-36D-3.5 ejection seat from Zvezda, which replaces the K-36DM of earlier production batches. The seat is somewhat lighter, cushioning was improved, and the ejection options have been enhanced, especially in extreme flight attitudes and low-level inverted flight. To enable the pilot to withstand high g forces, the seat was installed at an angle of thirty degrees. Maximum gross weight rose to 83,775 pounds, requiring twin nosewheels and airframe strengthening. The MKI is capable of carrying all of the weapons envisaged for the Su-30MK and it also has twelve hardpoints. As the Bars was not initially capable of its full operational spectrum, some of these weapons did not become available until later.

Added to the aircraft's arsenal was the BrahMos anti-ship missile, which at the moment is only envisaged for the Su-30MKI but can also be expanded to other versions. This weapon gives the Indian Air Force the ability to strike opponents far beyond its national borders. The rear cockpit is provided with basic flight controls so that the WSO can fly the aircraft in an emergency. The wing structure was slightly modified, increasing fuel capacity by 1,320 pounds. In addition to air refueling capability, the MKI can carry a refueling pod made in Great Britain in order to refuel other

The Bars N-011M radar of the Su-30MKI. *Irkut Corporation*

aircraft in flight. The aircraft was not just equipped with combat-relevant avionics, however. The Mk.3 equipment configuration includes a South African monitoring and analysis system, which monitors the condition of the aircraft and reports failures. It also records general changes, which are evaluated by ground personnel, allowing them to identify predictable failures or shortcomings.

Su-35S

Although the designation Su-35 had been used for a development line in the 1980s, and the resulting design flew in the late 1980s and early 1990s, the Su-27S was a completely new development of the Su-27. The Su-35S is an aircraft that falls between the fourth and fifth generations and possesses avionics systems that are used in part in modified form by the Sukhoi T-50. It appears that the most significant changes are inside rather than outside the Su-35S. It appears that while an effort was made to achieve a fundamental modernization of the Su-27, no drastic airframe changes were undertaken so as to keep costs down for potential customers.

On the other hand, the aerodynamics in particular, combined with thrust-vector control and modernization fly-by-wire system, appear to be so outstanding that, for example, the installation of canards and a major redesign of the vertical tail surfaces could be dispensed with. External changes are therefore limited to a reshaping of the nose section to accommodate the new Irbis-E radar with its more streamlined radome. The aircraft's rudders were enlarged and the rudder trailing edges are now vertical. Wing area was

The multi-role variant of the Su-30MKI, here carrying the BrahMos anti-ship guided weapon between the engine air intakes. *Irkut Corporation/Piotr Butovski*

increased by increasing wingspan from to forty-eight to 50.2 feet. The speed brake on the fuselage spine was eliminated completely, replaced by an additional fuel tank. Air braking on the ground is now accomplished by using the rudders as speed brakes. There are no longer radio antennas in the tips of the vertical tails. The tail "stinger" was also enlarged to accommodate more fuel.

Compared to the Su-27, total fuel weight rose by 4,630 pounds to 24,912 pounds. The Su-35S is the first variant of the Su-27 (with the exception of the Su-34) able to carry external fuel tanks (each holding 528 gallons) under its wings. Like preceding designs, the Su-35S was also given an air refueling probe for long-range missions. Fuel transfer rate in the air is 290 gallons per minute. The airframe was strengthened by increasing the number of titanium

components, in part to withstand higher loads, especially during extremely tight thrust-vector maneuvers, but also to increase airframe life. This is now 6,000 hours, with the first general overhaul at 1,500 hours. The undercarriage was also strengthened and twin nosewheels were adopted. The shape of the tail "stinger" was modified, changing the rear radar warning receiver resulting in a lance-like shape. The braking parachute is again housed in the tail "stinger," resulting in

deletion of the rearward-facing radar installed in the Su-27M. Where the Su-27M's braking chute was housed now accommodates a central TA-14-130-35 APU. While all other AL-31F engines had an APU on the accessory gearbox flange-mounted to the power plant, these two individual auxiliary power units disappeared from the engines of the Su-35S. The TA-14-130-35 starts both engines and supplies power and hydraulics on the ground if no ground equipment

Aircraft 901, the first prototype of the Su-35S with black anti-glare panel in front of the cockpit. *JSC Sukhoi*

is available (these are normally used to reduce wear on the onboard systems).

While Sukhoi made few changes to the Su-35S's exterior, its inner workings underwent significant changes. Here, too, the radar plays the key role, as it remains the primary detector of air and ground targets. Designated Irbis-E, it is a passive phased-array antenna (with an antenna diameter of 35.4 inches) from the developer NIIP. It is essentially a developed version of the Bars radar in the Su-30MKI and has been under development since 2004. The Irbis-E was tested in a Su-30MK2. Detection range was drastically increased and the Irbis-E is capable of detecting aircraft with a radar cross-

section of 32.3 square feet at up to 120 miles and up to 102 miles if the target is flying close to the ground. If the radar is operating in narrow scan mode, the Irbis-E is capable of detecting airborne targets at up to 240 miles. Stealth cruise missiles with a radar cross-section of 0.10 square feet can be detected at up to fifty-five miles. Thirty targets can be tracked at the same time and eight engaged simultaneously with active air-to-air missiles, and four of these eight targets can be engaged at ranges up to 180 miles. If semi-active air-to-air missiles are used, two targets can be engaged at the same time. The Irbis-E can also detect large ground targets at up to 240 miles, and up to four moving ground

Aircraft 902, the second prototype of the Su-35S with splinter camouflage scheme, which breaks up the contours of the aircraft. *JSC Sukhoi*

targets can be tracked and two engaged simultaneously. The electronic scanning angle is +/- 60 degrees in all directions and if the phased-array antenna is turned mechanically the azimuth angle is increased to +/- 120 degrees. In ground mode radar maps can be produced with a resolution of ten feet; in low-level flight the Irbis-E can function as a terrain-avoidance radar. The Irbis-E can detect tank concentrations at up to forty miles, ships to 240 miles, and bridges to 120 miles. The developer promises that in service, faulty modules (so-called LRU – Line Replaceable Units) can be replaced in thirty minutes, significantly reducing downtime during repairs.

Of course the Su-35S can continue to rely on the tried and tested infrared sensor. This is the much improved OLS-35, which in addition to the infrared seeker also has a laser target illuminator, tracker, and rangefinder, plus a TV camera. In pursuit mode the OLS-35 can detect air targets at a distance of fifty-five miles, closing targets at a minimum of thirty miles. The laser rangefinder measures reliably in air mode to twelve miles, and eighteen miles in ground mode, each with an

accuracy of +/- 15 feet. The OLS-35's scanning angle is +/- 90º in azimuth and +60º and - 15º in elevation. The OLS-35 can engage four air targets simultaneously. The Sura helmet-mounted sight is integrated as the third targeting system and is a modernized version of the sight that always caused such a sensation when German MiG-29s took part in foreign exercises. Some data is now displayed in the sight glass.

The cockpit underwent a radical change. It is now a true glass cockpit and has two central fifteen-inch multifunction displays and a new wide-angle head up display. The number of switches and buttons on the control stick and throttle lever was reduced, reflecting the HOTAS principle. Systems are operated mainly by switching elements of the HOTAS and the display screens. There are no analogue instruments left in the cockpit. The control stick is mounted on an electronic stump and no longer has any mechanical connections to the control surfaces. The stick is shorter and has less deflection travel than a conventional stick. The throttle lever was derived from that of the Su-37 and reacts only to pilot hand pressure. This decreased travel helps the pilot better control the aircraft at high g loads, as the smaller deflection paths require less force even at corresponding forces. The Su-35S has a so-called "dark cockpit," which means that warnings or reports do not appear until critical situations arise, relieving the pilot of the need to constantly monitor systems/conditions/his instruments. A new system in Russian aircraft is the oxygen generator developed by Zvezda. This extracts oxygen from the surrounding air and saves it in a container and consequently an unlimited supply is available. The crew is therefore not limited by the oxygen carried aboard the aircraft during long-range missions. Also from Zvezda is the new K-36D-5 ejection seat, a developed version of the K-36D-3.5. It has a greater adjustment range where the pilot's body size is concerned. The temperature range in which the seat can be operated (environmental temperatures based on different climate zones) has also been expanded.

Where possible this is based on experience with Su-30MK aircraft from India, Algeria, and Malaysia, as higher temperatures prevail there all year long, unlike in Russia. Some parts of the seat may have experienced increased wear due to the prevailing high temperatures. For cold climate zones, the K-36D-5 includes heated seats for the crew. Zero-zero ejection performance has been further improved. With the complete survival package, the seat weighs a maximum of 220 pounds. Ejection is possible at speeds and altitudes up to Mach 2.5 and 65,600 feet.

While the Su-35S is no typical stealth aircraft, design elements were integrated that reduce its radar signature. These extend from the use of radar-absorbing materials and paint to a special coating for the canopy (1/6th of the radar reflective area of the Su-27) to the possible addition of a plasma generator. The first information about this device was made public in 1999, when the Keldysh Research Institute released it. With a weight of just 220 pounds, the generator forms a plasma field of selected size and shape around an object, reducing its radar signature by a factor of one hundred. It is not known if the aircraft carrying the generator can still use its own radar.

Because of the device's low weight and power consumption the generator can be installed in the aircraft. In 2002, it was tested on a Su-27, which then completely disappeared from radar. Allegedly the device is already ready for installation as standard equipment on the Su-35S and MiG-35. If this is true, it would revolutionize the radar war. However, as the Su-35S continues not to have an active radar jamming system on board, it could be questionable whether this generator is actually available. Another possibility would be that the generator is installed only in domestically-based Russian aircraft for reasons of secrecy. Special attention was also paid to the engine air intakes, which were coated with an anti-radar material. The frontal aspect of engine turbine blades is an ideal radar reflector for enemy radars. In addition to this high-technology system, radar warning receivers are of course fitted providing 360-degree coverage.

The aircraft also has missile warning and laser sensors. The Su-35S's missile warning system operates in the UV band and detects the waveband of the plasma field from the exhaust gases of enemy missiles. This is, however, at the same time a disadvantage, for a UV sensor requires very high temperatures to be able to locate such a heat source. This means by implication that the UV sensor cannot detect a missile after its solid fuel has burned out. On the other hand the advantage of a UV system is that it is not influenced by heat echoes from the sun or other infrared sources. A further advantage is that UV waves are not absorbed by moisture in the atmosphere and the system can therefore detect incoming missiles in any weather. Should these come from the disturbing earth background, they are detected better by UV sensors than infrared devices.

Fixed antenna of the Irbis N-035 radar covered with protective foil.

Su-35S cockpit simulator.
United Aircraft Corporation/
Marina Lystseva

On the other hand a UV sensor cannot detect a missile against a clear sky as well as an infrared detector. The field of view of a UV system is also significantly narrower than that of an infrared system. UV systems are much simpler in design and also less costly than infrared or radar systems. The laser warning system advises the pilot if his aircraft is, for example, illuminated by a hostile laser rangefinder. This system also provides 360-degree coverage, its sensors located in the upper nose and beneath the tail "stinger." The navigation system includes a laser-gyro-stabilized inertial system as well as a satellite-supported system and radio navigation aids. For routine use the navigation system does not absolutely require external sources like those described above, making the Su-35S able to precisely determine its position autonomously over long distances, about twice as accurately as previous systems. The communications system was logically brought up to the latest digital standard and includes both VHF and UHF systems as well as a shortwave system. Data link allows selected material or communications to be transmitted in code to ground stations or friendly aircraft automatically or manually.

Almost the entire antenna array was redesigned, and there are no longer antennas in the tips of the vertical tails as on most Soviet/Russian combat aircraft. In addition to the familiar guided weapons (R-73, R-27, R-77, and air-to-surface weapons of the Kh family and all types of guided bombs), the Su-35S is capable of using long-range air-to-surface and anti-shipping guided weapons. These include the subsonic 3M-14AE for stationary ground targets, the subsonic 3M-54AE1 anti-shipping weapon, and the supersonic 3M-54AE anti-ship weapon. For many years a new long-range missile from Novator has been displayed on the Su-35S. Its designation is KS-172 and it is not simply an air-to-air missile. It is supposedly capable of engaging distant targets, especially AWACS aircraft, at ranges between 120 and 240 miles. Novator has not released further information, specifically with regard to the missile's performance parameters. The weapon is, however, larger and heavier than all previous long-range AAMs. As tests with the new RVV-SD medium-range missile have already been carried out using the Su-27SM3, its use on the Su-35S as well as of the also new RVV-MD (short range) and RVV-BD (long range) missiles

The new radome of the Su-35S without pitot. A missile-warning sensor is installed in front of the IRST. *JSC Sukhoi/KnAAZ/ Lukin*

Here the leading-edge root extensions demonstrate their full effectiveness in producing powerful vortices. The modified tail stinger is now spear-shaped. *Gilles Dennis*

may already have become standard on the Su-35S, finally replacing the R-27. To make the Su-35S with its new weapons system and weapons absolutely perfect, like its stablemate the Su-30MKI, it includes thrust-vector technology with all of its known advantages.

As the aircraft's gross weight has risen, an increase in thrust was necessary. From this came Product 117S, also called the AL-41F1. The Sukhoi, Saturn, and UMPO companies all provided funding for development of the new engine. The 117S is a much-modified AL-31FP with increased engine diameter, redesigned compressors and turbines, and a completely new digital engine control system. The combustion chamber was also redesigned. These changes result in an increase in thrust at full afterburning power to 31,923 pounds (sixteen percent more than the AL-31F) and 19,333 pounds at maximum dry thrust. One

important attribute of a power plant for a fifth-generation combat aircraft is supercruise, the ability to achieve supersonic speeds without afterburner. The 117S does not yet possess this ability, but it seems to have been included in the propulsion system of the T-50 and can possibly be retrofitted to the Su-35S. The first static trials took place in 2003, and flight testing began using the tenth prototype of the Su-27M in 2004. Total engine life increased to 4,000 hours, and the first main maintenance is due after 1,000 hours and the first general overhaul at 1,500 hours. The AL-41F was developed and produced by NPO Saturn, with UMPO sharing in production. Incidentally, the 117S is temporarily powering the Sukhoi T-50.

The first prototype of the Su-35S with the Bort number 901 took to the air at Zhukovsky on February 19, 2008. It was flown by Sergey Bogdan of Sukhoi. The nineteenth of

Su-35S with the newer blue-gray camouflage scheme and red protective covers over the nose optronics. *Sergey Chaikovski*

Armed with two S-13 rocket pods under the wings at the Pipetsk testing center. *Sergey Chaikovski*

February, was surely not chosen by chance, for Vladimir Putin and Dimitry Medvedev were to visit Zhukovsky on the twentieth and could thus see both the MiG-35 and the Su-35S. This first flight brought no problems to light. Aircraft 902, the second prototype, made its first flight in November of the same year. The first important contract for the Su-35S was signed in 2009, which was of importance both to Sukhoi

and the Russian Air Force. That same year a Su-35S prototype (Bort number 904) crashed because of engine failure during takeoff. Pilot Yevgeni Frolov was able to eject safely.

Forty-eight Su-35S aircraft are claimed to have been delivered by 2015. The first aircraft were flown to Aktyubinsk for service trials in 2011, after which they moved to Lipetsk. Conversion training of flight and ground crews took place there as well as the writing of documentation for air tactics and general flight operations. The need for several important changes became apparent during flight trials and these were made by the manufacturer KnAAZ (formerly KnAAPO). The first operational unit was the 23rd Fighter Regiment at Dzemgi near the Chinese border in the Far East. The first aircraft did not have the complete armaments suite envisaged by the Su-35S project. Those aircraft were later flown to the manufacturer and retrofitted there. The operational aircraft received a new tactical camouflage finish consisting of pale blue-turquoise undersides and dark gray upper surfaces.

All aircraft delivered after 2014, however, had pale blue undersides and pale gray and blue upper surfaces, with the borders between the two colors rounded instead of being

Above: The flight line at Lipetsk. Below: the yellow patches on the wingtips, vertical tail, and tail stinger are low-voltage formation lights. They shine weakly in the dark and help other aircraft orient themselves in formation. *Both, Sergey Chaikovski*

straight lines. Ultimately, the ground personnel as well as the pilots had to receive conversion training. This brought a major change, especially in diagnostic and evaluation technology, introducing laptops, tablets, and the most modern computer technology to the maintenance units. The Russian Air Force was confronted with this new technology for the first time when it introduced the Su-34 and Su-35S. Training on the new equipment was strongly supported by Sukhoi and

KnAAZ. A contract for delivery of a second batch of fifty aircraft to the Russian Air Force was concluded at the end of 2015, and by 2020, about one hundred Su-35S aircraft will be serving in Russia.

Su-34 (Su-27IB/T-10V)

At the beginning of the 1980s, the tactical air force of the Soviet Union demanded a multi-role aircraft that was to be very agile and fast and also have great range and payload. It was to be capable of deep-penetration attacks against enemy targets, even in the face of powerful air defenses. This required a high degree of survivability. These seemingly opposed requirements could only be met by creating a new fourth-generation aircraft. The new fighter-bomber was not to be as helpless against enemy fighters as those of the previous generation. What the air force wanted was a type that could both effectively strike ground targets and, if necessary, engage and even defeat enemy fighters. The modernization of existing designs would not have sufficed.

For decades Sukhoi had been responsible for tactical combat aircraft (Su-7, Su-17, Su-24, Su-25) and once again turned to his task. Logically, the designers examined the new Su-27, which possessed extraordinary maneuverability and range (speed was also more than sufficient). They needed to optimize the Su-27 so that it could operate at supersonic speeds at low altitude. Since the Su-24, it had been recognized that demanding low-level missions could only be handled effectively by a two-man crew. The Soviets believed that the crew of two should be seated side by side rather than in tandem. The presence of a second control stick in the WSO's position suggests that he can fly the aircraft if the pilot is disabled. The side by side arrangement requires fewer indicators, as it is possible to look from one seat to the other side. This configuration probably pays dividends, especially during long missions. The aircraft has a toilet and equipment to prepare food (more for warming food than actually preparing it). This would be much more difficult to achieve with a tandem cockpit. This concept was adopted from a project for a two-seat naval version of the Su-27, the Su-27MK2. The forward fuselage was no longer cylindrical in shape, but instead had a flattened cross-section. The fuselage sides were now vertical surfaces, which as a stealth feature reduced the radar reflective area.

The leading edge root extensions were redesigned to accommodate canards. To improve flight characteristics, the aircraft, now designated the Su-27IB (*Istrebitel Bombardirovchik*—fighter-bomber, internal name T-10V) was fitted with canards. These canards reduced gust loads in low-level flight. To make long missions as bearable for the crew as possible (the aircraft was required to remain in the air for several hours and take on tasks previously carried out by medium bombers), the aircraft was to have a pressurized cockpit that made it possible for the crew to fly without oxygen masks up to an altitude of 33,000 feet. The cabin pressure inside the cockpit was similar to that of a typical commercial airliner. These features required that the cockpit canopy be fixed; consequently, the crew cannot enter and leave the cockpit in the conventional manner.

Access to the cockpit is by way of a ladder attached to the nose gear and a hatch in the cockpit floor, the same as in bomber aircraft. The nose gear itself was reinforced and

The first prototype T-10V-1, identifiable by its Bort number 42. This aircraft still has single wheels on the main undercarriage legs and a short tail stinger. The second prototype, number 43, introduced twin mainwheels and the lengthened tail stinger.
Malcom Nason

Boundary layer fences were installed on the upper wing surfaces of production aircraft. *Svido Stanislav*

because of the aircraft's increased weight has twin tires. It is also mounted further forward to ease access to the cockpit. The nose gear retracts rearward. In the event of an emergency the crew can still abandon the Su-34 with their ejection seats. The ejection sequence is three times faster than that of the Su-24. To improve crew survivability, the entire cockpit is designed as a titanium capsule up to 0.67 inches thick and weighing approximately 3,300 pounds. Part of this armor also protects fuel tanks and part of the propulsion system. In fact, the cockpit is so designed to allow the crew to stand and even lie down. The ejection seats are fitted with massage systems to make long missions more bearable.

Allegedly not even the Tu-160 is as comfortable, which is the subject of many complaints from its crews (the extensive updating of the Tu-160 may well have overcome this shortcoming). Externally, it is also noticeable that the tail fins have disappeared. These are not required during operations at low altitude, nor are the adjustable air intake ramps, which are now fixed. The intake doors on the undersides of the forward air intakes have been deleted, replaced by auxiliary air inlet doors on the inner sides. The fixed geometry intakes result in a lower maximum airspeed of 1,180 mph at altitude;

however, they do save weight. This loss of airspeed is acceptable, as the Su-34 is intended for low-altitude operation. The removal of the tail fins is said to have favorably affected the aircraft's radar signature and also saved weight.

The first prototype, the T-10V-1, with the Bort number 42, took to the air for the first time in 1990, flown by Sukhoi test pilot Anatoli Ivanov. This prototype was converted from a Su-27UB and was used mainly for aerodynamic trials. The distinctive large tail "stinger" of the later Su-34, which contains additional fuel, was not installed on this aircraft. The first prototype had a self-defense radar mounted in the tail. This was intended to monitor the area behind the aircraft, and at that time (1990s) the media claimed that it could also be used with rearward-firing missiles. The current Su-34 has an APU in the last section of the tail "stinger," which probably supplies the aircraft's extensive electronics suite with power while on the ground. However, as the tail "stinger" is still marked in color and this suggests a small radome (at least the fairing of a technical system), a miniature tail radar could have been installed there, although a tail-mounted radar warning receiver is more likely. The braking parachute had to be moved from the tail "stinger" and is located several yards

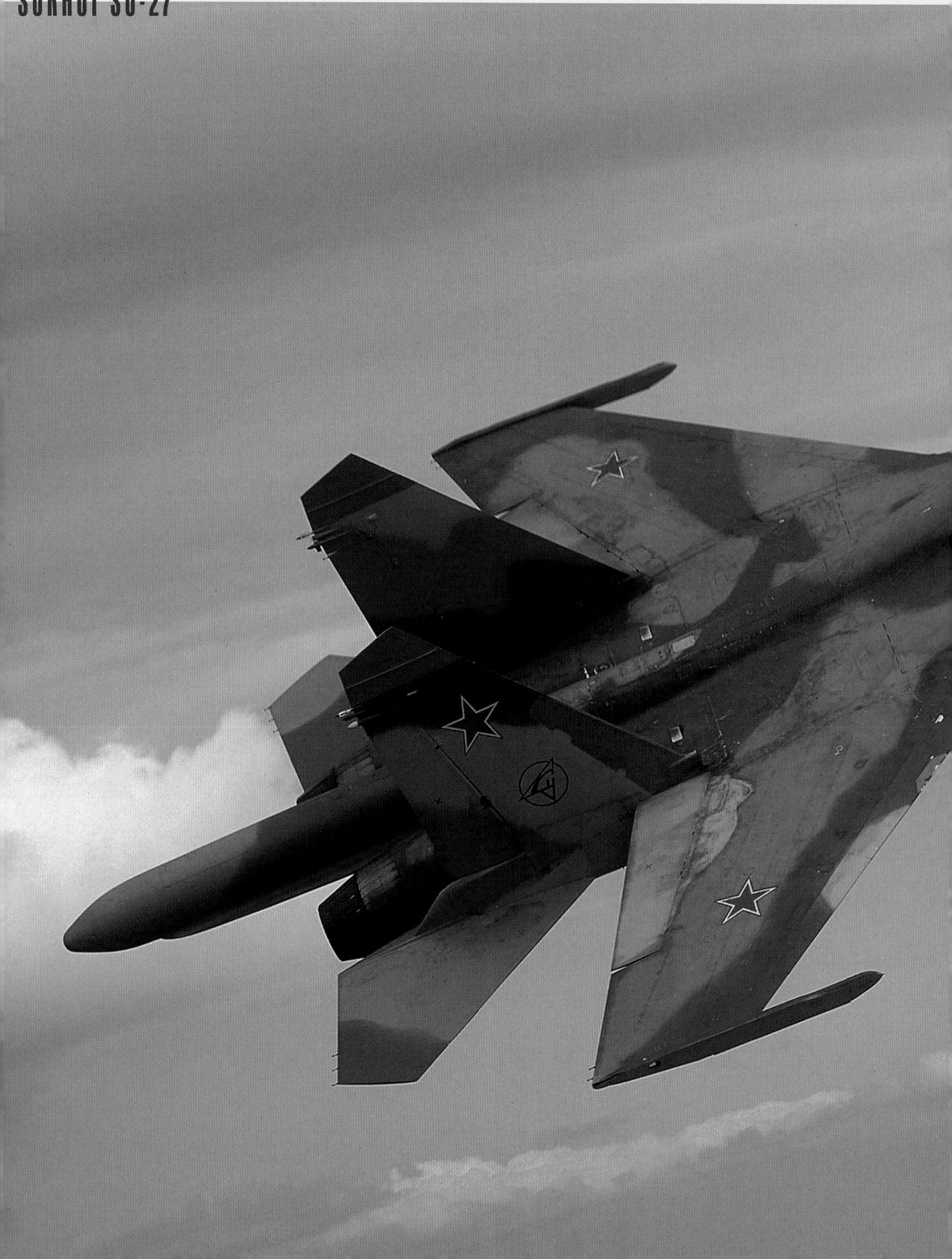

The fourth Su-34 prototype with the Bort number 45, here
in the ultimate configuration. The Bort number 349 was a
display number for foreign airshows.
United Aircraft Corporation

Aircraft 45 with Kab-500L guided bombs; Kh-31 air-to-ground guided cruise missile; and R-27, R-77, and R-73 air-to-air missiles. *United Aircraft Corporation*

further forward. A parachute container opens upwards and ejects the braking chute. The main undercarriage of the first prototype had single wheels, but the second prototype and the production aircraft were equipped as follows: two wheels of identical size in a tandem arrangement, rotating ninety degrees during retraction. This undercarriage configuration can deal with the aircraft's greater weight but also permits operation from unpaved fields. By rearranging the fuselage tanks, fuel capacity was increased to 26,455 pounds. A refueling probe was fitted and the inner hard points were connected to the fuel system, allowing external tanks to be carried under the wings (each 792 gallons). Incidentally, the Su-34 is the first member of the Su-27 able to carry such

tanks. The external tanks are self-sealing to a certain degree, as they are provided with a foaming material that expands and fills holes.

The radar once again forms the key element of the avionics system. Developed and produced by the Leninetz Factory in Leningrad, it has a passive fixed-array antenna, and scanning is achieved electronically, with no mechanical scanning. Scanning range is +/- 60 degrees in azimuth and elevation. Development began in 1987, and continued until the mid-1990s. It can detect, track, and engage both air and ground targets. The W004 operates in the three-centimeter (1.18 inch) waveband, and in ground tracking mode it can produce radar maps of the earth's surface and act as a terrain avoidance radar. Small ground targets like tanks can be detected at up to eighteen miles, fighter size aerial targets at up to fifty-five miles, and large land targets to 150 miles. This is an impressive performance for a radar developed in the 1990s.

In the meantime, it may have been replaced by a much improved or entirely new as-yet-unknown radar, possibly with an active fixed antenna. Information has not been forthcoming either from the manufacturer of the Su-34 or from Leninetz. Another targeting system is the Platan electro-optical system with a TV camera and laser illuminator, which is installed flush with the outer skin between the engine nacelles. A box with a window is lowered when the system is active. The system is designed primarily for use at medium to high altitudes, as its view angle is restricted. The system is similar to the Kaira carried by the Su-24, which has elements similar to those of the Platan system. It enables most attacks to be carried out in conditions of poor visibility, but not in bad

weather conditions with fog, rain, etc. In such conditions the radar must be used to search for and acquire data on targets, which makes the Su-34 much easier to detect. Use of the Russian Sapsan pod (manufacturer UOMZ), which integrates TV, laser, and FLIR sensors, is possible for low-level missions. A new Russian pod has been observed on the MiG-35 for some time.

Indian Su-30MKI aircraft use the Litening pod made in Israel by Rafael, and the Malaysian Su-30MKM the Damocles pod made by Thales of France. License production of the latter in Russia was considered but no agreement was reached (possibly because of an embargo). The third targeting system is the helmet-mounted sight, which previously gained worldwide attention during mock combats against German MiG-29s and Indian Su-30MKIs. Some emphasis was placed on stealth features for evading enemy radar detection. In addition to the features described above, a radar-absorbing paint finish has been used. According to Sukhoi, in low-level

The aircraft's flattened nose shape resulted in the Su-34 being nicknamed Platypus. *Sergey Chaikovski*

SUKHOI SU-27

True-to-life simulator cockpit of the Su-34 as used in operational service. *United Aircraft Corporation*

The 3,000-liter (792-gallon) external fuel tank is mounted between the engine air intakes. *United Aircraft Corporation*

The gray triangle between the leading edges of the engine air intakes is the Platan optical targeting system.

Vladislav Perminov

flight the Su-34 has the radar signature of a modern cruise missile (at least when viewed frontally).

A passive radar warning system is standard equipment. There is also an active jamming system in the form of various types of jamming pods (the *Sorbtsiya*, which has been around for quite some time, and a new model, the SAP-518) on the wingtips. A single large pod (SAP-14) is also carried beneath the central fuselage. The jamming pods operate in a frequency range of one to eighteen GHz, and large quantities of chaff and flares are contained in the tail "stinger." In the past there was talk of a missile-warning system being installed, but

examination of the airframe does not reveal any clues to suggest the presence of such a system.

The various systems used by the Su-30MKM and Su-35S allow them to be clearly recognized, which is not the case with the Su-34. The navigation system includes an INS with laser gyroscope and a satellite system with GLONASS (Russian satellite system) or GPS (American system). Routes can be precisely programmed and flown to within three feet. The cockpit underwent considerable modernization. While the first prototypes did have display screens in the cockpit, they were monochrome and just three were installed. Since then five modern color displays have been installed, along with newer digital operating consoles. The number of analogue instruments was drastically reduced, with just several backup instruments for the most important flight parameters remaining.

New weapons were vital if the Su-34 was to exploit its full combat potential. All guided weapons then considered modern, from the Kh-29 to the Kh-41 and the Kab-500 to Kab-1500 guided bombs, were all developed in parallel with the Su-27 and MiG-29, and some entered service in the 1980s, and others not until the 1990s. The Kh-29, for example, was successfully used against mujahedeen positions in tunnels in Afghanistan. Their accuracy made it possible to destroy tunnel entrances. The Su-34 was capable of carrying up to 17,637 pounds of weaponry, and the number of hardpoints was increased by two to twelve. The

Live R-73 and R-27 air-to-air missiles beneath the wings. This photo provides a clear view of the massive main undercarriage. *Sergey Chaikovski*

Su-34s lined up on the flight line. The blue-painted aircraft are from the first production batch. They are still missing the air outlets for the auxiliary gas turbine retrofitted in the tail stinger. *Sergey Chaikovski*

GSh-301 cannon from the Su-27 was retained with 150 rounds of ammunition. Gross takeoff weight rose to 99,210 pounds, about sixty percent greater than the gross weight of the Su-27. This increased weight made it absolutely necessary to strengthen parts of the airframe, the wing, and the vertical tail surfaces. More powerful engines also had to be installed if the aircraft was to possess the necessary degree of agility to deal with future threats. Some of the Su-34s now in service are equipped with the new and more powerful AL-31F-M1, each of which produces 30,350 pounds of thrust. The Su-34 does not have thrust-vector capability (which would be available as an option). Older production aircraft will have their worn-out AL-31F power plants replaced with the new engines.

A naval version was promised in addition to the ground attack variant. In addition to the adapted radar, a magnetic anomaly detector and a receiver for SONAR buoys were offered, both located in the tail boom. It was claimed that a submarine periscope could be detected at up to ninety miles. As some guided anti-shipping missiles could fly further than the Su-34's radar could track them, the guided weapons used data provided by satellites. In addition to the pure bomber version, an electronic warfare version was also tested. The necessary reconnaissance electronics were housed in a pod carried between the engines. Its primary role was to locate electronic command and control sites and attack them with the weaponry it carried. The Russian Air Force realized that it had to replace its Su-24s, some of which had been updated, with a new type if it was to meet current and anticipated threats.

In any case the Su-27IB, as the aircraft was still called, was built in the late 1980s, as a replacement for the Su-24. The first pre-production aircraft were handed over to the air force for testing in 2006. At the air force's state flight testing center in Aktyubinsk, and later at the Flight Testing and Combat Training Center at Lipetsk, the first five pre-production aircraft took part in extensive trials. The Su-34 met all of the air force's requirements, and Russia's economy now allowed the procurement of new equipment. The air force's first contract with Sukhoi was signed in 2008, calling for the delivery of thirty-two aircraft by 2012. In 2012, a second contract for ninety-two aircraft to be delivered by 2020, was signed.

After the first Su-34 pilots were trained at Lipetsk, operational activities began at air force bases in Voronezh, Morozovsk (near Rostov on Don), and in the Khabarovsk Region. So far there has been just one export customer, Algeria. This could in part be due to the fact that the Su-34 is not an inexpensive aircraft and that countries like India and China prefer a multi-role aircraft like the Su-30MKI or Su-35S. The procurement of the Su-34 was the first time since the collapse of the Soviet Union that new combat aircraft were purchased in significant numbers, providing an important instrument with which to ensure the sovereignty of Russia. At the time of writing there are about eighty-five Su-34s in service with the Russian Air Force, and all 130 aircraft ordered should be in service by 2020.

The braking chutes of this Su-34 will be jettisoned at a determined place on the taxiway, where they can be collected by ground personnel for reuse. The 3,000-liter external fuel tank is also visible here. *United Aircraft*

CHAPTER 6
Technical Description
(based on the T-10S variant)

Airframe

According to the Russian designation, the Su-27 is an aircraft designed according to the so-called integral concept, similar to that of the MiG-29. This concept combines the wings and airframe in such a way that both components, with smooth and edgeless joints, form a single lifting body. As the fuselage provides a considerable, if not the predominant, share of lift, wing loading drops in hard maneuvering, benefiting structural strength. This allows the aircraft to pull more Gs, which results in improved agility. Aluminum and titanium alloys are used as materials to the maximum degree possible. The wing root leading edges are extended forward to abeam the cockpit (LERX) and are typical for the Su-27 and its smaller sister the MiG-29. These leading edge root extensions produce powerful vortices over the upper wing surfaces and influence the flow of the boundary layer, which in turn reduces induced drag. Longitudinal stability also profits as a result. These vortices produce additional lift at high angles of attack, further improving agility. The wings have leading edge (Krueger-type) flaps (not leading edge slats as claimed in some English-language publications) and combined ailerons and flaps, or flaperons. The Krueger flaps can extend downwards up to thirty degrees, while the flaperons range of movement is +35°/-20°. The fly-by-wire system provides automatic interaction of the control surfaces. This is necessary on the Su-27, because the aerodynamic layout is designed to be unstable. The aircraft's center of gravity is not in the same place as the center of lift, and computer assistance is vital in maintaining control at all times and in all flight attitudes. The wings have wingtip launch rails that can carry short-range air-to-air missiles or jamming pods. Tailerons are mounted on the aircraft's tail to provide control about the lateral and longitudinal axes, and these provide differential tailplane movement (+15°/-20°). The tailerons are located directly at the foot of the vertical tail surfaces and are installed horizontally. Metal skinning on the tailerons is visible in some photos. If wing-launched weapons do not ignite in time but are released nevertheless, they can strike the tailerons and damage them. Twin tails were selected for the vertical tail surfaces, for experience had shown that these were better for optimization of directional stability. A single tail would have to have been much larger to achieve the required stability, which would have been associated with higher material loads in close combat. The vertical tails were mounted precisely vertically. For a further optimization of directional stability and to counter spins, ventral fins were installed beneath the roots of the vertical tails. The smaller vertical tails also reduced the radar reflective area. The vertical tails of the Su-27UB and the Su-30 versions and the Su-27M and Su-34 were enlarged, explaining their greater overall height on the ground. A twin-engine layout was adopted to obtain the required engine thrust for a minimum thrust-to-weight ratio of 1:1. A further advantage is quite clearly the increased safety should an engine be lost during flight.

The engines are housed in individual nacelles beneath the fuselage and make possible the carriage of additional

Here the prototype of the Su-27SKM shows the clean aerodynamic lines of the Su-27 design. The camouflage originates from the Su-30KI project. *United Aircraft Corporation*

weapons there. The air intake shafts are angled, which combined with placement of the power plants under the fuselage, provides better air supply to the engines when the aircraft is flown at high angles of attack. Internally, the intakes have folding titanium grilles, which are very fine and prevent foreign bodies from being sucked in by the engines. This grille only opens into the intake flow when the undercarriage is loaded and the engine is operating. To further improve suction performance at high angles of attack there are automatic, shutter-like doors on the undersides of the forward air intakes. Aluminum and titanium alloys are used to a large degree in the airframe, with significantly less of the latter (for example, on the underside of the central fuselage with the

wing-bearing section and important load-bearing elements). Composite materials are only used in covers over electronic systems, like the radome and other antenna covers, plus some panels of the external skin. The airframe is of semi monocoque construction. The prominent tail "stinger" houses various items of equipment, fuel, a braking parachute, radar warning receiver, and chaff and flares. To provide the pilot with a good all-round view, he has a raised canopy with nothing in the rear to obstruct his view. The one-piece windscreen, and compared to previous designs, provides a better forward view. Three mirrors are placed on the windscreen frame to improve rearward view. The Su-27 has a total of ten hardpoints, three per wing, one under each

This Ukrainian Su-27UB shows the arrangement of the engine air intakes beneath the integral lifting body. *Chris Lofting*

The large distance between the
engine air intakes allows weapons,
such as the R-27 and R-77 air-to-air
missiles, to be carried there.

engine air intake, and two in tandem between the engine air intakes. Weapons on the wing stations are fired directly from there, while those under or between the air intakes are first dropped from the weapons pylons and then ignited. This is to ensure a clean and safe separation of weapons from the aircraft. Heavy weapons like the Kh-59M are also dropped from the wing stations and then ignited.

Fuel System

The main task of the fuel system is obviously to supply the engines and the auxiliary power unit with fuel. Fuel is also used to cool the engine lubricating oil and the GP-21 hydraulic drive system (see Power Supply) and for cooling air tapped from the engines for the environmental system. The Su-27's fuel system can accommodate a total of 20,723 pounds of jet fuel, housed in two airframe tanks with a total of 18,518 pounds of fuel and two integral wing tanks with 2,200 pounds. The Su-27's integral layout makes possible this enormous fuel capacity, as there is additional space in the fuselage-wing join areas. Neither the F-15C (approx. 13,227 pounds), which is the Su-27's American counterpart, not the F-14, nor any other comparably agile combat aircraft can carry such a quantity of fuel. Of course this is the maximum amount, which is not always carried, and standard fuel is 11,552 pounds. The Su-27UB has the same total fuel capacity, and it can be flown with 13,448 or 18,739 pounds of fuel. The internal tanks are pressurized with air taken from the engines' low-pressure compressors, preventing foaming and boiling at high altitudes. The tanks were originally coated with polyurethane foam as fire protection. Because of an embargo in the 1980s, the Soviet Union was temporarily unable to obtain the material, and a self-sealing mixture was added to the tanks. The Su-27 has no piping in the wings for the carriage of external fuel tanks, this being provided later for the Su-34 and Su-35S. As well, no refueling probe was installed, something present on all later versions except the Su-27UB. In case of an emergency landing with too high a quantity of fuel, it is jettisoned via the engines. A switch in the cockpit releases fuel through the afterburner nozzles without igniting it. The jettisoning of fuel stops automatically when 3,300 pounds of fuel remain. Fuel delivery and pressure pumps are installed in the fuel tanks and engines themselves, and on both accessory gearboxes, so that if the airframe pumps fail the engine-mounted pumps will draw fuel from

these tanks, although this results in operating limitations. Fueling on the ground takes place via a central filling point, which can also be used to drain fuel for maintenance purposes. If in an emergency no refueling truck with pressure fueling hose or similar equipment should be available, the aircraft can be refueled manually through a fueling hatch atop the fuselage. The pilot has fuel gauges in the cockpit as well as fuel consumption and range indicators. He also receives visual and acoustical warnings of a malfunction or low fuel state.

Power Plants
Development of the AL-31F

After the basic technical data for the new Su-27 had been determined, it was unavoidable that the designers also find a new power plant. Obviously this had to be significantly more powerful than existing engines but more economical to operate as well. As well, for the first time a Soviet military jet engine was to be a turbofan. Sukhoi had a small selection of power plants to choose from: the AL-31 from the Lyulka OKB (headed by Arkhip Lyulka), the D-30F6 from the Solovyov OKB (headed by Pavel Solovyov), and the R59F-300 from the Tumansky OKB (headed by Sergey Tumansky). After an assessment of the competing designs by the ZIAM (Central Institute of Aviation Engines), the Lyulka Design Bureau (Saturn Engineering Plant) was tasked with development and construction of the AL-31F (internal designation Product 99). Since the end of the war, the majority of designs produced by Sukhoi had been powered by engines made by Lyulka, and the two design bureaus had a long history of working together. New was the fact that for the first time Sukhoi was to design a turbofan engine. It is worth mentioning that Arkhip Lyulka had developed a theoretical engine design with an axial compressor even before the Second World War. The AL-31 was to achieve a thrust-to-weight ratio of at least one and have a minimum specific fuel consumption which was to be twenty-five percent less than that of the AL-21F-3, which powered the Su-17M4 and Su-24. It was for these reasons that the OKB chose to design a turbofan engine with a three-stage low- and nine-stage high-pressure compressor and single-stage high- and low-pressure turbines. Turbine inlet temperature was to be increased by 212° F compared to that of the AL-221F-3. To be able to achieve such high temperatures, new materials had to be used for the high-pressure turbine blades, a task that was

The AL-31FP from the developer/manufacturer Saturn, recognizable by its downward-hanging nozzle.

given to the VIAM (Research Institute for Aviation Materials). A so-called monocrystalline blade was to be developed, which, because of its inner crystalline structure, required no additional cooling. By then the Soviets had received more detailed information about the power plants of the F-15 and F-16, and the specs were close to those of the AL-31F. To gain an advantage, the designers saw themselves forced to design a four-stage low-pressure compressor, an eleven-stage high-pressure compressor, and make both turbines two-stage. In 1974, an engine was run on the test bench and it was found that it did not and could not achieve the required performance figures. The designers went back to the original number of stages, although a four-stage low-pressure compressor seemed unavoidable. This configuration resembled that of an engine that had already completed flight tests. It was the RD-33 by Klimov, which was to be used in the also new MiG-29. For time and cost reasons the Sukhoi designers finally took

compressor components from the RD-33, which led to the AL-31F compressor. Preparations for the mass production of monocrystalline turbine blades were also initially unsuccessful. The turbine blades therefore had to be cooled with air drawn from the high-pressure compressor; however, this reduced thrust and increased fuel consumption. In addition to cooling, the leading edges of the turbine blades and the guide apparatus were given a special heat-protective coating. All of this threatened the success of the entire T-10 project, for without the required power plants it would be impossible to achieve the desired agility. These delays were also the reason why the first prototype was powered by modified AL-21F-3 engines: there were simply no AL-31Fs available. To avoid delays in flight testing, trials had to begin with the AL-21F-3 engines, even though they produced less thrust, consumed more fuel, and were heavier than the anticipated AL-31F. When, in 1979, the T-10-3 was equipped with the first pair of

AL-31F engines and was as good as ready to fly, the LII (Gromov Flight Research Institute) refused to authorize the first flight with the AL-31F. The reason was the AL-31F was subject to too many restrictions and thus could not have carried out a reasonable test flight. The AL-31F engines were removed again, and in a breathtaking five months the Lyulka OKB, together with the manufacturer Saturn, overcame the majority of the AL-31F's shortcomings. In August Vladimir Ilyushin made the first flight in the T-10-3 with the AL-31F engines. The T-10-4, also with AL-31F engines, followed in October. In the process, the aircraft accessory gearboxes, previously installed in the forward engine area, were moved to positions underneath the power plants. This to some degree eased maintenance on the ground and improved fire safety. Should fuel leak from engine accessories, it would not touch hot parts of the engine. However, these advantages were offset by a serious disadvantage, namely that this arrangement caused prominent bulges on the lower engine fairings and increased drag. It was decided that the engine accessory gearboxes should be moved to positions over the engines on the future prototypes. This was done on the T-10-7 and T-10-12. To prevent engine damage from foreign objects ingested during takeoff, landing, or taxiing, grilles were installed in the air intakes to catch foreign objects. The T-10-7 and T-10-12 were the first prototypes of the redesigned Su-27 (T-10S), causing it to become the combat aircraft we recognize today. During subsequent trials, no serious problems arose with the AL-31F and it later earned the reputation of being one of the best power plants in the world.

The AL-31FN was derived from the AL-31F. It was redesigned for use in the Chinese J-10. For space reasons the aircraft accessory gearboxes had to be moved from atop the engines to underneath them. Salyut delivered large numbers of these engines to China.

Technical Description

The AL-31F is a twin-shaft turbofan engine with a bypass ratio of about 0.6. The low-pressure compressor has four stages with adjustable guide vanes for optimal flow to the compressor blades. The high-pressure compressor has nine stages and the inlet guide vanes of the first three stages are also adjustable. Overall compression ratio is about twenty-three, and maximum air flow rate is 242 pounds per second. The annular combustion chamber joins a single-stage high- (maximum turbine entry temperature 2,537° F) and low-pressure turbine. The jet pipe contains afterburner segments and ends in a variable convergent-divergent nozzle. Specific fuel consumption at maximum dry thrust is 20 g/kN.s and at maximum afterburner 53 g/kN.s. The AL-31F weighs approximately 3,307 pounds, and its air intake measures 35.4 inches in diameter. The engine was controlled elctro-hydromechanically by the KRD-99 analogue limit controller, the NR-31 fuel pump, and the RSF-31 nozzle and afterburner controller. Actual engine control took place mechanically by the throttle lever in the cockpit, which was linked by control rods to the NR-31. The engines are accommodated in straight air intakes under the middle/rear of the lifting body. The air intakes were designed to provide optimal airflow to the engines and less to minimize radar signature, the compressor blades of the low-pressure compressor being open to enemy radars, making excellent reflectors. At the mouths of the air intakes are variable intake ramps, which are also supposed to optimize airflow and prevent wave drag. On the outer lower edges of the air intakes there are thrust bearings, which lock the extended main undercarriage. In addition to the engine accessory gearboxes mounted on the engines to power engine components (pumps, gearing), an aircraft accessory gearbox is mounted atop the front of the AL-31F. The Su-27 thus has two of these (one per AL-31F). Flange-mounted on these are hydraulic and fuel pumps as well as direct current (DC) and alternating current (AC) generators. Also located there is the GTDE-117 gas turbine engine (starter turbine, or APU). This starter turbine can be used on the ground to provide the aircraft with power and/or hydraulic pressure if no external ground equipment is available. The aircraft batteries start an electric motor mounted on the turbo starter. It revs up the latter via a mechanical connection until the turbo starter ignites and turns on its own. By way further mechanical connections it powers the aircraft accessory gearbox and the systems mounted there. The aircraft accessory gearbox is mechanically connected to the engine accessory gearbox and the turbo starter thus also starts the AL-31F. Conversely, once started, the engines power the corresponding systems via the gearboxes. Of course, not all of the systems operate the whole time the engine is turning, and those that are not required are separated from the power flow by various couplings. For installation, the engines are not adapted specifically for the left or right side and are removed horizontally, rearwards onto a removal vehicle. The two aircraft accessory gearboxes do not have to be removed with the engines; however it is necessary to release the existing connections.

Should a fire break out in the engine compartments, these are fought by the aircraft's own firefighting system. Warning sensors alert the pilot or technician on the ground (the latter is in the cockpit during engine run-ups), informing him in which engine compartment it is burning, and he operates the appropriate switches to manually extinguish the fire (with the medium Halon). Technologically, new production methods flow into newer versions of the AL-31F. Salyut, for example, introduced BLISK (bladed disc) technology into the improved AL-31F-M3. Whereas previously a compressor stage

consisted of a rotor disc onto which were installed many individual compressor blades, this component is now a single piece. This technology saves weight, as the attachment parts for the individual blades are now unnecessary. Furthermore the blades' fracture strength is increased, as there are no longer joints between the disc and blades.

The AL-31F Series 2, which is used in the latest versions of the Su-27, has a maximum service life of 1,500 hours, while that of the improved AL-31F-M1 is 4,000 hours, as is the 117S of the Su-35S. The first major overhaul takes place at 500 hours for the AL-31F, and after 1,000 hours for the AL-31F-M1 and 117S. As the AL-31F-M3 and the 117S are both made by Salyut and produce the same thrust, they would seem to be one and the same engine, which, meanwhile, is also called the AL-41F1.

The empty engine bays. *Sergey Burdin*

The first thrust-vector nozzles, the oversize rectangular design with flat outlet. *JSC Sukhoi*

Thrust Vectoring

In the mid-1980s, Soviet engine designers sought ways to further increase the Su-27's agility. Designing a thrust-vector nozzle (a thrust nozzle that could be swiveled vertically or laterally) offered such a possibility. Lyulka Saturn began working on such a design in 1986, under the leadership of Viktor Shepkin. The chief designer was Anatoli Andreyev. A nozzle was created that could swivel vertically +/- 15 degrees. The design itself looked rather unusual: a sort of box was placed over the engine outlet, and two horizontal movable plates, one above the other, formed the thrust nozzle exit. These jet plates were moved by the hydraulic system. A Su-27 with prototype thrust-vector nozzles (T-10-26/LLUV-KS) flew for the first time on March 21, 1989. It was flown by pilot Oleg Tsoi of Sukhoi. A second aircraft, a Su-27UB, joined the test program in 1990. Flight testing revealed that a nozzle of rectangular construction had drastically lower infrared emissions, which would make it more difficult for enemy locating systems to detect it. Thrust also dropped drastically, however, by fourteen to seventeen percent. This was caused by the flow passing from the circular combustion chamber and turbine exit into the rectangular area of the thrust-vector nozzle. Compounding this was the weight of the entire thrust-vector nozzle, which was simply too great, combined with the reduced thrust. In the 1980s, the Soviet Union did not yet have carbon fiber components, which could have been used for the vector nozzle, and so it was made of metal. The Lyulka project for a flat nozzle was put on ice, and it turned to the classic round nozzle. One problem concerned the transition from the rigid jet pipe to the movable nozzle. This had to be sealed in such a way that neither the afterburner flow at approximately 3,630° F nor the pressure of the exhaust

stream damaged the seal. It was also necessary to integrate control of the vector nozzles into the Su-27's fly-by-wire system to achieve maximum agility in air combat. Both problems were solved, and on April 2, 1996, Yevgeni Frolov took the eleventh prototype of the Su-35S program (T-10M-11/Su-37) into the air on its first flight. The maneuvers flown by Frolov clearly demonstrated the superiority of an aircraft with thrust-vector capability over conventionally-powered machines. On the AL-31FU of the Su-37, the complete nozzle and part of the jet pipe are movable, but only in the vertical plane. This is sufficient, however, for the Su-37 to fly maneuvers far beyond anything possible with a conventionally-controlled aircraft. Another design was necessary to enable the exhaust gas jet to also be deflected to the side and further increase agility. Salyut further developed the AL-31FU to become the AL-31FP, which is installed in the Indian Su-30MKI, the Algerian Su-30MKA, and the Malaysian Su-30MKM. In addition to structural improvements, as well as up to +/- 15° of vertical movement, the vector nozzle can also be swiveled laterally, further improving maneuverability. In the original arrangement, however, at full lateral deflection the exhaust gas stream would strike the tail "stinger." They could not simply remove it, as it housed important equipment (braking chute, chaff and flares). The danger of damaging or even destroying the tail "stinger" was countered with an unconventional arrangement of the nozzles. If one looks at the tail of the Su-30MKI from behind, it becomes apparent that the nozzles are splayed outward, causing the exhaust gases to pass laterally and below the tail "stinger," and in doing so imparting lateral torque to the machine. On the Su-37, the vector-nozzle positioning cylinder is powered by the aircraft's hydraulic

Here, complete AL-31FP engines are seen during packing by the manufacturer. Note the large portion of the nozzle that is completely movable. *United Engine Corporation/gelio-livejournal.com*

Production AL-31FP engines with the entire movable thrust nozzle section, here installed in the Su-27KUB for test purposes.

AL-31F Specification

Length	16.24 ft.
Diameter	4.2 ft.
Weight	3,350 lb.
Air Flow-Through Rate	242 lb./sec
Maximum Thrust	17,310 lb.
Maximum Afterburning Thrust	27,650 lb.
Maximum Fuel Consumption	12,786 lb.
In Maximum Afterburner	52,030 lb.
Maximum Degree of Compression	23

In contrast the AL-31F-M1 from the developer/manufacturer Salyut, where only the thrust nozzle petals divert the exhaust gas stream.

system, while on the AL-31FP in the Su-30MKI, positioning actuation is integrated into the engine's fuel system. The AL-31FP is about 210 pounds heavier and 15.75 inches longer than the AL-31F, and time between overhaul for the vector nozzles is 500 hours.

The complete nozzle module of the AL-31FP is still not movable, however. Inspiration for a more compact design came from an unexpected source — namely from Klimov. The design bureau in Petersburg developed a three-dimensional, axisymmetric vectoring nozzle for the RD-33 engine of the MiG-29. Klimov called the system KLIVT—Klimov Vectoring Thrust. Salyut bought the technical documentation from Klimov and adapted the design. The result was the AL-31F-M1 with a thrust vectoring nozzle. The engine was tested in Su-27s of the LII (Bort numbers 595 and 598). Like those of the RD-3MK, the nozzle petals themselves were controlled to deflect the exhaust stream

and not the entire nozzle module as on the AL-31FP. The advantage of this variant is a weight savings, simpler construction and repair, and faster deflection of the petals than a complete nozzle module. The AL-31F and its variants are built by UMPO in Ufa, NPO-Saturn (merging of OKB Saturn/Lyulka) in Rybinsk, and by Salyut in Moscow. The AL-31FP can be retrofitted into older versions of the Su-27. This requires no significant modifications to the airframe, although the fly-by-wire system must receive an appropriate update.

Hydraulic and Pneumatic System

The hydraulic system operates the aerodynamic control surfaces and flaps, the lowering and retraction of the

The AL-31F-M1 was tested in the Su-27 operated by the LII. Note the three bulges on the ring around the thrust nozzle, probably housing actuators.

undercarriage, the air intake ramps and folding intake protective screens, wheel braking and nosewheel steering, operation of the canards and the air refueling probe (Su-30SM, Su-35S, Su-34, Su-30MK versions, Su-33). The tail hook and folding mechanism of the Su-33 are also hydraulically powered. The NP-112 axial piston pumps provide 4,060 psi operating pressure for two separate and independent systems. One pump is flange-mounted to each aircraft accessory gearbox, with each gearbox in turn powering one of the hydraulic systems. These two systems are divided into the first and second systems. Although both systems are separated from one another, both simultaneously supply the most important control surfaces such as the rudders, flaperons, tailerons, Krueger flaps, and, when installed, the canards. Should one system fail, the other automatically takes over control of the control surfaces. The first system supplies the following systems/components:

- undercarriage
- the ramp in the port intake and the folding screens in both intakes
- nosewheel steering
- main undercarriage wheel braking (normal and emergency)
- extension/retraction of the refueling probe, arrestor hook, and folding mechanism (when fitted)

The second system supplies the main undercarriage wheel brakes, operation of the speed brake, and the ramp in the starboard intake. The speed brake measures twenty-eight square feet and is located on the fuselage spine. It can be extended at speeds up to 620 mph. All two-seat versions and the Su-27M have a larger 32.3-square-foot speed brake. The emergency hydraulic system consists of a hydraulic accumulator, which is constantly kept under pressure when the primary hydraulic system is operating and is only used in a serious emergency. Should both hydraulic systems fail, the hydraulic accumulator supplies the most important control systems for a few seconds to maintain a normal flight attitude. The crew must then eject, as no further hydraulics are available. During flight testing, the AL-31F proved to be so reliable that the simultaneous loss of both engines with their associated gearboxes and hydraulic pumps was effectively excluded. The T-10 prototypes powered by the AL-21F had electrically-powered emergency hydraulic pumps.

The pneumatic system is used for emergency lowering of the undercarriage, the normal opening and closing of the canopy, and pressurization. In an emergency the arrestor hook of the Su-33 is extended pneumatically as is the air refueling probe of Su-27s thus equipped. System operating pressure is 3,045 psi.

Undercarriage

The nose and main undercarriage units each have single wheels, while the heavier variants like the Su-35, the Su-30MK versions, and the Su-33 and Su-34 have twin wheels in the nose. The mainwheels are braked hydraulically, while the nosewheel is unbraked. To prevent foreign objects from the runway from being thrown into the engine air intakes, a mudguard is fitted to the nosewheel. The complete undercarriage retracts forward. Should the hydraulic system fail and normal lowering of the undercarriage is not possible, the pneumatic system is engaged. It is controlled from the cockpit and the undercarriage lowered. Should the pneumatics fail, after being unlocked manually the undercarriage drops under its own weight and the slipstream fully opens and locks it in the down position. Part of the main undercarriage locking system is located on the outer lower edges of the engine air intakes. This configuration allows the design of the main undercarriage legs to be simplified, which in turn saves room in the undercarriage well as well as weight. Wheel base is nineteen feet and the track width fourteen feet. Because the crew enters the cockpit of the Su-34 through the nosewheel bay, the undercarriage was changed and retracts rearwards. Wheel base is 21.6 feet. Braking is accomplished by a multi-disc brake system, and fans installed in the hubs of the mainwheels prevent overheating. Should overheating nevertheless exceed the allowable level, tin fringes melt and release the high tire pressure caused by the heat, preventing the tires from bursting. The ground crew recognizes the melted spots on the ground and the affected tire is changed. To monitor tire wear, several small depressions are placed in the outer surfaces. This allows ground personnel to recognize in time when a tire requires changing.

Flight Control System

The flight control system ensures that the Su-27 can be flown safely to its limits within the allowable parameters. As the Su-27 was designed to be unstable about its longitudinal axis, a fly-by-wire system was absolutely necessary. To prevent a complete loss of this system, control about the lateral axis was made quadruple redundant. The pitch and roll controls, however, were mechanical by means of control rods from the joystick and pedals to the hydraulic cylinders of the corresponding surfaces. Pitch and roll control was made triple redundant. The flight control system can be used in three modes. In the Takeoff/Landing and Flight mode, the system automatically selects one of the two operating modes based on the position of the undercarriage (lowered or raised) and is the most commonly used mode. The Direct Control mode engages automatically in the event of a problem with the flight control system. This control mode places high demands on the pilot if he is to control the aircraft safely, for pitch stability decreases, damping performance changes, and roll becomes more difficult to handle because of increased joystick sensitivity. In addition to the automatic selection, this operating mode can also be selected manually on the left switch console. In the crash of the Indian Su-30 it is likely that this switch was inadvertently operated by the pilot, causing the crash. Incidentally the Direct Control mode is selected to perform the cobra maneuver. There are several limiters to maintain the maximum allowable angle of attack (max. 30°) and g load (9 g); however, these can be overridden by the pilot if required (for example, during air combat). The Krueger flaps automatically adjust their setting angle to match the angle of attack, providing increased lift especially in air combat. This improved agility, allowing tighter turns to be flown. In addition to controlling flight, the flight control systems perform other important tasks. Data from the flight control system is necessary for the navigation and weapons systems and the ground control link, as well as for control of the autopilot, recovery from dangerous flight attitudes to horizontal flight, automatic climb and descent, control by ground installations or AWACS, the return flight to home base, and the automatic approach to land. The main control

Ukrainian Su-27 with extended speed brake and open braking-parachute container. The T-10's nosewheel leg is farther forward and retracts rearward. *Chris Lofting*

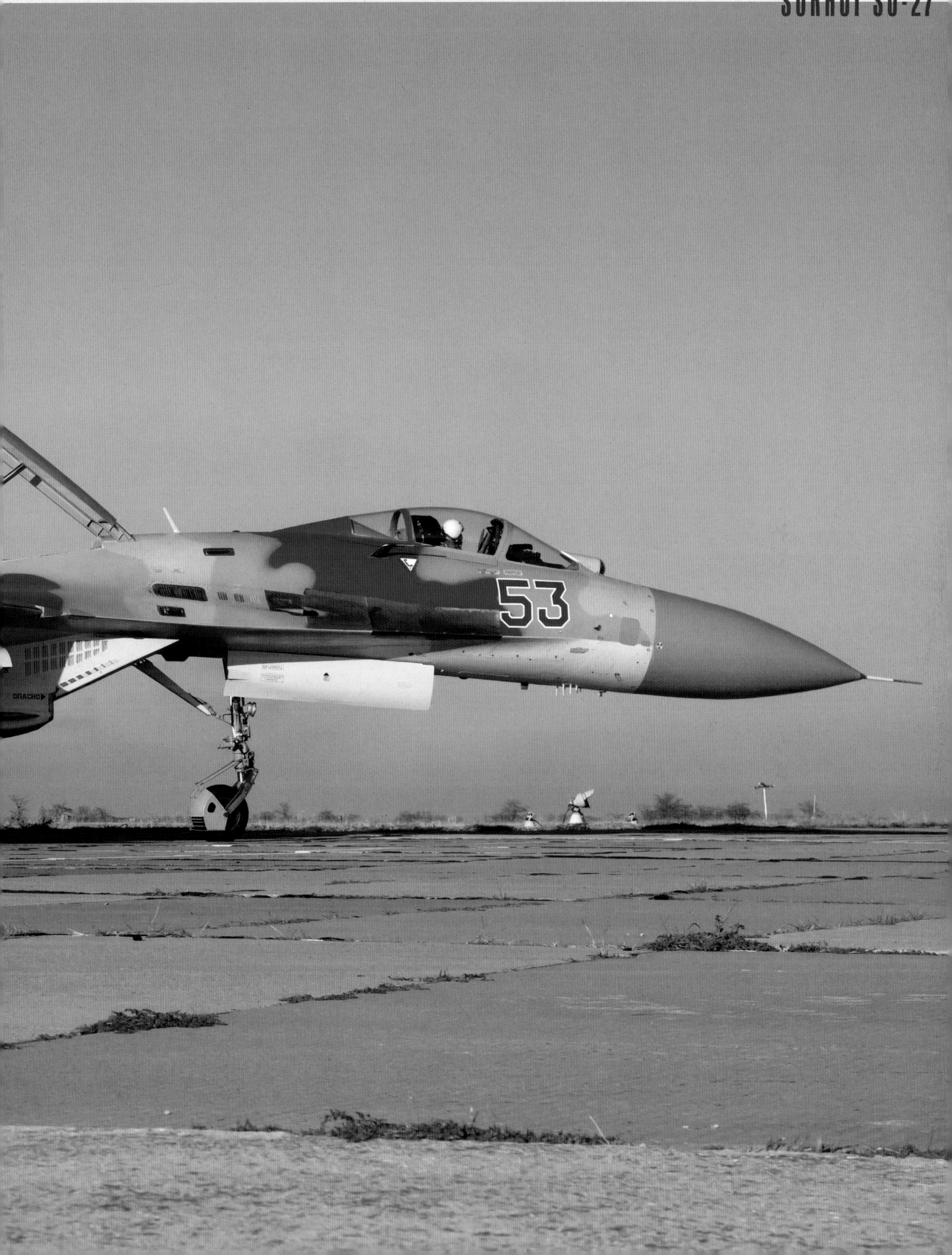
53

element is the classic control stick arranged centrally in the cockpit, controlling the flaperons and tailerons, while the foot pedals control the rudders. The thrust levers are horizontally sliding elements. There are several switches on the control stick, mainly for operation of the cannon, air-to-air missiles, and other weapons. The autopilot system is also operated from there and the automatic flight operation mode can be switched off from there. Trimming the longitudinal and lateral axes is accomplished with a joystick-like button on the control stick. A target assignment button is used to select a target on the HUD. The undercarriage brake lever is on the back side of the hand grip. Controls on the throttle lever allow for hardpoints to be selected and operate the speed brake and drag chute. Another button allows the pilot to transmit. This layout is also called HOTAS (Hands On Throttle And Stick) and means that several very important controls are located on the stick and throttle lever and that the pilot does not have to take his hands off these primary control elements.

Radar

Probably the greatest challenge facing the Soviet military aircraft industry in developing fourth-generation combat aircraft at the end of the 1960s/beginning of the 1970s, was the development of radar and digital computer technology. The west had a lead in this field and the Soviets were determined to catch up. The effects of the Second World War were not felt as deeply in any other country as they were in the Soviet Union. Scarcely had the German armed forces been defeated when the next enemy, the USA, was already in the starting blocks. The reason was the opposing ideologies of the two states, which led to tensions to proxy wars and almost to an exchange of blows. After the Second World War the Soviet Union had much work to do to return to where it had been before the war, as well as keep up with the rest of the world. By the end of the 1940s, both sides realized that intercontinental ballistic missiles tipped with nuclear warheads would represent the ultimate weapon. Both states began an armaments race, with the USA in more favorable conditions from the beginning. It had not been devastated by the war and its industries had not been flattened. The Soviets raised enormous funds with which to accomplish this, but priorities had to be set as its resources were not limitless. After the war, funding for missiles and the atomic weapons industry received top priority, and several other areas had to

get by with less. Poor political decisions certainly played a role in the Soviet Union falling behind from the outset in the fields of electronics and computer technology. Of course it was more difficult for the Soviet Union than for other countries that were not part of the communist block to acquire these technologies, if these were developed or sold in the west. The first intensive research into digital computer technology began in the late 1960s, with many companies and research institutes in the Soviet Union taking part. The first digital computer for Soviet combat aircraft was produced in the early 1970s. Two targeting systems—a new radar and an optical complex—were to be created for the new MiG-29 and Su-27 fighter aircraft. The Su-27's radar was to be superior to the APG-63 envisaged for the brand-new F-15. This was only possible with digital computer technology. It is interesting that NIIR and NIIP Institutes were integrated into the present-day Phazotron Company, which builds radars primarily for the MiG-29/MiG-35. The NIIR developed the radar for the MiG-29, while the NIIP was responsible for that of the Su-27. In 1978, it was agreed that the two radars should have common components to standardize development, production, and later maintenance in service. So NIIR developed part of the radar, while NIIP produced other elements. The NIIP, however, came to the conclusion that, in order to be superior to the APG-63, a radar had to be produced that combined a mechanically movable slot antenna and a fixed phase antenna. The APG-63 was moved solely by hydro-mechanical means, which had disadvantages compared to a fixed antenna, where the radar beams were aimed electronically. However, development of the associated digital computer, software, and fixed antenna proved much more complicated than had been assumed. The components that were created did not deliver the desired parameters for a radar superior to the APG-63. In 1982, therefore, it was decided to initially shelve work on the radar with fixed antenna for the Su-27 and fall back on a conventional flat antenna. Moreover, it was decided to use a larger version of the radar antenna from the MiG-29's radar, the N-019, for the Su-27. This brought with it the advantage of standardizing elements in both radars, but the above-named advantages were not enough. The computer the NIIR had developed for the fixed-antenna radar was replaced and the Ts-100 from the Institute for Digital Computer Technology was used instead. The redesigned N-001 radar was ready for flight trials and these were completed one year later. Another year passed until the

An aircraft of the QRA (Quick Reaction Alert) from Kilp Yavr with its radome removed and part of the radar antenna unit (on the right in the photo disassembled), revealing the actual radar antenna. *Andrey Zinchuk*

radar was thought ready for service use, but even with the larger antenna and new computers the original target of a 120-mile detection range against fighter-size targets was not met. The N-001 achieved just half of this goal. The NIIP saw itself forced to develop a new radar, the significantly more powerful N-011, which was tested in the Su-27M. After further changes to the N-001, primarily to address a high failure rate, which would have drastically limited us of the Su-27, it was not until 1991, that the radar was ready for service use.

In design terms the N-001 is a twist-cassegrain impulse Doppler radar and, as previously said, it has a high degree of commonality with the smaller N-019 of the MiG-29, specifically the smaller antenna (diameter 3.6 feet) and the Ts-100 digital computer. It operated in the 3-cm (1.18-inch) waveband and has an average transmitting power of 1 kW

and has look down/shoot down capability (better detection of targets against ground interference). Maximum search range against targets with a radar reflective area of 32.3 square feet is sixty miles for closing targets and thirty-nine miles in pursuit mode. Lateral antenna sweep is +/- 60 degrees. In target pursuit mode the N-001 can simultaneously track ten targets and engage the most dangerous (the fastest and closest target). It has sometimes been claimed that later modifications enabled the N-001 to engage two targets. In addition to purely detecting and tracking targets, the radar can also be used to guide semi-active radar-guided air-to-air missiles. The original N-001 was designed solely for aerial combat and had no noteworthy ground attack capability. Using emitted and reflected radar emissions, the radar is capable of calculating the radar reflective area of its target and displays this in the HUD with corresponding symbols. By

The red components on the side of the nose are part of the radome folding mechanism. *Andrey Zinchuk*

The lighter areas on the top of the tail stinger show the position of the chaff and flare cassettes. *Olav C. de With*

The Lipetsk Falcons releasing flares. *Sergey Chaikovski*

means of a data-transfer system, the Su-27 can receive target information from external sources like AWACS or ground stations, which is displayed on a display screen in the cockpit. Without using his own radar, the pilot can approach or engage targets without revealing his position. The IFF

(Identification Friend or Foe) works with the radar and is fully automatic. The radar is especially well-protected against electronic jamming.

Self-Defense Systems

The Su-27 has a radar warning system, which warns the pilot when his aircraft is detected by enemy radar. The system's receivers are installed on the outside of the engine air intakes and in the tail "stinger." These can be identified by their white-gray dielectric patches (on early aircraft, whose radomes were painted green, these patches were also green). The tail "stingers" of early production aircraft were more cylindrical and had no rearward-facing radar warning antennas. The side-mounted radar warning receivers were removed from the tail "stinger" of the Su-27K and a receiver was placed in the tip of the cone. The radar warning receivers on the engine air intakes were eliminated from the Su-30MK

Sorbtsiya jamming pod on the wingtip of an Su-27P.
Right: The IRST module.

and were integrated into the leading edges of the wing, which probably provided better all-round coverage. Lateral coverage was 360 degrees, vertical coverage +/- 30 degrees. There was a radar warning system indicator in the cockpit, informing the pilot visually and acoustically as to the approximate direction and hemisphere, the type of radar illumination (fighter aircraft, short-, medium- or long-range ground-based air defense systems, AWACS) and the particular type of aircraft (F-15, F-16, etc.). Different indications and tones tell the pilot whether his aircraft is constantly or only occasionally being illuminated, and whether the enemy radar has locked on. The pilot receives corresponding tones and indications that are unmistakable. A chaff and flare dispensing system is installed in the Su-27 to counter radar- or infrared-guided missiles. This is located in and on the sides of the tail "stinger" and the chaff and flares were ejected from there.

A total of ninety-six cartridges are carried, always with two flares and one chaff packet in each cartridge. The firing sequence can be selected on a control panel, which also monitors the number of cartridges remaining. On the Su-27K these cartridges have been moved to the upper side of the aircraft between the engines, as there is no longer space for them in the shortened tail "stinger." Chaff and flares are released by pressing a button on the left side console. The redesigned tail "stinger" began appearing on production aircraft in 1987, previously having been more cylindrical and containing a small number of chaff/flare cartridges. Active jammers like the Sorbtsiya are mounted on the wingtips. One pod usually serves as receiver and analysis station, while the other transmits the correspondingly adjusted jamming signals. In addition to these conventional defense systems,

Not an Su-27 going down in flames, but the massive release of flares at the completion of the Tailslide. *Chris Agnew*

On the Su-27P/S the IRST is still located centrally in front of the cockpit. *Andrey Zinchuk*

for several years an active system called President-S has also been offered, which can be retrofitted to aircraft in service. It is a towed decoy that is intended to divert radar-guided missiles by producing false radar images. It is attached to the airframe and when needed is reeled out up to 450 feet on a cable. The decoy weighs just eleven pounds.

Optronics – IRST/LR

The Su-27 has a second location device, an infrared seeker/tracker with integrated laser rangefinder (IRST/LR), a smaller version of which is also seen on the MiG-29. The IR is a passive system, producing no emissions itself, and detects heat rays (light in the infrared band) from exhaust gases and possible airframe heating from fast-moving targets or incoming missiles. The system produces no emissions that would allow the enemy to detect the Su-27. Should clouds or

Here the IRST has been moved to the right because of the installation of an air refueling probe on the left side of the nose (here a Su-35S). *JSC Sukhoi*

other phenomena cause the IRST to lose its target, the radar automatically switches to this last target, for during operation of the IRST the radar antenna constantly follows without transmitting (when the radar is in use the IRST also follows in

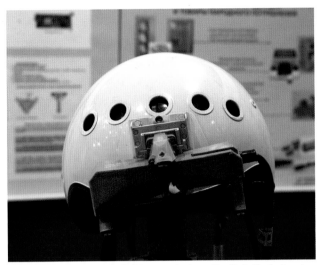

The helmet-mounted sight mounted on the Sch-7a helmet, here with the sight glass folded away.

Here the sight glass (slightly red colored) is in the extended position on the modernization Sura helmet-mounted sight.

case the radar should lose the target). If the helmet-mounted sight is used, the infrared seeker heads of the aircraft's missiles turn in the direction the pilot is aiming, as do the radar and IRST. The system always uses the optimal search method (IRST or radar), to avoid betraying the aircraft's position. The IRST's maximum range in search mode is thirty miles if the enemy aircraft's engines are facing the sensor and nine miles if it is on a reciprocal course. The IRST also includes a laser rangefinder, which measures the precise distance to the target for use of the cannon, the radar being too imprecise for this role. This reduces the amount of ammunition used. The laser's range is up to 1.8 miles for air targets and three miles for ground targets. For reliable use, the IRST/LR requires conditions of good visibility. Meteorological conditions such as clouds and fog seriously hamper its performance.

Whereas the first sights had only a green targeting circle in the sight glass, the Ukrainian manufacturer offers an update that provides additional displays in the sight glass.
Arsenal Special Device Production State Enterprise

Helmet-Mounted Sight

The first air force to use helmet-mounted sights for its pilots was the South African Air Force in the 1970s. A simple system for the South African Mirage F1AZ was developed there and was used with short-range infrared-homing AAMs to shoot down Soviet-made combat aircraft flown by Angola. The Soviets immediately recognized the advantages of such a system and developed their own. The Arsenal Factory in Kiev was responsible, and it began developing the helmet-mounted sight at the same time that design work began on the MiG-29 and Su-27.

By the mid-1980s the helmet-mounted sight for the new Su-27 and MiG-29 fighters was ready and was designated the Sh-3UM-1, while nowadays it is called the Sura. Maximum importance was placed on effectively engaging targets, less on extensive displaying of information. The resulting helmet-mounted sight was a typical Soviet product: simple and yet highly effective. In size and shape the sight itself resembled a dental mirror. In the center of the transparent disc was a small green circle, which was to be placed over the target. The circle was electronically placed over a unit on the front of the helmet. This unit also physically accommodated the aiming disc, which folded out of the way when not needed. The unit also included three laser diodes which shine onto rotating prisms installed on the base of the HUD at the sides. This system determines where the pilot is looking.

Previously, during close air combat, the aircraft's longitudinal axis had to be pointed quite precisely at the target in order to place it under fire. Not so with the Sura! It makes it possible for the pilot to look up to sixty degrees from the aircraft's longitudinal axis to switch the seeker heads of his R-73 (R-74, RVV-MD) short-range air-to-air missiles to the target before launching them. It is therefore possible to open fire sooner than if he had to first point the aircraft's nose at the target. Western pilots first learned to their discomfort about this time savings and resulting advantage when they went up against German MiG-29s after the reunification of East and West Germany. The Germans acquired the helmet-mounted sights from the NVA (National People's Army), and in combination with the improved R-73 short-range air-to-air missile they defeated their Western opponents in air exercises. The results were repeated when the Su-27 flew against Western combat aircraft. The Western air forces were so shocked and amazed that it was not until they learned about the Soviet helmet-mounted sights that they began developing their own. A much improved version of the Sh-3UM-1, now called the Sura, has been available since 2000. It is used by the Su-30MKI/MKM and MKA. Other versions are the Sura-K for the Su-30MKK, Su-30MK2, Su-27SM, and Su-27SK. The Sura-M is reserved for the Su-30SM and Su-35 and is lighter than the Sura-K — thirteen pounds compared to the previous twenty-two (this includes the entire system, even the associated computer modules). The manufacturer, Arsenal, has offered updates for the Sura, Sura-M, and Sura-K. These include additional indications in the targeting sight such as target heading with the help of an arrow, altitude, speed, and range to the target. The actual helmet sight and several electronic modules are replaced. The helmet-mounted sight weighs 13.75 ounces, and the Sura-M's view angle is +/- 70° in azimuth and +65°/-35° in elevation.

Electrical System

The main producers are two alternating current (AC) generators, each of which is flange-mounted on one of the aircraft accessory gearboxes. They produce 115/200 V at 400 Hz. A GP-21 hydraulic drive system was installed on each AC generator. If one AC circuit failed, the other

automatically went to 150 percent of its normal output but was limited to two hours of operation. The second power system consisted of direct current generators (DC) for twenty-seven Volts, rectifiers, and transformers, which in part converted DC to AC current. Two nickel-cadmium batteries supplied power to the cockpit on the ground and ultimately the turbo starter for starting the engines. If the DC system fails, for a limited time the batteries deliver current to selected systems, including for the AC transformers. The nickel-cadmium batteries cannot be charged during flight, as this takes place at a battery charging station on the ground. During normal operations, the aircraft receives electric power from ground equipment, both stationary and mobile, to preserve battery power. The aircraft's batteries are heated to prevent capacity from dropping in low temperatures like those encountered at high altitudes. To prevent the electrical systems from being damaged, there are circuit breakers. During maintenance and servicing, some circuit breakers are pulled to prevent the associated systems from being accidentally activated, causing injury to personnel or damage to equipment. The Su-30MK/SM and Su-35S have revised electrical systems to meet the higher power requirements of their avionics.

Air Data System

The air data system supplies the aircraft control, navigation, engine, and weapons systems with the necessary air pressures. The system also supplies data to the ejection seat, the cockpit pressurization system, the flight data recorder, and cockpit instruments with data. These come from the main pitot tube that is fitted to the tip of the radome. If this should become unserviceable, there are two backup tubes, one on each side of the fuselage beneath the canopy. On the Su-27M and Su-35S the main pitot tube has been moved from the tip of the radome to the side of the fuselage nose. Angle-of-attack and yaw angle sensors and temperature probes also supply the air data system, which turns air values into electric ones for use by various systems. All sensors are metal and heated to prevent icing.

Navigation

The navigation system determines the aircraft's position in the air and its geographical location over land. This is done with the aircraft's inertial system and land-based navaids.

The flight control system, the cockpit instruments, and the head-up display all receive the necessary information from the navigation system. In cooperation with the aircraft control system, the flight is carried out to the preprogrammed airfield and, if necessary, an automatic landing approach is carried out to a height of 150 feet. The navigation and air data systems deliver information to the weapons system, to make possible the precise use of weapons. Finally, the fuel and range indicators also receive data from the navigation system. The system consists of a short-range radio navigation and landing system (RSBN for Russian types), the air data system, and the associated conversion and computer systems. The RSBN system involves stationary radio beacons transmitting signals, which are received and processed by the Su-27. With this system it is possible to program flight routes and carry out an automatic approach to a height of 150 feet (even when this mode is selected, the pilot must land the aircraft manually), provided the airfield is equipped with an instrument landing system. Other elements of the navigation system include the ARK-19/-20 radio compass, the A-611 radio beacon receiver, the A-035 radio altimeter, and an SO-69 transponder. The ARK-19/-20 radio compass determines the heading to be flown from radio signals from ground-based radio stations and comparing them to the aircraft axes. A mast antenna and a loop antenna in the fuselage spine receive the signals, reception range depending on the Su-27's altitude, and the transmitting power of the beacon. The radio altimeter with its transmitting and receiving antennas is installed in the nose of the aircraft. It is designed to provide the pilot with precise altitude information above the ground, but only up to a maximum altitude of 3,300 feet. The barometric altimeter is based on local barometric pressures and is too imprecise to avoid collisions with the terrain. The pilot can select a minimum flight altitude on the radio altimeter instrument, and if the aircraft descends below this altitude the pilot receives a warning signal. The A-611 beacon receiver is installed to allow the pilot to better find airfields with transmitting radio beacons. The beacon transmits an inner and an outer circle, and when the Su-27 penetrates one of these the aircraft's pilot receives indications via his headset. The SO-69 transponder transmits information on the aircraft's identification, altitude, and speed to air traffic control as soon as the aircraft is within ground radar coverage and is interrogated. Air traffic control uses these signals to safely and efficiently coordinate air traffic. In combat situations, identification friend or foe is carried out in the same way, and it also helps ground controllers direct the action from the ground. Laser gyros and/or satellite navigation systems were introduced when the Su-27K and later aircraft of the Su-30MK family appeared.

Communications System

Voice communication, commands from ground control stations, data transfer to other operational aircraft, and ground stations, as well as acoustical signals to the pilot by onboard systems are accomplished by the communications system. The Su-27 has two radio systems, the VHF R-800 and HF R-864, their transmitters and receivers housed in the tips of the vertical tails. The radio signals are encoded. Radio communication range is up to 900 miles (again dependent on altitude). The pilot can also communicate with the second member of the crew and technicians, the latter by means of a cable connection used when the machine is on the ground. Crew conversations are recorded and can be replayed later for evaluation, for example in the event of an accident. The communications system also includes the R-855UM emergency radio set, which is used to locate the crew or aircraft after an ejection or forced landing. The pilot is capable of communicating with the crews of search and rescue helicopters or aircraft. Range is up to thirty miles if the SAR aircraft are flying at a minimum altitude of 1,800 feet. The radio set can also be used as a beacon, with a maximum range of forty-two miles. The battery delivers power for at least twenty-four to fifty-five hours, depending on the mode of operation. The emergency radio is located in the seat shell in the NASS-7 survival kit. It is contained in an automatically inflated buoy-like case. This case is made of orange material for easier location and floats. When the case inflates, the antenna rights itself and the battery begins supplying power. The emergency radio set can be removed by the pilot, in order to be transported by him on land.

Environmental Control System

The environmental control system provides temperature control and pressurization of the cockpit, supplies the ventilation and anti-G systems, cools the avionics and radar, and prevents the windscreen and canopy from fogging. Bleed air is taken from the seventh stage of the high-pressure compressor, which because of the compression of the air in the engine is already at a temperature of several hundred degrees. This is cooled significantly in the air-air cooler before passing through a fuel-air cooler. The air is then dried and fed to the turbo-cooler, where it is ultimately cooled to 41 degrees F. Engine bleed air at about 390 degrees F is added to achieve the temperature selected for the cockpit, which had previously been set at the correct air pressure by pressure machines. The pilot can select a cockpit temperature between 60 and 77 degrees F. Warm air is blown onto the canopy to prevent it from fogging. The environmental control system also cools the avionics, but significantly lower temperatures are required because of the heat produced by the avionics. Air piping delivers cooling air to or into the avionic packages. If the cooling system fails, overheating equipment shuts itself down to avoid or at least minimize damage. Indicators advise the pilot of the loss of the affected avionics. The radar is also liquid cooled using an alcohol mixture. It is an individual closed system. Elements of the radar, the IFF and other HF components are air-pressurized, as is the radar liquid cooling system.

Oxygen System

The oxygen system supplies the crew with oxygen or an enriched oxygen mixture during flight, during ejection, or when the main oxygen system fails. It also helps start the engines, including air restarts. The gaseous oxygen is contained in pressure bottles, and each system (crew supply, engine/turbo starter) is a separate system so that the loss of one system does render the other inoperable. The main system provides the crew with the necessary supply of oxygen in all flight conditions and altitudes when the cockpit is pressurized. Oxygen is supplied by the crew's oxygen masks, which are connected to the oxygen system by ORK quick-release connectors (attached to the ejection seats). The air breathing oxygen system automatically available makes four modes of operation:

- oxygen-air mixture (altitude of 0 to 6,500 feet: pure surrounding air; 6,500 to 26,250 feet: oxygen-enriched)
- pure oxygen breathing (26,250 to 39,370 feet)
- over-pressure breathing
- emergency supply
- helmet ventilation

In the cockpit, a combined analogue instrument informs the crew of the actual cockpit altitude, the amount of oxygen remaining, lung function, and the differential pressure of the cockpit in relation to the atmospheric pressure. The Ekran warning indicator issues a warning if cockpit altitude exceeds 39,370 feet or if the oxygen supply falls below fifteen percent. The crew also receives a message from the voice warning system. If the system malfunctions the crew can operate it manually using a control panel on the left rear instrument console. The emergency oxygen supply comes from a 0.7-liter pressure bottle in the seat pan of the K-36. It is activated either by the pilot manually pulling a handle on the right side of the seat, or automatically if he ejects. The engine oxygen system is there to facilitate an engine restart in flight should one or both engines fail. As well, when the cannon or missiles are fired, oxygen is sprayed into the combustion chambers to prevent powder gases from causing the burn process in the combustion chambers from failing. Should a compressor pump manifest itself, the engine's anti-surge system again ensures that additional oxygen is injected. The turbo starter also receives oxygen to ensure that it ignites. To ensure that future missions are not limited by the amount of oxygen carried on the aircraft, Zvezda, which also produces outstanding ejection seats, created the BDKU-130 onboard oxygen generator system. The oxygen bottles are eliminated, as the necessary oxygen is taken from the compressed bleed air from the engine compressor. This air is subsequently dehydrated and cleaned, allowing the aircraft to fly through chemically-, bacterially- or nuclear-contaminated air. The advantage of such a system compared to the previous oxygen bottles is that operational duration is theoretically unlimited, as it is no longer restricted by the amount of oxygen carried in the aircraft. Another advantage is the system's low weight and reduced space requirements. The filling and maintaining of the oxygen bottles is also no longer required during routine operations, which reduces operating costs. The system is designed to provide sufficient oxygen for a crew of two up to an altitude of 65,600 feet. At present it is used in the Su-30MKI/MKM/MKA, Su-35S, MiG-35, MiG-29K/KUB, and the MiG-29UPG. Simultaneous with the development of the oxygen generator, the emergency oxygen system of the K-36 ejection seat was also redesigned. Originally there was an oxygen bottle in the seat pan. This has been replaced by a chemical oxygen generator, making the system literally maintenance-free.

Pilot Equipment

Appropriate clothing is required to ensure that the crew is capable of performing under all flight conditions. Some of the blood can be forced from the upper body into the legs, especially under high g forces during close combat. The effects range from tunnel vision to loss of consciousness as the brain is not receiving enough oxygen-enriched blood. To prevent this, crews wear either the PPK-3 anti-g pants or the complete WKK-15 anti-g suit. Air pockets are integrated into both, and these are connected to tubes by way of the ORK, forcing air into the pockets and exerting pressure on the legs, arms, and chest. This allows blood to remain in the body core and brain. This is supported by special pressure breathing for the pilot. If missions at altitudes from 39,000 to 65,000 feet are expected, the pressure suit is used, while the anti-g pants are used for missions up to 39,000 feet. The suit, however, permits the pilot to better endure high g-forces at all altitudes. The ZSH-7A or the newly-developed ZSH-10 helmet is worn with the suit or pants. The latter is lighter and more ergonomic than its predecessor the ZSH-7A. The helmet provides protection for the head during ejection, accepts the helmet-mounted sight as well as the headset, oxygen mask, and sun visor. The oxygen mask provides the pilot with the necessary oxygen or oxygen mixture during maneuvers. The ZSH-7A helmet is used not only by the Russian Air Force, but by other Sukhoi users as well and will probably be gradually replaced by the ZSH-10.

K-36 Ejection Seat

The K-36DM is a so-called zero-zero seat, which means that it allows the pilot to safely escape the aircraft at zero speed in the air or on the ground from a height of zero feet. It also enables the crew to abandon the aircraft safely at speeds up to 870 miles per hour. The operating envelope of the K-36DM extends to the aircraft's service ceiling of 65,600 feet. Located in the seat cushion is an emergency oxygen bottle, emergency rations, a life raft, and other survival equipment needed to allow a pilot to survive in the wilderness for a time. In the event of a water landing, the oxygen masks and emergency oxygen allow the crew to breathe under water for a brief time. This means that they can go down with the aircraft as deep as sixty-five feet and still reach the surface. An emergency radio set (from the emergency kit in the seat pan) is provided to assist in locating the downed crew. It can

be used either for voice communication or as a radio beacon. Range varies between ten and forty miles and depends on the height of the search aircraft. The K-36DM's firing sequence takes place electrically, but it is designed to be mechanically redundant so that ejection can take place if the electrical system fails. This is part of the reason for the seat's very high reliability (ninety-seven percent). The seat weighs approximately 265 pounds (including the emergency kit in the seat pan) and is thus somewhat lighter than its predecessor and comparable to seats made by the British manufacturer Martin Baker. The Su-27's seat is installed at an angle of seventeen degrees. The actual ejection process is initiated by pulling the handle between the pilot's legs. The Su-27's canopy is not blown, instead it is pyrotechnically unlocked and raised, after which the powerful airstream opens the canopy further and blows it away. On the ground the canopy is raised by the seat as it moves upwards. In an emergency, on the ground the canopy can be manually opened from the outside. The jettisoned canopy pulls a connecting line (between the canopy and the seat) releasing the ejection seat for firing. The pilot's limbs are restrained for a safe ejection from the aircraft. As soon as he pulls the ejection handle, the arm limiters turn ninety degrees horizontally, fixing the arms against the seat and preventing them from being thrown outward. At the same time the seat's leg restraint belts pull the legs toward the seat and the knees are raised. The hip and shoulder restraints also engage, fixing the pilot's entire body in place. If this fixing in place was not completed, the pilot's arms and legs would be torn off, broken, or severely damaged, as his limbs would probably strike or become caught on something in the cockpit during ejection. When fully extended, the extending telescopic tubes (approx. 5.25 feet), one on each side of the headrest, release small parachutes which turn in opposite directions as the seat falls. This concept stabilizes the attitude of the seat and pilot as they fall, namely with the front of his body facing the earth. In its various versions, the K-36 is used in the Su-22, Su-24, Su-25, Su-27 (and its versions), the MiG-29, MiG-31, and the Tu-160 long-range bomber. It was even used in the Soviet Buran space shuttle and the Yak-41 VTOL aircraft. The latest versions of the seat, the K-36D-3.5 and K-36D-5, are used by the Su-30MK and the latest versions of the MiG-29. The seats are lighter (220 pounds instead of 227) and have better ejection sequences than their predecessors. Their service life is 5,000 hours or thirty years. The K-36D-5, which

K-36DM with pilot dummy in the configuration immediately prior to ejection. *NPP Zvezda*

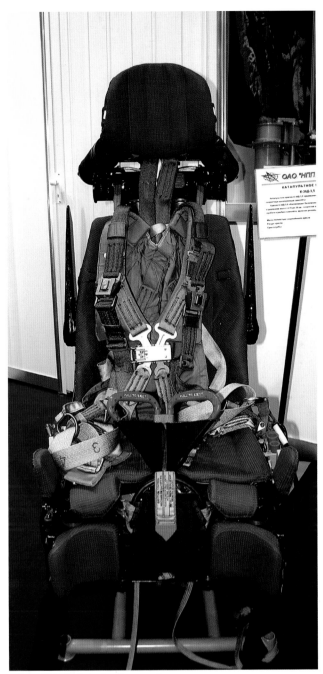

New K-36D-3.5 ejection seat.

K-36DM Specification

Weight	265 lb.
Ejection Height	approx. 210 ft.
Number of Rocket Stages	2
Second Stage Thrust	7,420 lb.
Maximum Acceleration During Ejection	18-20 g
Duration of Maximum Acceleration	0.12 – 0.15 sec.
Seat Height Adjustment	6.3 in.
Parachute Area	645 square ft.

ergonomics. Multifunction screens displaying various information, primarily from the radar, appeared for the first time. The main indicators in the Su-27 are primarily analogue and vertical tape instruments combined with the windscreen device (Head-Up-Display) and the display screen (cathode ray principle), which is in the upper right part of the instrument panel (Head-Down-Display or HDD). The Head-Up-Display shows information important for flying the aircraft and operating the weapons systems; the HDD displays information from the radar and IRST, while in navigation mode it shows flight routes and associated facilities. It is only an indicator screen, not an operating screen like modern devices. The principle flight instruments (barometric altimeter, airspeed indicator, vertical speed indicator/turn, and bank indicator and compass) are concentrated in the center of the instrument panel. They are outlined in white to make it possible for the pilot to quickly find them. One advantage of analogue instruments is that when the pilot looks at the instrument a pointer or bar is in a certain area of the indicator scale, and the brain can immediately determine via the eyes whether the parameter is in a critical or normal range. Digital instruments often show a value as a number, which the brain must process. To optimize the thought process, many displays have symbols in different colors (green, yellow, red, blue). The advantage of digital displays is that they can display significantly more information than round instruments, but to avoid sensory overload, only momentarily important indications can be displayed. Furthermore, display screens are no longer purely indicators, today they can be used to operate various systems. Both the crew in the air and the technicians on the ground use these display screens to control aircraft systems. Since the Su-30MKI, this technology has found growing use in versions of the Su-27. While the instrument panel is used primarily to monitor the systems, to the left and right of the pilot's seat of

has a heated seat and backrest, is installed in the Su-35S and T-50.

Cockpit Configuration

In the 1970s, cockpit configuration in the Soviet Union was still very conventional, but the same was true of Western aircraft manufacturers. At the beginning of the 1970s, however, the F-14 brought about a change in cockpit

Standard cockpit of the Su-27P/S. *Vitaly V. Kuzmin*

the Su-27 there are switch consoles, from where a wide variety of systems are controlled. These are very numerous and make the pilot's task much more difficult in ticklish combat situations, in part because he must turn his gaze to the control consoles and briefly take his eye off his target. Through the use of modern computer technology, in recent years the aircraft has itself taken over some of this workload, reducing the pilot's workload.

Warning and Information Systems

The Su-27 has a variety of indicator and information systems that inform the pilot during flight or the technician on the ground of dangerous or critical conditions or certain operating conditions. The first and most important of these is the EKRAN display unit. It is located on the right edge of the instrument panel. The text messages are produced by burning pixels onto a metal-coated foil roll, which looks like an old analogue reel of film. Roughly 260 different warning reports are available. These are preprogrammed and appear on the display unit. If, for example, a fire were to break out in the port engine compartment, the message "Fire LH Engine" appears. Only the most important message appears on the display screen. If additional warning messages are received by the EKRAN, the pilot or technician can display them in turn by pressing a button. After every flight or major operation (such as engine runs) by the aircraft, the EKRAN roll is removed for analysis and a new roll installed. Up to sixty-four reports can be shown on one roll. If the EKRAN itself has a malfunction, the ERROR field illuminates. Another system for the crew or technicians consists of labeled illuminated lights and these are concentrated primarily in a place near the EKRAN. Lights of different colors are used, for example green for engaged systems, yellow for warning signals, and red for dangerous conditions. If a critical light field lights up, the Master Caution light begins to blink. Pressing on the light causes the blinking to change to a steady light. The Su-27's final warning device is a voice warning system. The messages are delivered in a woman's voice (according to psychologists this has calming effect on pilots) and was nicknamed Natasha by the Soviets, while the Germans gave the name Rita to this system in their MiG-29s. Up to forty-six preprogrammed warning messages (on magnetic tape) can be received by pilots or in the nose-protecting helmets worn by ground crews. Another information system is the flight data recorder (often wrongly called the Black Box, as it is orange). Parameters (roughly 500) are saved on a magnetic tape, specifically aircraft operations, actions by the pilot, and flight data (angle of attack, speed, altitude, etc.). After every flight or major maintenance process, such as engine test runs, the data is uploaded and evaluated. This is done to determine if the technical system is functioning improperly or is developing a tendency to do so. The data also reveals if the pilot has flown his aircraft beyond allowable limits. Provided it survives, after an accident, the flight data recorder's tape can be read, revealing the cause. The recorder is housed in a very robust container so that its data can be evaluated even after a crash. The manufacturer guarantees that about ninety-five percent of the data can be retrieved if the recorder has spent a maximum of two days in liquid, three days in salt water, fifteen minutes at temperatures up to 1,800 degrees F and 10 ms of accelerations of up to 32,150 ft/sec^2. The flight data recorder is usually switched on manually from the cockpit, but it also turns on automatically under conditions likely to require a major industrial repair (for example, engine revolutions over eighty-five percent or unloading of a main undercarriage and lowered tailerons.

CHAPTER 7
Weapons

New Weapons for the Fighters of the Fourth Generation

In order to equal or surpass the new generation of Western combat aircraft, it was not enough to only develop new aircraft and detection systems. New weapons were required as well. In 1973, the Soviet Air Force requested a medium-range family of missiles for the future MiG-29, and long-range missiles for the Su-27. Both radar and infrared seeker heads were to be used. The new air-to-air missiles were given the designations K-27R (radar) and K-27T (infrared). The later long-range variants were given the suffix E for a larger rocket engine. The Vympel and Molnya design bureaus submitted their designs, and after thorough evaluation Vympel was selected to develop the K-27 family of missiles. Vympel had two different designs. One envisaged the use of purely aerodynamic control to maneuver the missile and a second with canard surfaces with forward-honed leading edges. TsAGI was also involved and it recommended the version with canards. The K-27 was the first missile of its kind anywhere to have inertial guidance. This type of guidance is in operation from time of launch until the semi-active radar seeker head is activated. Nevertheless, correction signals for guidance of the K-27 are sent by the Su-27's radar. Among the advantages of the K-27's inertial guidance system was increased range. The planned mixed load of radar- and infrared-guided K-27s meant that in combat the pilot could select the version best suited to the situation, radar or infrared. This also made it more

difficult for the enemy to select and employ appropriate countermeasures. At that time the lighter K-27 was thought to be just as effective as the American AIM-7Sparrow, while the heavy K-27 variant with larger rocket engine was rate superior to the Sparrow. The initial versions of the K-27 have been in the Soviet Air Force inventory since 1984, and its designation was changed to R-27. A new short-range missile was also requested in 1973. Once again the competition was between Vympel and Molnya. Vympel entered the race with a design for a much-improved R-13 (which had its origins in a captured Sidewinder and had been developed into several versions). The R-14 proposed by Vympel had purely aerodynamic control, combined with a wide-angle infrared seeker head. Molnya entered the newly-designed K-73, which was to have a seeker head with a narrower search angle than that of the R-14 as well as a wingless configuration. Evaluations of the capabilities of foreign missiles and its own experience led the air force to decide that Molnya should introduce a wide-angle seeker head for its K-73. In 1976, the K-73 underwent another redesign after serious shortcomings were found. A combination of aerodynamic control with, for the first time, thrust-vector control plus cruciform-shaped fins gave the missile an agility that surpassed anything before it. At that time the USA was also developing a wingless missile with thrust-vector control, but the project was abandoned after results proved unsatisfactory. The K-73 ultimately prevailed as the R-73, its capabilities proved in numerous mock combats between

Fully armed with R-73 short-range missiles on the two outer-wing hardpoints and R-27s on the remaining hardpoints.

Chris Lofting

German-flown MiG-29s and opponents from allied air forces. The Su-27 also had the opportunity, especially the Indian Su-30MKI, which flew against American F-15s and F-16s, as well as French Mirages. The Soviet designers created a short-range air-to-air missile, which, at the moment is still the best anywhere (including further developments).

Many of the independent OKBs have meanwhile merged to form large companies. The former Raduga OKB, which developed many guided weapons for aircraft (including the entire Kh air-to-surface missile family), is now part of the Tactical Missile Corporation. The developer/manufacturer of the 3M-14 and 3M-54 was the Novator OKB, which is now part of the Almaz Antey concern, which is known for its extremely capable S-300 and S-400 series of surface-to-air missiles. The Vympel OKB, which developed air-to-air missiles, is now also part of the Tactical Missile Corporation. Such mergers have also taken place in other sectors of the armaments industry, and the manufacturers of combat aircraft, helicopters, and aero-engines have each merged into umbrella groups.

R-73 (AA-11 Archer)

The R-73 missile, which entered service in the 1980s, has dominated the short-range air-to-air missile sector up to the present day. It is used against highly-agile air targets at short ranges but is also capable of striking ground targets. The IR seeker head has a field of view of forty-five degrees and in conjunction with the helmet-mounted sight can engage targets far off the aircraft's longitudinal axis (see Helmet-Mounted Sight). The R-73 can engage targets from near ground level or at up to 65,600 feet and at speeds up to approximately 2,175 miles per hour. It is capable of successfully engaging targets turning at up to 12 g. Its special feature is its control system, which combines aerodynamic surfaces with thrust-vector control. Thus it is still the most agile short-range air-to-air missile in the world, although some Western models (for example, the IRIS-T and MICA) are now supposed to at least be its equal. The R-73 is a fire-and-forget weapon, which means that after it is fired it tracks and pursues its target independently. Opposing fighter pilots who came up against the R-73 while participating in exercises were left with a bitter aftertaste. Once captured by the helmet-mounted-sight, escape from the R-73 was impossible. This combination proved to be the most dangerous close combat system of all. The R-74 is a developed version and has an improved field of view of sixty degrees and a more sensitive seeker head. The RVV-MD is the latest guided weapon in the R-73 family and also has a field of view of sixty degrees. It is supposed to have a combined infrared and radar seeker head. Its resistance to electronic and optical countermeasures is rated very high.

R-27 (AA-10 Alamo)

The R-27 is a medium-range missile and uses either semi-active radar guidance or passive IR seeker heads. Its engagement range extends from altitudes of 65,000 to 88,500 feet and maximum target speed of 2,175 miles per hour. The R-27 can be fired from aircraft maneuvering at up to 5 g and still shoot down its target. The semi-active radar variant of the R-27 was supposed to be replaced by the R-27AE; however, its use came with the significant disadvantage that the target must be illuminated by the aircraft's radar until the missile impacts. This seriously limits the maneuverability of the attacking fighter, which can become a target itself. Development and production of the active R-27AE has been cancelled in favor of the R-77. If the R-27R (or R-27ER) is electronically jammed on its way to the target, it then automatically tracks toward the jammer to engage it. A larger rocket engine has been added to improve range. This is recognizable by its larger diameter, which does not extend over the entire length of the missile. The suffix E added to the

designation means Extended, identifying the larger engine. The field of view of the radar-guided version's seeker head is fifty degrees, while that of the infrared version is fifty-five degrees. The heat-seeker's designation is R-27T or ET, and lock-on to the heat source takes place at a maximum range of eighteen miles. The R-27R/T entered service in 1984, together with the MiG-29, as the Su-27 did not enter service until two years later. The Russian military began receiving the extended-range R-27ER and R-27ET in 1987.

R-77 (AA-12 Adder)

The R-77 was born of the necessity to create a medium-range fire-and-forget guided missile that did not have to be illuminated by the aircraft's radar continuously until impact. The design goes back to 1982, possibly inspired by the appearance of the American AAM-120 AMRAAM air-to-air missile. The R-77 is designed for medium ranges with an active radar seeker head and thus meets the conditions of the fire-and-forget principle. Nevertheless, it can receive correction orders from the launch aircraft and be assigned to another target, guidance during the final phase of flight being provided by the missile's own active radar. One interesting feature is the missile's grid tail fins, which were also used by the Soviet SS-20 (RSD-10 Pionier) medium-range nuclear

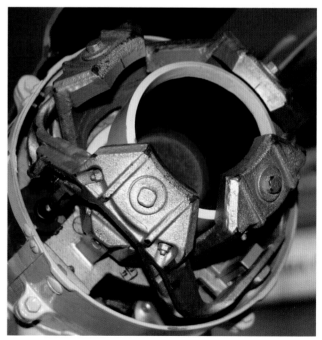

The secret of the R-73's agility is its thrust-vector control.

In the center is the Russian "close combat terror" of Western fighter pilots, the R-73 short-range air-to-air missile.

missile and currently on the Iksander short-range missile. Combined with the missile's aerodynamic control surfaces, these give the R-77 such a degree of maneuverability that it is capable of engaging targets maneuvering at up to 12 g. A laser proximity fuse detonates the fragmentation warhead at the desired range. The R-77 can be used at altitudes from 65,000 to 82,000 feet, with a maximum target speed of up to 2,240 miles per hour. Despite its excellent performance, curiously the R-77 does not appear to have entered service with the Russian Air Force in large numbers if at all, for neither the MiG-29 nor the Su-27 are capable of operating the missile with their original radars. The first aircraft to be capable of using the R-77 were the MiG-29S and Su-30MK. The R-77 is also not to be found in Russian Air Force photos of its fighter aircraft. Why this is so is not known. Perhaps there were so many R-27s left from Soviet times that it was not required, but this seems questionable given the limited storage times for such weapons. Or perhaps cost alone was why this modern weapon did not enter service in large

numbers, though this is not very illuminating with regard to the missile's capabilities. And the possibility that the R-77 was procured in numbers, but the Russians do not wish to reveal it to the outside world, is also not very convincing unless it can be traced to the manufacturer. The published photos of Russian combat aircraft deployed to Syria show aircraft armed with the R-27 and not the R-77. Its successor, the RVV-SD, is already undergoing trials. It has an extended range of sixty-five miles and was tested on the Su-27SM3.

GSh-301

The AO-17A cannon was originally intended for use in both the MiG-29 and the Su-27. It was a heavier caliber (30 mm) twin-barreled derivative of the GSh-23. The weapon had a weight of 220 pounds and a maximum firing rate of 3,000 rounds per minute. Muzzle velocity was 2,788 feet per second. Designated the GSh-30, this cannon was later installed in the Su-25 and the Mi-24 attack helicopter. It was

Infrared-guided R-27T missiles on the inner-wing pylons and radar-guided R-27R missiles under the engine air intakes. On the wingtip hardpoints are mounted R-73 air-to-air missiles. *Sergey Chaikovski*

thought, however, that at 220 pounds the gun was too heavy for the Su-27 and MiG-29. A twin-barrel 30 mm naval cannon was redesigned to have just one barrel, which was shortened by 19.7 inches. The result was the GSh-301. It can be used against air and ground targets, and its effective range is 650 to 2,600 feet in air combat and 3,900 to 5,900 feet against ground targets. Maximum firing rate was halved from the original 3,000 rounds per minute to 1,500 to 1,800, while muzzle velocity remained the same. The use of a single barrel halved the cannon's weight to about 110 pounds. The shells weighs approximately thirty ounces, while the projectile weighs fourteen ounces. The aircraft carries high-explosive and armor-piercing ammunition, the AP round capable of penetrating up to 1.6 inches of armor plate. The ammunition is belted and stowed in a magazine box. The cannon itself is mounted in the starboard LERX, while the ammunition box is

placed behind the nosewheel bay. The spent casing ejector chute is directly behind the starboard LERX, casings being ejected over the forward air intake. The gun is cooled internally by water vapor and externally by ram-air. For precise use, the cannon is coupled to the aircraft's laser rangefinder.

The GSh-301's ammunition capacity is 150 rounds, which at first glance seems too little in comparison to Western cannon; however, it is actually envisaged just as a backup in aerial combat. It does, however, have a larger caliber than most Western cannon. It thus has a more destructive effect on the target, having much more kinetic energy than, for example, a 20 mm round. The larger caliber also means a larger casing with more propellant. Firing trials have shown that on average just five to seven rounds are required to destroy an enemy fighter. The gun's light and simple design comes with a drawback, however, namely with regard to

The red guided weapon is an R-77 medium-range air-to-air missile, here on the prototype Su-27SKM. *United Aircraft Corporation*

The grid tail fins of the R-77.

Chapter 7: Weapons

GSh-301 automatic cannon with associated ammunition box and 150 rounds of belted ammunition.

operating life. The barrel must be replaced after 1,000 rounds have been fired and the entire cannon after 2,000 rounds. But as the cannon is very accurate, training on it is very short. To protect the airframe from muzzle blast a heat-proof steel component is added. It also absorbs some of the enormous recoil forces. Ammunition can be fired in continuous fire mode or in bursts, the length depending on how long the firing button is pressed.

Kh-29 (AS-14 Kedge)

The Kh-29 is designed for use against hardened or armored ground targets and vessels. Two different seeker heads are available, with semi-active laser or TV guidance. Use of the semi-active laser guidance mode requires the target to be illuminated by the launching or accompanying aircraft or by

personnel on the ground. The missile's seeker head receives the reflected laser beam and follows it to the target. A condition of use is that no cloud or fog be present to absorb the laser beam. When TV guidance is used, the rocket must be steered to the target by the weapons operator/navigator, during which deviations of six to ten feet are not exceeded. An alternate method is for the weapons operator to mark the target on the TV picture on the display, after which the seeker head guides the weapon to the target using contrast recognition. In this mode the missile is accurate to within six to nine feet. During the autonomous part of the missile's flight the pilot or weapons operator can manually transmit corrective data to the weapon. This weapon played an important role in attacking high-priority ground targets in the Soviet wars in Afghanistan and Chechnya.

Kh-31 (AS-17 Krypton)

The Kh-31 was developed to attack shipping (Kh-31A) and air defense radars (Kh-31P). The basic design of both versions is identical up to the warhead and seeker head. The Kh-31 has a solid-fuel booster, which accelerates the missile to the ramjet engine's ignition speed. The solid fuel accelerator and the ramjet engine share a common combustion chamber. The Kh-31 flies to the target at its very high speed of 2,900 miles per hour, making it difficult to combat. This speed is only possible at high altitudes, however, and the missile's maximum speed at low level is about Mach 2.7. The Kh-31A anti-shipping version is capable of destroying ships with displacements up to 4,960 tons. It has an active radar seeker head and is a fire-and-forget weapon. At extreme low level the Kh-31 can be used in sea state conditions up to five. The Kh-31P anti-radar version is designed to neutralize air defense, air traffic control, and early warning radars and is said to be very effective against the Patriot missile system. It has a passive radar seeker, which receives signals from the enemy radar and then guides toward the transmitter. It is thus also a fire-and-forget weapon. The missile has a large frequency range in order to be able to detect as many enemy radars as possible or continue tracking despite rapid frequency changes by the ground radar. There are longer range versions of both variants. This was achieved by improving the engine and increasing fuel capacity, resulting in a slight increase in length. The weapons are designated Kh-31AD and Kh-31PD.

Kh-35E (AS-20 Kayak)

The Kh-35 was developed as an anti-ship missile capable of sinking vessels up to the size of a cruiser. The weapon was developed in the mid-1980s, and entered service with the Russian military in the early 1990s. Rightfully, it must be said here that the first Russian aircraft able to carry this weapon were the MiG-29SMT 9.19 and the Su-27SM, which entered service with the Russian Air Force very late. The missile has an active seeker head, which automatically switches on during the approach to the target, thus making it a fire-and-forget weapon. Prior to switching on its seeker head, the missile receives target data from the launching aircraft and navigates to the target using its inertial navigation system. The Kh-35's radar seeker head automatically detects the target at about twelve miles from its target, then self-guides the rest of the way. Depending on sea state, the missile flies

The GSh-301 is installed in the Su-27's starboard LERX. The area in front of the muzzle is protected by heat-proof steel skin.

Hugh Dodson

Chapter 7: Weapons

The Kh-29T, in this photo the orange-white-painted weapon with the TV seeker head.

at between ten and forty-five feet. When launched from a helicopter, a solid-fuel booster accelerates the missile during the launch phase before its jet engine starts on reaching ignition speed. The Kh-35 flies at about 680 miles per hour. There are also ship- and land-based versions of the Kh-35. The improved Kh-35UE has twice the range of the Kh-35, and its seeker head has in improved detection range of up to thirty miles. In addition to active radar guidance, the missile also has passive radar and satellite guidance.

Kh-38

The Kh-38 is a new family of medium-range cruise missiles with a range up to about twenty-five miles and can be considered the successor to the Kh-25. The cruise missile flies at about twice the speed of sound and can be fitted with active and passive radar seeker heads, as well as satellite and infrared guidance.

Kh-41 (AS-22)

The Kh-41 came from the P-80 or the improved P-270 (NATO designation SS-N-22 Sunburn), which was carried by warships of the Soviet fleet (*Sovremenny* Class). It was in turn developed from the P-120 (NATO designation SS-N-9), which was originally carried by *Charlie II* and *Papa* class nuclear submarines. It is an anti-ship missile that can also be launched from the air. Power is mixed, a solid-fuel engine firing during launch to accelerate the cruise missile to the speed required to start the ramjet engine. The missile flies at more than 30,000 en route to the target. It is guided by its inertial navigation system. For the final approach to the target, the Kh-41 descends to sea level and switches on its radar. The low altitude at which it flies above the sea (thirty to sixty feet), the earth's curvature, which does not reveal the missile until a few dozen miles from its target, and its high speed of Mach 2.2 leaves little time for radars to detect the Kh-41. During the final approach to the target, from a range of 5.5

miles the Kh-41 also carries out independently a variety of maneuvers at up to 10 g to further complicate the task of the enemy air defenses. Because of its size, the Kh-41 has to date only been carried by the Su-33. As the range of the Kh-41 exceeds the detection range of the Su-33's radar, external target data had to be fed to the Kh-41 for initial guidance to the target. Range depends on the flight profile and drops rapidly if it flies exclusively at wavetop height. Maximum range can be achieved if the flight to the target is mainly carried out at higher altitudes.

"Yakhont/BrahMos"

The Yakhont (Russian designation P-800, NATO designation SS-N-26) is an anti-ship weapon and can be considered the successor to the Kh-41. Similar to its predecessor in size and performance, it also has mixed solid-fuel and ramjet propulsion. The air intake is located just behind the nose of the missile and is fitted with a cover that is jettisoned during launch of the cruise missile. The shock cone contains the targeting radar, this arrangement of the radar in the air intake cone resembling that of the MiG-21. The missile's reduced weight compared to the Kh-41 is in part due to a simplified propulsion system and the use of modern electronics. In cooperation with the Indians, the Yakhont was developed into a version that, in addition to the air-launched version, allows the cruise missile to be fired from submarines, from land, and from ships. The last two variants, designated BrahMos, have a solid-fuel accelerator. The name BrahMos is derived from the names of the Brahmaputra and Moskva Rivers and symbolizes the cooperation between India and Russia. The BrahMos is intended primarily for use by the Su-30MKI, but it can also be used ay all other modern Sukhois. Range varies depending on launch platform and the air-launched version has the greatest range. While the BrahMos has a similar flight profile to that of the Kh-41, the flight to the target is made at heights above 33,000 feet and not until the final approach to the target does it descend to fifteen to sixty feet above the surface of the sea. The high flight altitude has the disadvantage of early detection by the enemy, but this height (less air resistance than at sea level) seems necessary to achieve great range combined with an attack speed up to Mach 3. The BrahMos can switch on its active/passive radar at a distance of fifty miles from the target. The BrahMos enables the launching aircraft to attack a target from a safe distance without having to penetrate the flotilla's air defense zone.

Kh-58 UshKE (TP)
(AS-11 Kilter)

The Kh-58 has existed since the late 1970s, and was originally conceived for use by the MiG-25BM. Over the years a variety of versions of the Kh-58 were developed. It is an anti-radar missile for use against enemy radars (stationary and mobile).

The guided weapon with the black radar head is the Kh-31. The pointed tips of the narrow cylindrical structures on the outside of the missile are the protective covers over the ramjet cruise engine's air intakes and are jettisoned when the missile is launched.

For this purpose it has a passive radar seeker head that covers a broad spectrum of the most different-known radar sources. For radars operating in pulse mode, it covers the range between 1.2 and 11 GHz, and in continuous mode, the A-Band. The passive seeker head emits no radar pulses that could be detected by the enemy and steers automatically toward the radar source. Meanwhile, air defense radars detect approaching cruise missiles, but as the Kh-58 flies very fast in the end phase of flight (greater than 2,400 mph) and has a limited radar signature (radar-absorbing paint), the task for the radar being attacked is made significantly more difficult. Should the Kh-58 be detected in time, the target radar might switch off and change position. This is partially countered by an active radar that engages automatically, but not on the Kh-58UShKE (TP). This is the most modern version at the moment and also has heat sensors to ensure destruction of the enemy radar even if it is switched off. The missile fins are foldable to enable it to fit into the weapons bays of the Sukhoi T-50. An external radar receiver that detects enemy radar emissions is carried both for the Kh-31 and Kh-58 (and versions). The Kh-58UShKE has smaller dimensions than the preceding versions, which makes it even more difficult to detect. The Kh-58 could be carried by the Su-17M4 and today by the Su-24, Su-25, and MiG-31.

Kh-59M/MK/MK2
(AS-18 Kazoo)

The Kh-59 is a versatile guided weapon that can be fitted with a variety of seeker heads. The first guided weapon in this family is the Kh-59M. It has a TV seeker head and is used against stationary land and sea targets. The Kh-59M transmits the television picture to the aircraft from which it was launched. These signals are received by an APK-9E Tekon pod and displayed on the WSO's (or that of the pilot for single-seat aircraft) display screen as a television image. The WSO or pilot can also transmit correction signals via the APK-9E to change the missile's flight path if required. The missile is manufactured by the Ukrainian company Arsenal, which also produces the Sura helmet-mounted sight. The APK-9E weighs about 570 pounds. The Kh-59M's TV seeker head is replaced by an active radar seeker head on the Kh-59MK and it is primarily envisaged as an anti-ship weapon, although it can be used against land targets. Range is 2.5 times greater than that of the Kh-59M. This may be because the

Kh-59M receives its guidance signals by way of the APK-9E, which has a maximum transmitting range of about eighty-five miles. The radars carried by aircraft that carried the missile also had a limited range for ship targets.

Flight altitude over the surface of the sea is thirty to forty-five feet, while in the final approach phase the missile flies at twelve to forty feet. The seeker head's active radar switches on at ranges up to fifteen miles from the target. The most modern variant carries the designation Kh-59MK2 (similar to the Kh-59MK cruise missile); however, its design is completely new. The Raduga development company wanted to create a guided cruise missile comparable to the Western Storm Shadow and Taurus. Accordingly, great importance was given to stealth configuration, so the missile body is rectangular and the head has angled surfaces. The wings are not deployed until the missile separates from the launching aircraft. These measures allow the Kh-59MK2 to be carried by the T-50 – another aircraft with internal weapons bays. It is intended for use against stationary targets for which the coordinates are known and can be transmitted to the cruise missile. Guidance to the target is by means of inertial guidance (INS) in combination with the Glonass system (Russian GPS), and the missile approaches the target at subsonic speed. Either a daylight TV sensor or a FLIR, which is unaffected by weather or light, is used for final guidance to the target. The TV seeker head as a CEP (Circular Error Probable) of fifteen feet, the FLIR nine feet. If the target cannot be detected by either the TV sensor or FLIR, satellite reception provides precise guidance to the target. The missile warhead weighs 680 pounds, while the entire cruise missile weighs about 1,700 pounds. Altitude above the ground varies between 150 and 900 feet depending on terrain. In addition to the large Sukhoi, the Kh-59MK2 can also be carried by the smaller MiG-35.

3M-14AE/3M-54AE (Club-S)

In the 1980s, the Novator OKB designed long-range guided weapons specifically for submarines, these being launched from the twenty-one-inch torpedo tubes. This resulted in the 3M-14 and the 3M-54. The 3M-14 was developed into the 3M-14AE. It is intended for use against stationary ground targets and flies at subsonic speeds. For use with combat aircraft like the Su-27, the 3M-14AE is stowed in a canister that is suspended from the innermost wing hardpoints or

The Kh-31 guided anti-ship weapon. On the tail of the weapon shown here there is a launch booster, needed if the weapon is fired from a helicopter for example.

between the engines. The canister is dropped and as it falls the cruise missile is ejected and ignites its engine. Altitude varies between 150 and 450 feet depending on the terrain profile, while over water it is about sixty feet. The radar seeker head begins searching for the target at about twelve miles from the target. From the 3M-54 was derived the 3M-54AE for use from combat aircraft. There is one version (EM-54AE1) that attacks enemy ships at subsonic speed and one (3M-54AE) that achieves Mach 2.5 in the final phase of flight. The cruise missile flies to the target at subsonic speed, but in the final flight phase (twelve miles from target) the supersonic component separates and continues independently to the target. The 3M-54AE and AE1 have radar seeker heads that can acquire the target from a distance of forty miles. The somewhat smaller warhead is due to the larger radar and greater fuel weight for the supersonic capability. The cruise missile's inertial guidance system, which receives target information from the aircraft prior to launch, guides the missile to the target. During the cruise phase the cruise missile can receive and process GPS signals for course correction.

Because of a general agreement between Russia and the USA, the range of exported air-to-ground cruise missiles is limited to 180 miles and that of the types used in Russia is considerably greater.

The huge Kh-41 Moskit anti-ship missile.

Guided Bombs

The Kab-500L and Kab-1500L are laser-guided bombs with total weights of 500 and 1,500 kilograms (1,100 and 3,300 pounds). Laser guidance requires the target to be illuminated until the bomb arrives. This can be accomplished with a targeting pod on the aircraft or an illuminator installed in the aircraft. An accompanying aircraft can also provide laser illumination. People on the ground can also illuminate the target with a portable laser illuminator and the reflected beams are received by the bomb's seeker head. The bomb then guides itself to the target and corrects the flight path using the outgoing and incoming laser beams. This guidance method can only be used in clear weather, as clouds, fog, rain, snow, or heavy mist absorbs the laser.

The Kab-500Kr and Kab-1500Kr are television-guided bombs weighing 1,100 and 3,300 pounds. Television cameras are mounted in the nose of the bomb and transmit a television picture to a display screen in the cockpit. The pilot or weapons system officer fixes the target using a marking on the display screen. The seeker head remains on the marked target using contrast recognition and the bomb guides itself to the target using movable fins. Good visibility conditions are also required here. Because of their accuracy, laser- and television-guided bombs can be used against targets like bunker systems, bridges, command posts, and other pinpoint targets, where a high degree of accuracy is required.

Since 2000, the Russians have also had a 500-kilogram (1,100 pound) Kab-500S satellite-guided bomb in their arsenal. The weapon receives signals both from the Russian Glonass and American GPS systems. Target deviation is twenty to forty feet for the authorized area and becomes more precise if the full coded information is transmitted. This

The modern anti-ship weapon, the Yakhont, godfather of the BrahMos.

Pre-production Su-30MKI with the Kh-59M and the associated APK-9 guidance pod under the port engine air intake. *Irkut Corporation*

The Kh-59MK guided weapon cannot be used by the Su-27K in the background of this photo. The pale-gray cylinder beneath the Kh-59MK is the missile's jet engine.

The launch container for the 3M-14AE guided weapon. Only the weapon's radar seeker head projects from the container.

In the foreground is the Kh-58 UshKE anti-radar missile. The version with additional heat sensors has the suffix TP.

results in a significantly lower target deviation, far less than the twenty to forty feet. This system allows guided bombs to be used in bad weather or at night. In Syria, these bombs were used by the Su-34. To enable the use of laser-guided weapons without an external laser illuminator, the Russian optics plant UOMS developed the SAPSAN-E targeting pod. It has infrared capabilities and a laser rangefinder plus target illuminator, tracker, and receiver for illuminated targets. The infrared capability also makes it possible to use other guided weapons in conditions of poor visibility. The pod weighs 550 pounds. A 550-pound guided bomb (Kab-250) with the above-described guidance methods was created, primarily

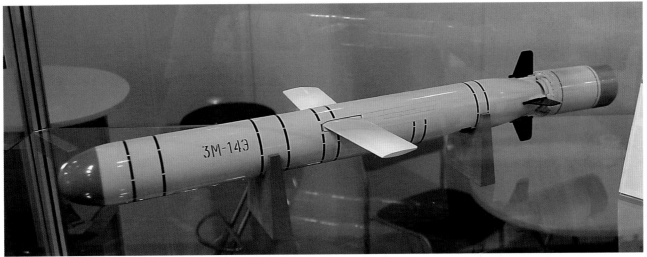

The 3M-14E cruise missile. It is the submarine-launched version of the 3M-14AE, here with a launch booster on its tail.

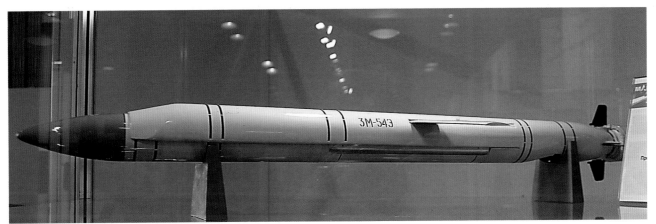

This is also a submarine-launched version, the 3M-54E. The 3M-54 with the suffix AE is carried by combat aircraft.

The Kh-59MK2 stealth cruise missile. *Vitaly V. Kuzmin*

Glide Bombs

After the USA created the ability to aerodynamically change conventional free-fall bombs to give them a range of several dozen miles (depending on release altitude and airspeed), engineers in Russia also recognized the potential. Bazalt, a weapons developer and manufacturer, fitted the PBK-500 cluster bomb container with extendable wings, giving it a potential range of up to thirty miles (from a release height of 30,000 feet). Designated the PBK-500U, it is loaded with sub-munitions that guide themselves to the target (by radar or infrared) after release. A satellite receiver is included, to guide the PBK-500U precisely to the target area so that it can release its sub-munitions there. The possibility of providing the PBK-500U with a propulsion system to increase range even further has also been considered. This would make it possible to build large numbers of economical guided

for stowage in weapons bays, but it can also be used by the Su-27 (with the appropriate equipment).

The massive Kab-1500L laser-guided bomb.

Here the protective cover is removed from the TV seeker head of a Kab-500Kr guided bomb, which is mounted on a Su-34.
Russian Defense Ministry/Vadim Savitsky

The new Grom guided weapon. *Vitaly V. Kuzmin*

weapons, as expensive propulsion units do not always have to be installed for greater range.

UPAB-1500

This weapon is a new development and was first revealed in 2005. It is a television-guided bomb, which unlike the Kab-1500Kr, has deployable wings, which can give it a range of up to forty miles when dropped from about 30,000 feet. Instead of a conventional pair of wings, the weapon had four wings arranged in a cruciform configuration. It is likely that TV seeker heads and satellite receivers are fitted, laser guidance being limited by the laser illuminator's inadequate range.

A noticeable feature of some of the TV-guided weapons is a grid in the glass of the seeker head. Its purpose is to screen against electronic jamming. All guided bombs are released from heights between 3,000 and 45,000 feet at speeds of 340 to 680 miles per hour. The optical seeker head comes from companies in the Ukraine and are purchased by Russia for use in its guided weapons. The official boycott resulting from the present political situation may complicate the mutual use relationship. The Russian Air Force has been offered a targeting pod for missions with TV-guided weapons. It has

the same sensor head as the TV-guided weapons, but the pod is simply not dropped. Instead it is used by the weapons system operator or pilot to acquire and engage targets.

Grom

The Grom guided weapon is offered in two versions; a guided cruise missile (Grom E-1) and a glide bomb (Grom E-2). These guided weapons are based on the Kh-38. They are stand-off weapons, about which no range or flight parameters have been released. Guidance is provided by a combined inertial guidance and satellite receiver system.

Unguided Weapons

In addition to these guided weapons, the Su-27 can use a wide variety of unguided munitions. In addition to large-caliber rockets there is also a huge palette of free-fall bombs for a variety of purposes. Cluster bomb containers can also be used by the Sukhoi, the sub-munitions being released near the target and guiding themselves to the target.

Color Profiles

A.

B.

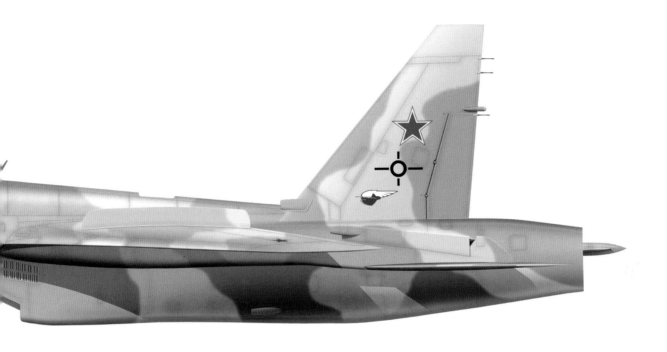

A. The very first prototype of the Su-27, the T-10-1.
B. Aircraft from the T-10S series of prototypes, the T-10-17 with inert weapons.

SUKHOI SU-27

A.

B.

A. The completely unpainted P-42 record-setting aircraft.
B. Su-27P armed with R-27 AAMs. On the vertical tail is the stylized archer of the Sukhoi Design Bureau.

A.

B.

A. Su-27UB with the green dielectric panels over electronic components, a typical feature of Soviet combat aircraft.
B. Su-27P of the Russian Air Force with redesigned tail stinger.

Color Profiles

SUKHOI SU-27

A.

B.

A. Third prototype of the Su-27M (Su-35).
B. Su-27K carrier aircraft armed with R-73 and
R-27 AAMs and the huge Kh-41 Moskit cruise
missile between the engine air intakes.

SUKHOI SU-27

A.

B.

Color Profiles

A. Revised camouflage scheme for the Su-27K.
B. Su-27KUB

SUKHOI SU-27

A.

B.

A. Su-34 armed with the Kh-31 for the anti-shipping role.

B. Su-35S with the noticeably changed vertical tails.

A.

B.

0   3

A. Russian Su-30SM
B. Algerian Su-30MKA

Color Profiles

A.

B.

A. Angolan Su-27
B. Ethiopian Su-27

A.

B.

0   3

A. Chinese J-11

B. Chinese Su-30MKK armed with R-27 air-to-air missiles and the Kh-59M with its APK-9 guidance pod under the engine air intake.

A.

B.

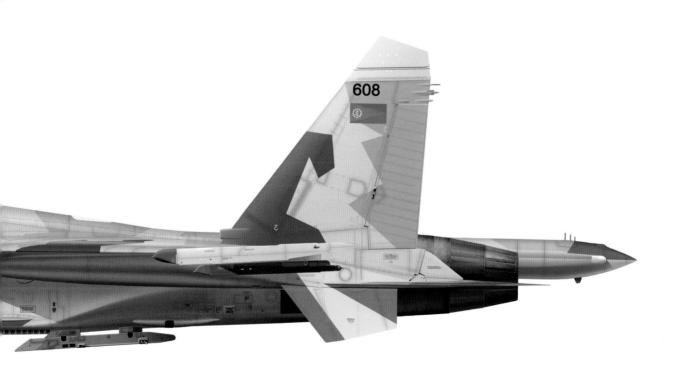

A. Chinese J-15 carrier aircraft.
B. Eritrean Su-27 with the striking Ukrainian camouflage scheme and a false cockpit painted under the nose.

A.

B.

A. Indian Su-30MKI with R-73 and R-77 AAMs plus Kab-500L laser-guided bombs (beneath the engine air intake trunks).
B. Indonesian Su-27SK

A.

B.

Color Profiles

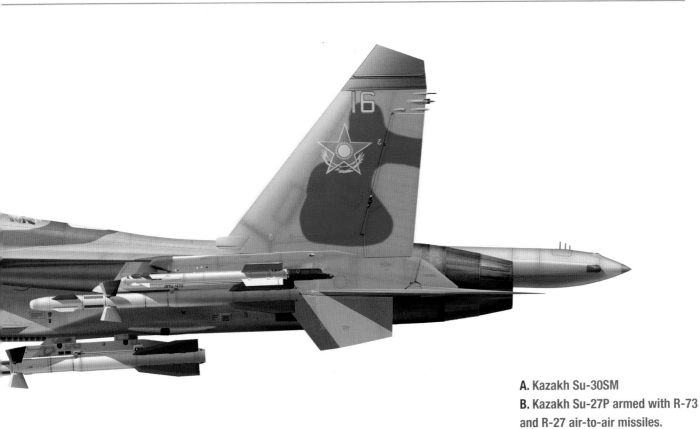

A. Kazakh Su-30SM
B. Kazakh Su-27P armed with R-73
and R-27 air-to-air missiles.

SUKHOI SU-27

A.

B.

0 — 3

A. Malaysian Su-30MKM with the Damocles targeting pod for the Kab-500L laser-guided bombs carried by the aircraft.
B. Ugandan Su-30MK2

SUKHOI SU-27

A.

B.

A. Ukrainian Su-27P (built before 1987) with typical armament of R-73 and R-27 AAMs.
B. Uzbek Su-27P

SUKHOI SU-27

A.

B.

A. Venezuelan Su-30MK2
B. Vietnamese Su-27SK

A.

0   3

A. White Russian Su-27P

Appendices

Specifications

Designation		Su-27S/P	Su-27UB	Su-30	Su-27K	Su-27KUB	Su-27M
OKB Code	T-10	T-10S	T-10U	T-10PU	T-10K (Su-33)	(Su-33)	T-10M (Su-35)
Overall Length (ft)	64.6	71.85	71.85	71.85	69.5	72	64.6
Wingspan (ft)	48.2	48.2	48.2	48.2	48.2 (27.4 folded)	52.5	48.2
Wing Area (ft²)	635	667	667	667	732 (less canards)	753 (less canards)	667 (less canards)
Height (ft)	19.3	19.3	21	21	18.7	19.3	21
Max. Gross Weight (lb)	56,659	61,729	67,240	72,752	72,752	–	74,957
Weapons Load (lb)	–	13,227	8,818	8,818	14,330	–	17,637
Fuel Weight (lb)	19,841	20,723	20,723	20,723	20,944	20,723	22,597
Power Plant	AL-31F	AL-31F	AL-31F	AL-31F	AL-31F Series 3	–	AL-31FM
Max. Dry Thrust/	17,085/	17,085/	17,085/	17,085/	–	–	–
Max. Afterburner	24,730	27,651	27,651	27,651	28,101	–	28,101
Max. Speed at Sea Level/	870	870	870	870	808	–	870
33,000 ft in mph	1,385	1,553	1,320	1,320	1,429	–	1,553
Range on Internal Fuel	1,926	2,423	1,864	1,864	1,864	2,175	1,988
Service Ceiling	57,415	60,695	57,415	57,415	55,774	–	59,055
Max. Climb Rate (ft/min)	–	59,055	–	–	–	–	–
Max. G Load	–	9 g	9 g	9 g	9 g	9 g	9 g
First Flight	1977	1981	1985	1988	1987	1999	1988

Designation	Su-27SK	Su-30MKK	Su-30MK2	Su-30MKI	Su-30SM	Su-35S	Su-34
OKB Code				/-A/-M			(T-10V)
Overall Length (ft)	71.85	71.85	71.85	71.85	71.85	71.85	76.4
Wingspan (ft)	48.2	48.2	48.2	48.2	48.2	50.2	48.2
Wing Area (ft²)	667	667	667	667 (less canards)	667 (less canards)	–	667 (less canards)
Height (ft)	19.3	21	21	21	21	19.3	20
Max. Gross Weight (lb)	72,752	85,539*	85,539*	85,539*	85,539*	76,060	99,208
Weapons Load (lb)	13,228	13,227	8,818	8,818	14,330	–	17,637
Fuel Weight (lb)	19,841	17,637	17,637	17,637	17,637	17,637	17,637
Power Plant	AL-31F	AL-31F	AL-31F	AL-31FP	AL-31FP	AL-31F-M1	AL-31F-M1
Max. Dry Thrust/	17,085/	17,085/	17,085/	17,085/	17,085/	19,783/	18.434
Max. Afterburner	27,651	27,651	27,651	27,651	27,651	32,597	30,349
Max. Speed at Sea Level/	870	870	870	870	839	870	870
33,000 ft in mph	1,553	1,320	1,320	1,320	1,317	1,490	1,180
Range on Internal Fuel (mi)	2,300	1,864	1,864	1,864	1,864	2,237	2,485 (with external tanks)
Service Ceiling	60,695	57,415	57,415	57,415	56,758	59,055	49,213
Max. Climb Rate (ft/min)	–	–	–	53,150	–	55,118	–
Max. G Load	9 g	9 g	9 g	9 g	9 g	9 g	7 g
First Flight	1991	1999	2002	1997	2012	2008	1990

* Maximum allowable takeoff weight ("overload"). Normal maximum takeoff weight is about 76,060 lb.

Radar Designation	N-001	N-001VE	N-011	N-011M Bars	N-011R	Irbis-E	B-004
Max. Range (mi) (radar reflective area 32.3 ft²)	62	68	62	93	155	250	56
Max. Tracked Targets	10	10	13	15	25	30	–
Number of Targets Engaged Simultaneously	1-2	2	4	4	12	8	–
Installed in	Su-27S /-UB/-K	Su-30MKK /-MK2	Su-27M	Su-30MKI MKA, MKM	Su-30SM	Su-30S	Su-34
Creation of Ground Maps		*	*	*	*	*	*

Guided Weapons Overview

Designation	Weight (lb)	Explosives (lb)	Range/Target Deviation (mi)	Guidance
R-73	231.5	16.5	18	infrared
R-77	385	49.6	50	active radar
R-VV-SD	419	66	68	active radar
R-27T	540	86	31–43	infrared
R-27TE	765	86	43–60	infrared
R-27R	558	86	31–43	semi-active radar
R-27RE	783	86	43–60	semi-active radar
Kh-29TE	1,521	705	12–19	TV
Kh-29L	1,455	705	5–6	laser
Kh-31A	1,345	207	43	active radar
Kh-31AD	1,576	243	75–100	active radar
Kh-31P	1,323	192	68	passive radar
Kh-31PD	1,576	242	112–155	passive radar
Kh-35U	1,146	320	81	active radar
Kh-35UE	1,213	320	162	active radar, GPS
Kh-38	1,146	max. 551	25	laser, radar, IR, GPS
Kh-58UShKE (TP)	1,433	330	152	passive radar, infrared
Kh-59M	2,050	705	71	TV
Kh-59MK	2,050	705	177	active radar
Kh-59MK2	1,698	683	180	INS, satellite, optical
3M-14AE	3,086	992	3731	active radar
3M-54AE1	4,299	882	3731	active radar
Kh-41	8,752-9,149	705	87–155[3]	active radar
Yakhont/BrahMos	5,512	661	3731	active radar
KAB-500L	1,100	430	13–23 ft	laser
KAB-1500L	3,300	463–1,433	13–23 ft	laser
KAB-500Kr	1,146	220–309	13–23 ft	TV
KAB-1500Kr	3,362	970	13–23 ft	TV
KAB-500S	1,235	430	23–39 ft	satellite
UPAB-1500	unknown	unknown	230	TV
Grom-E1	1,146	551	unknown	–
Grom E2	1,146	551 + 287 (2 warheads)	unknown	–
SAPSAN-E[2]	551	–	–	FLIR, TV, laser
Litening[2]	456	–	–	FLIR, TV, laser
Damocles[2]	584	–	–	FLIR, TV, laser

1 Because of an agreement between Russia and the USA, the range of exported stand-off weapons is limited to 180 miles.

2 Targeting pod

3 Depending on flight profile

Designers and Test Pilots

Pavel Sukhoi
July 22, 1895 – December 25, 1975
Head of the design bureau from the time of its founding, also held other positions in different OKBs (Tupolev), especially during the Second World War and until the death of Stalin in 1953. Pavel Sukhoi led the OKB that bore his name until his death.

Yevgeni Solovyov
January 1, 1931 – July 7, 1978
Test pilot with Sukhoi from 1959 to 1978; died in a crash during testing of the T-10-2.

Mikhail Simonov
October 19, 1929 – March 4, 2011
Chief designer of the T-10/T-10S project from 1977 to 1979. Deputy Minister for the Aviation Industry from 1979 to 1983, designer general of the Sukhoi OKB from 1983 to 1999.

Nikolai Sadovnikov
October 25, 1946 – July 22, 1994
Test pilot with the Sukhoi OKB from 1979 to 1988, made the first flight of the T-10-3 from the Nitka-T1 Complex and of the T-10-25 from the T2 complex. First flight and testing of the first T-10U-1 prototypes, set several records in the P-42. In 1987, together with I. Votinsiev, he made nonstop long-range flights in the Su-27UB (just under 8,700 miles/15 hours). Crashed in the T-10K-1 in 1988. He ejected, but the back injuries he suffered ended his flying career.

Mikhail Pogosyan
Born April 19, 1946
First deputy chief designer from 1992 to 1998; chief designer of the S-37 (Su-47). In 1999, became general designer and later CEO of the Sukhoi company and then general director of the United Aircraft Corporation.

Viktor Pugachev
Born August 8, 1948
Test pilot with Sukhoi from 1980 to 2001. First arrested landing at the NITKA-T1 Complex, first flight of the T-10K-1 prototype and intensive deck trials. First landing by a Soviet carrier aircraft on an aircraft carrier (with the T-10K-2 prototype on the Tbilisi), demonstration of the Cobra Maneuver. First flight of the Su-27KUB; today holds a responsible position in aircraft development programs.

Vladimir Ilyushin
March 31, 1927 – March 1, 2010
Test pilot with the Sukhoi OKB from 1957 to 1981. First flights by the T-10 and T-10S prototypes in 1977 and 1981. The same year he crashed while flying the T-10-7 and survived, but since then he has not been active as a test pilot.

Oleg Tsoi
Born May 16, 1944
Chief test pilot with Sukhoi from 1984 to 1997, first flight in a thrust-vector aircraft anywhere in the world on March 21, 1989 (T-10-26). First flight and testing of the Su-27M, set several records flying the P-42.

Vyacheslav Averyanov
Born September 15, 1959
Company pilot with KnAPPO from 1986 to 1989, became test pilot with the Sukhoi OKB in 1989. Tested Su-27M and Su-37 prototypes. First flight and testing of the Su-30MKI. Since 2007, test pilot and flight instructor with the Irkut Aircraft Corporation.

Alexander Komarov
November 12, 1944 –
December 23, 1981
Test pilot with the Sukhoi OKB from 1971 to 1981. Killed in a crash during a test flight in the T-10-12.

Sergey Bogdan
Born March 27, 1962
Flew the Su-33 from the *Admiral Kuznetsov*, test pilot with Sukhoi since 2000. Tested the Su-30MK family and the Su-27M and Su-27SM single-seaters. First flight in the Su-35S; chief test pilot at Sukhoi.

Igor Votinsiev
Born March 6, 1953
Test pilot with the Sukhoi OKB since 1980. Tested the Su-27, Su-30, Su-33, Su-34, and Su-27. In 1987, made non-stop long-distance flights in a modified Su-27UB together with N. Sadovnikov (just under 8,700 miles/15 hours). Then chief test pilot at Sukhoi. Altitude-payload record in the Su-34 in 1997. Now works as deputy of the Sukhoi flight testing center in Zhukovsky.

Sergey Kostin
Born March 8, 1971
Test pilot with Sukhoi since 1991. Test-flew the Su-27M, Su-27SM, Su-30, Su-34, and Su-35.

Yevgeni Frolov
Born May 17, 1951
Test pilot with the Sukhoi OKB since 1983. Tested aircraft from the Su-27 to the Su-27M. First flight and testing of the Su-37 and Su-27SM, set several records in the P-42. Presently works with Sukhoi in flight simulation.

Taras Arzebarski
Born December 3, 1978
Test pilot with Sukhoi since 2005. Tested the Su-27SM, Su-34, and Su-30MK versions, as well as the Su-35S. Instructor for foreign Su-30MK pilots.

Bibliography

Books

Antonov, Vladimir, Yefim Gordon, Mikolai Gordyukov, et al. *OKB Sukhoi: A History of the Design Bureau and Its Aircraft.* Leicester, UK: Midland, 1996.

FliegerRevue Extra 20–21.

Fomin, Andrey. *Su-27 Flanker Story.* Moscow: RA Intervestnik, 2000.

Gordon, Yefim. *Su-27 Flanker.* Shrewsbury, UK: Airlife, 1999.

Gordon, Yefim. *Flankers: The New Generation.* Hinckley, UK: Midland, 2001.

Gordon, Yefim, and Alan Dawes. *Russian Air Power.* Shrewsbury, UK: Airlife, 2002.

Morin, Arkadi, and Nikolai Valuyev. *Sowjetische Flugzeugträder.* Berlin: Brandenburgisches Verlagshaus, 1996.

Various authors. *Airforce Monthly* magazine.

Various magazines: *Takeoff, Aircraft Magazine, Aerospace,* and *Orbis Publishing* (www.take-off.ru).

Internet

www.acig.info
www.aerospace.boopidoo.com/philez/Su-15TM PICTURES & DOCS/Overscan's guide to Russian Military Avionics.htm
www.ag-friedensforschung.de
www.ainonline.com
www.airforce-technology.com
www.arsenalcdb.com.ua
www.asian-defence.net
www.ausairpower.net/
www.bangaloreaviation.com
www.defence-today.com.au
www.defenceweb.co.za
www.defensenews.com
www.diepresse.com
www.eanswers.com/
www.in.rbth.com/
www.info.kopp-verlag.de
www.knaapo.ru
www.ktrv.ru
www.lifefistdefence.com
www.liquisearch.com/helmet_mounted_display
www.mariwoj.pl/
www.medium.com
www.milavia.net
www.naval-technology.com
www.ndtv.com/india-news
www.niip.ru
www.npo-saturn.ru
www.pravdareport.com
www.radar-mms.com
www.reuters.com
www.ruaviation.com
www.russianknights.ru
www.salut.ru
www.sinodefence.com
www.sukhoi.org
www.take-off.ru
ww.tass.ru
www.uacrussia.ru/en
www.uk-odk.ru
www.558arp.by/en
http://defence.pk
http://indiatoday.intoday.in/story
http://naviny.by/
https://rhk111smilitaryandarmspage.wordpress.com
http://turcopolier.typepad.com
http://vayu-sena.tripod.com/
su27flankerfamily.wordpress.com/
su-27flanker.com

Photo Credits

JSC Sukhoi, KnAAZ, UAC (United Aircraft Corporation), Irkut Corporation, UEC (United Engine Corporation), JSC 558. Aircraft Repair Plant, Arsenal SDP State Enterprise, NPP Zvezda, Russian Defense Ministry, Alexey Micheyev, Charles Agnew, Hugh Dodsun, Olav de With, Oleg Revin, Peng Chen, Rob Schleiffert, Sergey Chaikovski, Chris Lofting, Svido Stanislav, Vitaly V. Kuzmin, Dimitri Jurijew, Andrey Zinchuk, Gilles Dennis, Resa Wahyu Giang, Jose Ramirez, Nguyen Phuong, Wojciech Kowalski, Malcom Nason, Sergey Burdin, Vladislav Perminov.

Artwork

Frank Krüger, Manfred Meyer, and Talgat Ashimov.